OECD Economic Surveys

Russian Federation

2009

OECD

ORGANISATION FOR ECONOMIC CO-OPERATION AND DEVELOPMENT

The OECD is a unique forum where the governments of 30 democracies work together to address the economic, social and environmental challenges of globalisation. The OECD is also at the forefront of efforts to understand and to help governments respond to new developments and concerns, such as corporate governance, the information economy and the challenges of an ageing population. The Organisation provides a setting where governments can compare policy experiences, seek answers to common problems, identify good practice and work to co-ordinate domestic and international policies.

The OECD member countries are: Australia, Austria, Belgium, Canada, the Czech Republic, Denmark, Finland, France, Germany, Greece, Hungary, Iceland, Ireland, Italy, Japan, Korea, Luxembourg, Mexico, the Netherlands, New Zealand, Norway, Poland, Portugal, the Slovak Republic, Spain, Sweden, Switzerland, Turkey, the United Kingdom and the United States. The Commission of the European Communities takes part in the work of the OECD.

OECD Publishing disseminates widely the results of the Organisation's statistics gathering and research on economic, social and environmental issues, as well as the conventions, guidelines and standards agreed by its members.

This work is published on the responsibility of the Secretary-General of the OECD. The opinions expressed and arguments employed herein do not necessarily reflect the official views of the Organisation or of the governments of its member countries.

Also available in French

Cover illustration: © Pat O'Hara/The Image Bank/Getty Images.
Corrigenda to OECD publications may be found on line at: *www.oecd.org/publishing/corrigenda*.

Table of contents

Boxes

Tables

Figures

This Survey was prepared in the Economics Department by Geoff Barnard, Roland Beck, Paul Conway and Tatiana Lysenko, under the supervision of Andreas Wörgötter. Substantial contributions were provided by the following individuals: Irina Knyazeva, Mikhail Matovnikov, Hanna Peltonen, Marcel Salikhov, and Larisa Smyrnich. Research assistance was provided by Corinne Chanteloup and secretarial assistance by Josiane Gutierrez.

The Economic Survey of the Russian Federation was discussed at a meeting of the Economic and Development Review Committee on 9 April 2009.

The Survey is published on the responsibility of the Secretary-General of the OECD.

This book has...

StatLinks

A service that delivers Excel® files from the printed page!

Look for the *StatLinks* at the bottom right-hand corner of the tables or graphs in this book. To download the matching Excel® spreadsheet, just type the link into your Internet browser, starting with the ***http://dx.doi.org*** prefix.

If you're reading the PDF e-book edition, and your PC is connected to the Internet, simply click on the link. You'll find *StatLinks* appearing in more OECD books.

BASIC STATISTICS OF THE RUSSIAN FEDERATION

(2008, unless otherwise specified)

THE LAND

Area (thousand sq. km)	17 098
Agricultural area (thousand sq. km)	2 223

THE PEOPLE

Population (millions, beginning year)	142.0
Inhabitants per sq. km. (beginning year)	8.3
Average annual population growth (per cent, 1998-2008)	–0.3
Employment (millions, 2008)	68.5
By sector (per cent of total)	
State and municipal enterprises and organisations	31.4
Private sector	57.3
Mixed form of ownership	11.3
By branch (per cent of total)	
Industry	20.8
Agriculture and forestry	10.0
Construction	8.1
Services	61.1
Unemployment rate (per cent of labour force, end-year)	7.8
Inhabitants in major cities (millions)	
Moscow	10.5
St. Petersburg	4.6
Novosibirsk	1.4
Nizhnii Novgorod	1.3

GOVERNMENT/ADMINISTRATION

Bicameral Parliamentary system (The Federal Assembly)	
Council of the Federation (upper house)	169 seats
State Duma (lower house)	450 seats
Number of registered political groups in the State Duma	4
Regional government	
Subjects of the Federation	84
of which: Republics	21
Krais (territories)	8
Oblasts (regions)	47
Autonomous *oblast*	1
Autonomous *okrugs* (areas)	5
City of Moscow	
City of St. Petersburg	

PRODUCTION

GDP (RUB billion, current prices)	41 668
GDP per capita (USD, market exchange rate)	11 811

PUBLIC FINANCE

General government revenue (per cent of GDP)	38.4
General government expenditure (per cent of GDP)	33.6
Domestic public debt (per cent of GDP, end-year)	3.4

FOREIGN TRADE AND FINANCE

Exports of goods and services (USD billion)	522.9
Imports of goods and services (USD billion)	368.2
Central bank gross foreign exchange reserves (USD billion, end-year)	427.1
Gross external public debt (per cent of GDP, end-year)	2.0

THE CURRENCY

Monetary unit: Rouble	
Currency units per USD (period average):	
Year 2008	24.9
December 2008	28.2

Executive summary

The global crisis has put a sudden end to the strong recovery of the Russian economy since the financial crisis of 1998. *A slowdown was becoming increasingly likely, given the erosion of favourable factors such as undervaluation of the rouble and spare production capacity and labour resources, but the severity of the crisis is a function of overlapping internal and external factors:*

- *Collapsing prices of oil and other commodities have resulted in a sharp turnaround in the terms-of-trade, which no longer support domestic demand.*
- *The drying-up of access to international capital markets hit some Russian banks and corporations hard, and a sudden deterioration of Russia-specific and more general emerging market risk premia increased financing costs steeply.*
- *The sharp depreciation of the rouble against the dollar in particular (related to falling oil prices and the deterioration in the private capital account) greatly increased the burden of foreign currency corporate debt, which has risen considerably in recent years.*

The government and central bank responded swiftly to the onset of the crisis, providing liquidity and capital to the banking system and seeking to boost aggregate demand. The government is ready to accept a large fiscal deficit in 2009 and can do so because of accumulated reserves saved in better times. Aggressive fiscal stimulus should aim at maximising the multiplier effect on domestic demand. Such stimulus should be cast in a credible medium-term framework, to safeguard fiscal sustainability. Monetary policy in the short term should make financial conditions as easy as possible, which means inter alia not resisting fundamental pressures for depreciation of the rouble. Maintaining the functioning of the banking system is of prime importance, but that is consistent with allowing considerable consolidation of the sector.

Looking beyond the crisis, a broad-based and comprehensive policy package is needed to put in place a more robust growth model. This Survey makes recommendations in four important areas where co-ordinated reforms promise considerable synergy effects:

- Economic rents from natural resource extraction should be captured and mostly saved by the government, but without unduly discouraging exploration and development, and the tax structure should be further reformed to enhance economic efficiency (without worsening equity – equity concerns will be addressed in more detail in the forthcoming *OECD Labour Market and Social Policy Review*).
- There should be a gradual switch to inflation targeting in order for monetary policy to complement fiscal policy and create a sound, price-stability oriented macroeconomic policy framework which also allows Russia to resist Dutch Disease pressures.
- *The banking system should be made more efficient and less crisis-prone.* Making prudential supervision counter-cyclical, facilitating effective competition by allowing further consolidation of the sector and reducing the state's role as an owner of banks would be important steps to that end.

- *Product markets are overly regulated, hampering competition, innovation and productivity growth.* Pervasive state involvement should be reduced, barriers to entry eliminated and public administration reform stepped up. Russia could also benefit from lower barriers to foreign direct investment and reduced levels and dispersion of import tariffs.

ISBN 978-92-64-05433-2
OECD Economics Surveys: Russian Federation

Assessment and recommendations

The global crisis brought a sudden end to a decade of strong economic performance…

Between the financial crisis which struck Russia in August 1998 and the global crisis which broke out in earnest in September 2008, the country had the strongest decade of growth in its history, with real GDP nearly doubling. This strong increase in output, coupled with the vigorous real appreciation of the rouble, driven mainly by the surge in energy and raw material prices, meant that nominal GDP measured in US dollars rose almost 7-fold during that period, more than in any other major country. A wide range of other economic and social indicators also saw dramatic improvements during those ten years. Total factor productivity grew strongly, real wages soared, and unemployment and poverty rates fell sharply. Strong current account surpluses, combined with a swing in the private capital account from large net outflows to even larger net inflows, pushed international reserves to nearly USD 600 billion, behind only China and Japan. The transformation of the government finances was particularly marked. After defaulting on part of its debt in 1998, the federal government ran a string of surpluses and almost extinguished public debt while building up foreign assets amounting to 13% of GDP by end-2008. The picture for inflation was more mixed, but for most of the past decade inflation was on a trend decline, falling from 85% in late-1998 to single digits by mid-2007. At that time, a combination of surging international food and energy prices and very rapid money supply growth in Russia pushed inflation back up to 15%, before it began to fall again in late-2008 as energy and commodity prices collapsed and money supply growth came to a sudden halt.

… which in recent years was boosted by transitory factors…

While stronger macroeconomic policies and structural reforms both contributed importantly to the good economic performance through mid-2008, a good deal of the impetus to growth came from transitory factors, as was outlined in the *2006 Economic Survey of Russia*. Initially, there was the 50% real depreciation of the rouble at the time of the 1998 crisis, which sparked a recovery driven by import substitution and facilitated by substantial underutilisation of capital, allowing rapid growth to occur without high rates of investment. Then, both during 1999-2000 and to an even greater extent from 2003 to mid-2008, the terms of trade improved sharply, driven mainly by a rising oil price. The loosening of conditions in international capital markets, with declining spreads for emerging market borrowers and rising net inflows combined with low interest rates in advanced countries, gave a further impulse to the strong increase in domestic demand in Russia.

... so that the quality and sustainability of growth were already in question before the global crisis hit Russia

The contribution of transitory factors to growth in recent years increasingly raised questions about the sustainability of the expansion, particularly as some of the favourable factors (such as oil prices and the compression of borrowing spreads for emerging markets) exceeded or approached record levels. Although investment grew robustly, it remained low in relation to GDP compared with other rapidly catching-up economies, and the economy began to show signs of overheating as capacity utilisation rates rose and labour shortages emerged. Real GDP growth was increasingly driven by booming domestic demand, while the balance of payments and the government budget both became increasingly reliant on oil, with non-oil current account and fiscal deficits rising steadily. There is wide agreement, including within the government, that a shift to a new more self-sustaining growth model is needed. The government's Russia 2020 growth strategy, which aims for innovation-driven growth and reduced reliance on the production of raw materials, was developed in 2008 while oil prices were still high and rising, but the crisis struck before that strategy could even begin to be translated into concrete policy actions. It is therefore important to return to the structural reform agenda both within the context of anti-crisis measures and beyond.

The origin of the crisis was multifaceted...

The continuation of rapid growth had certainly become increasingly vulnerable to a decline in oil and gas prices, but a normal oil price downturn would probably have been consistent with merely a growth slowdown rather than the severe recession which is now under way. The size and speed of the decline in oil prices that began in July 2008 were greater than any previous episode, and the effects were exacerbated by similarly extreme falls in the prices of other export commodities. Financial turmoil, including the disruption of emerging market access to international capital markets, was also exceptionally severe. At the same time, world demand collapsed in the last quarter of 2008, dramatically shrinking world trade, which hit the volume as well as the price of Russian exports of metals and natural gas. The impact of these external shocks on the Russian economy was aggravated by domestic vulnerabilities, including fragile confidence in domestic banks and the currency.

... and a broad-based response is needed

The strategy for Russia in tackling such a big economic crisis needs to be broad-based, including a range of fiscal and monetary policy measures to support aggregate demand and maintain the functioning of the banking system. As in other countries, policymakers in Russia should seek measures that maximise the immediate demand effect; minimize distortions; protect macroeconomic stability and fiscal sustainability *via* a clear exit strategy from stimulus measures; and, where possible, yield longer-term efficiency gains while achieving short-term demand management goals. Designing a response that best conforms to these principles, including finding the right balance where there are trade-offs between them, is the overarching near-term policy challenge.

The policy response was immediate and vigorous

The authorities' reaction to the onset of the crisis was broadly in line with that of many OECD economies, although the response in Russia was unusually rapid and large, reflecting in part the substantial resources available to the authorities after years of fiscal and balance of payments surpluses. Liquidity and capital were provided to the banking system, deposit insurance limits were increased, and a number of expansionary fiscal measures were announced. All told, quantifiable announcements in the first months of the crisis were equivalent to about 13% of GDP. These measures were initially thought to be more than adequate to address the consequences for Russia of the global financial crisis, but it has become increasingly clear that Russia is facing a deeper and longer downturn than was imagined a few months ago. As the stock of available resources has dwindled while the cost of some initial measures has risen (notably the combination of limiting depreciation of the rouble while providing ample liquidity to banks) new measures are being more carefully weighed, especially with respect to possible risks to fiscal sustainability.

Maintaining the functioning of the banking system will be critical

Demand-support measures will be less effective to the extent that the financial system is not operating smoothly. This implies that maintaining the functioning of the banking system is of prime importance. While liquidity shortages did trigger turmoil at the onset of the global crisis, the main threat to credit growth now appears to be solvency problems, arising from the declining capacity of borrowers to repay bank loans. Banks risk breaching regulatory capital requirements if, as expected, the downturn brings an upsurge in non-performing loans. Such capital shortages can force deleveraging as banks shrink their balance sheets to meet capital adequacy requirements. Banks may also be unwilling to lend as credit risks on new lending rise in an environment of negative real GDP growth both domestically and abroad. The challenge is to maintain capital adequacy and prevent a sharp curtailing of lending flows financing new activities, while minimising moral hazard and the cost to taxpayers.

Monetary policy should become counter-cyclical

Just as monetary conditions during the period of strengthening oil prices were too easy, as balance of payments strength fed through to money supply growth *via* the central bank's exchange rate-oriented monetary policy, so they risk becoming too tight in a context of falling oil prices and capital outflows. Intervention to support the rouble in the months following the onset of the crisis meant sharply falling reserves, and this was accompanied by a large fall in M2 since September 2008. Real interest rates are becoming positive for the first time in years just as aggregate demand is collapsing due to adverse external shocks. In addition, the resistance to depreciation delayed a compensatory stimulus for non-oil tradable when the oil price fell. The stepwise widening of the exchange rate band allowed some breathing space for firms with heavy foreign currency liabilities and possibly prevented a sharper weakening of confidence in the rouble and, thus, a run on deposits. But the costs were heavy, as expectations of further depreciation encouraged capital flight. The central bank's communication policy should foster the recognition that the real exchange rate eventually has to move in line with large swings in fundamentals such as oil prices. This episode revealed the weakness in the monetary policy framework and illustrated that holding to a fixed exchange rate or managing a float for an extended period is difficult, as serious conflicts with fundamentals are likely to arise sooner or later, particularly in a commodity-dependent economy.

Fiscal stimulus should be aggressive, but cast in a medium-term framework that safeguards sustainability

The main short-term challenge for fiscal policy is to maximise the fiscal multiplier while managing moral hazard and risks to long-term fiscal sustainability. *The former tends to suggest expenditure measures, possibly in the form of transfers to low-income households or lower levels of government, rather than general tax cuts.* Temporary measures, such as one-off transfers or temporary tax rebates, can be one effective way of maximising the short-term demand impact. Measures that are hard to reverse, such as raising entitlements or cutting tax rates, could undermine long-term sustainability. The current crisis is increasingly looking like a more extended downturn than originally foreseen, which may make infrastructure spending more attractive than otherwise, particularly since there is evidence that the fiscal multiplier is highest for such spending. The threat to fiscal sustainability would appear to be less of a problem in Russia than in many OECD countries, given low levels of gross public debt and substantial public financial assets. Nonetheless, the federal deficit will be very large in 2009, and could remain at high levels for several years. Moreover, Russia faces underlying negative demographic trends and particularly serious environmental degradation problems, which could entail major fiscal costs in the future. As in other countries, therefore, *it will be important for Russia to set its stimulus efforts in a medium-term context and credibly chart a return to a sustainable public debt path.*

Looking beyond the crisis, Russia needs to find a better growth model

At some point the crisis will end, and oil prices will probably recover sooner rather than later. In the medium term, Russia will face the challenge of putting in place a healthier model for sustained catch-up growth. This should be one based on innovation, investment, the accumulation of human capital and coherent implementation of the rule of law within a well regulated and competition-enhancing market economy, rather than one largely driven by strong but temporary improvements in the terms of trade and the increasing reliance on state corporations with inadequate governance structures as well as *ad hoc* support of selected banks and corporations. To this end, there is considerable scope for major progress in a wide range of areas. For example, education performance is mediocre; the healthcare system is deficient in a number of respects; innovation policy does not get the most from Russia's considerable potential; administrative reform is needed to improve the efficiency of the public service; and some important prices, notably for natural gas, remain distorted, making the economy more energy-intensive than it should be. Many of these topics have been addressed in past *Economic Surveys*, and much of that earlier analysis remains valid. Particular challenges discussed in this *Survey* include macroeconomic management, including the priorities for monetary and fiscal policy, the development of the banking system, and product market regulation reforms to widen the scope for competition.

A switch to inflation targeting would free monetary policy of tensions between different objectives

The central bank's welcome intention to shift over time to an inflation-targeting regime would address the tensions which have beset monetary policy in recent years. Inflation targeting has proved a successful framework for a wide range of countries, including those with a high degree of commodity dependence. Also, it has often worked well even when some factors, advanced as pre-conditions for making the transition to inflation targeting, have not been fulfilled. Nonetheless, there is a good case in Russia for taking a gradual approach to such a transition, as certain important conditions, some of which go beyond technical preparations on the part of the central bank, requiring political support, remain unfulfilled. Too little is yet known about the ability to forecast inflation and the response of inflation to changes in policy interest rates. To that end, *the Central Bank of Russia's recently introduced inflation reports, which are a welcome innovation, should be improved to become less descriptive and more analytical.* Also, inflation targeting would undoubtedly work better if Russia had deeper financial markets and greater central bank independence. *The unexpected return to budget deficits should be used to issue more domestic government debt, providing banks with more paper for refinancing and establishing a benchmark for the financial sector.*

Fiscal policy should be the main instrument for managing the real exchange rate effects of oil price fluctuations

Reorienting monetary policy to achieving inflation objectives implies that insulating the economy from large fluctuations in oil prices will largely fall to fiscal policy, especially as regards the mechanisms for taxing and saving oil. During the recent period of high oil prices reserves amounting to about 13% of GDP were accumulated in two funds, one to smooth oil-price-dependent revenue fluctuations and the other to provide for a stream of income to boost long-term national welfare. *In periods of oil price weakness, allowing the lower prices to be reflected in larger non-oil deficits financed by running down the Reserve Fund will offset part of the pressure for depreciation. Using fiscal policy to lean against real exchange rate pressures arising from oil price swings helps to insulate the non-oil economy from such swings and is welcome.*

The tax structure should be improved to enhance growth

Russia has made major improvements to the structure of its taxation and to tax collection. Tax bases have been broadened, rates cut, and compliance improved. Nonetheless, scope remains for further reform that could speed up convergence to advanced country income levels. *Oil and gas taxation should be adjusted to capture economic rents without unduly harming incentives for exploration and development. In particular, export taxes on crude oil and oil products should be removed in the medium term, and tax rates harmonised to achieve a better balance between the taxation of economic rents from oil and those derived from other non-renewable natural resources, including natural gas. The government should address problems with VAT refunds directly, rather than bow to demands to cut rates, given that VAT is a relatively efficient tax. Russia has scope to increase the revenue share of property taxes, which OECD research suggests is the least growth-unfriendly form of taxation*. Corporate profit tax, which is found to be particularly harmful for growth performance, is already at low levels after the most recent cut to 20% but, subject to satisfactory overall revenue collection, further reductions should not be ruled out. Economic efficiency would also suggest exploring *ways of reducing the comparatively high tax wedge, which again is relatively growth-unfriendly*. Apart from the possibility to further improve economic efficiency, considerable scope also remains to alleviate poverty, which despite some progress during the recent episode with exceptionally high growth is still far more prevalent than in OECD countries. This may require more redistribution than can be achieved at the moment with a flat tax rate for personal income, a regressive unified social tax and relatively low real estate and wealth taxation. This issue will be dealt with in the forthcoming *OECD Labour Market and Social Policy Review*.

The banking system should be made less crisis-prone…

Russia's banking sector has suffered repeated crises since the start of transition. Policy makers face two broad regulatory challenges in seeking to improve the stability of the banking system: to converge on existing best practice as regards the implementation of prudential supervision and (a challenge shared with many other countries) to address defects in bank regulation which amplify economic cycles and give insufficient weight to liquidity considerations. In the cyclical upswing Russian banks on average maintained but did not increase capital cushions above the minimum standard, and many therefore risk falling below the minimum as loan losses rise as a result of the recession, unless new capital can be found. As in OECD countries, there is a need for a more macro-prudential approach to financial supervision, which takes more account of systemic risks, in addition to focusing on bank-specific ones. *Capital requirements and/or provisioning rules should be made counter-cyclical and capital requirements should be allowed to vary across banks to reflect each bank's contribution to systemic risk. In addition, stress tests should include assessments of shocks which hit across the banking system*. There will be ongoing efforts to reform international rules to strengthen existing supervision approaches, and *Russia should actively participate in these discussions while proceeding with own reforms to bolster financial market stability*.

… and more efficient

Russia's financial system, despite its recent rapid expansion, is still relatively underdeveloped, leaving considerable scope for financial deepening to contribute to long-term growth. A number of reforms would contribute to such deepening. First, although Russia has many banks, competition overall is weak, especially at the regional level. *Consolidation of the sector would help, as this would lift more banks above a minimum efficient scale, which is necessary to contribute to effective competition. Over the long term, competition and efficiency would be improved by streamlining the state's involvement in the sector*. Here, as with state-owned enterprises in other sectors, policy goals are mixed with commercial ones, mandates are unclear, and institutions with sub-optimal corporate governance arrangements are given major roles. *Beyond being boosted by competition, banking efficiency would benefit from improvements in the rule of law, faster convergence to international financial reporting standards, and measures to lengthen the effective duration of bank liabilities (notably, repeal of the Civil Code provision that allows withdrawal of all household deposits on demand regardless of their contractual term).*

Product market regulation is overly restrictive, suggesting considerable scope for raising potential growth

The OECD's product market regulation (PMR) indicator for Russia reveals that, despite liberalisation in some areas, such regulation is, on average, highly restrictive. The overall level of regulation is significantly higher and restricts competition to a greater extent than in any OECD country – including the emerging market economies within the OECD area. All three of the high-level sub-components of the overall PMR index are high in Russia relative to comparator countries, although there is considerable regulatory heterogeneity in lower-level sub-components.

Pervasive state involvement in business is one major factor inhibiting stronger competition

Reflecting the legacy of the Soviet era as well as the backlash after the chaotic early years of transition to a new system, state control in the Russian economy is extensive, *via* both direct state ownership and control over economic activity. State-owned enterprises are found across a wide range of sectors and often occupy a dominant position in their industry. Furthermore, there is a pervasive blurring of the line between the public and private sectors, arising not only from the extensive role of state-owned enterprises but also by close ties between government (at all levels) and major private firms. One reflection of this phenomenon is the unusually important role of current or former politicians and senior bureaucrats in business, which gives rise to multiple, distorting and costly conflicts of interest. Recent initiatives to strengthen the obligations for politicians and senior bureaucrats to publicise their incomes and financial assets are welcome. The special-status state corporations, most of which were established recently, are exempt from some reporting and monitoring obligations. *These exemptions should be removed. Furthermore, the extent of the problems posed by the unclear governance of these institutions, which are neither under full political surveillance nor privately owned, should be carefully monitored.* The PMR indicators also signal a high level of government involvement in the private business sector. In part, this reflects a prevalence of command-and-control-type regulation. *Significant benefits in terms of economic performance could be yielded by reducing political interference in the operation of state-owned enterprises (SOEs) and private sector firms. This should include separating the activities with non-commercial policy objectives of SOEs and consolidating them to the relevant government department; improving standards of transparency and disclosure in SOEs; imposing an effective firewall between public and private professional activities to avoid conflicts of interest; disposing of golden shares in SOEs and private firms; increasing the independence and accountability of government representatives and accelerating appointments of independent and accountable directors on SOE Boards; intensifying privatisation (once SOE corporate governance has been improved); reducing the list of strategic firms and sectors; and using regulatory alternatives to command-and-control regulation and direct intervention.*

Barriers to entry could also be reduced…

Russia performs well in some regulatory areas related to barriers to entry, including regulatory and administrative opacity and the system of licensing and permits. However, the administrative burden that the government places on entrepreneurs starting a new business, whether they are corporations or sole traders, is still very high and acts as an obstacle to new entry. This could be indicative of more widespread inefficiencies in government administration and reflect ongoing difficulties in reforming the public administration, creating new regulatory institutions and implementing market-orientated forms of regulation. *Many measures could be taken to reduce barriers to entrepreneurship and increase competition, including: further public administration reform and cutting red tape; increasing the transparency and accountability of public administration; carrying out Regulatory Impact Analysis to assess significant new regulatory proposals; breaking the dependence of regional governments on a limited number of local firms for revenue raising; providing for more vigorous and uniform implementation of competition law; minimising uncertainty and the need for subjective decision making within the government administration so as to reduce corruption opportunities; and continuing work to make network industries more competitive, with stronger regulation.*

… with considerable scope for liberalising trade and foreign investment

Russia's average import tariff rate is somewhat higher than in most other middle-income countries and significantly higher than in OECD countries. Further, despite the implementation of a programme to simplify the rate structure in 2000-01, the dispersion in tariffs has actually increased since the beginning of the 2000s, indicating a less uniform structure. Lowering tariff protection and tariff dispersion to OECD levels would be both beneficial for economic performance and helpful in speeding Russia's accession to the World Trade Organisation (WTO), which has been under negotiation for more than 15 years. WTO membership would in turn exercise some leverage for making more progress with competition-enhancing reforms. As to foreign direct investment (FDI), inflows have, until recently, been robust, but barriers to foreign ownership are estimated to be high in Russia compared to OECD countries. In part, this reflects the enactment in May 2008 of the law on strategic industries, which defines 42 sectors in which control by foreign investors requires prior authorisation from a government commission. Although this law increases transparency and is less *ad hoc* than the previous regime, its sectoral coverage is broader and notification delays longer than OECD-recommended practice. The emergence of large state-controlled conglomerates with dominant market positions also acts as a barrier to FDI inflows. The scope for foreign investors to acquire equity in these conglomerates or participate in government procurement contracts in the sectors they occupy is strictly limited. Beyond explicit barriers to FDI, the overall regulatory environment in Russia is perhaps the most significant impediment to greater inflows of FDI. *The government should increase the openness and predictability of the foreign investment regime, review the list of strategic sectors and ensure a level playing-field between domestic and foreign firms with respect to government procurement and access to subsidies.*

ISBN 978-92-64-05433-2
OECD Economic Surveys: Russian Federation

Chapter 1

Stabilisation and renewed growth: key challenges

The Russian Federation enjoyed a decade of strong growth between the 1998 financial crisis and the intensification of the global economic crisis in September 2008, but has since been gripped by a severe recession. The main near-term challenge for policy-makers is to manage the consequences of the economic downturn and limit its severity and duration. Looking beyond the crisis, the overarching challenge is to put in place a sounder growth model, one driven by innovation, investment, and the accumulation of human capital. This will ultimately require reforms in many areas, but this chapter focuses on a limited number of key challenges: 1) further strengthening the macroeconomic policy framework; 2) improving the functioning of the financial system; and 3) raising the levels of competition throughout the economy via streamlined state involvement and lower barriers to entry.

The most immediate challenge for the Russian Federation is to cope with the economic and financial crisis that took hold in 2008. As in many other countries, the Russian authorities have been grappling with the question of what mix of macroeconomic and structural policies will most effectively limit the decline in demand in the near term while also favouring longer-term growth, safeguarding fiscal sustainability, and controlling inflation. Decision-making has been complicated by the speed with which the situation has been changing, with the global slowdown continuing to surprise by its severity.

Beyond the horizon of the current economic slump, Russia faces a host of economic challenges. These include sharply negative demographic trends, poor health outcomes, and adverse environmental indicators. In addition, despite the strong growth of the past decade *per capita* incomes are still a small fraction of the OECD average. Achieving a long period of strong catch-up growth would both bring the direct benefits of higher incomes and provide resources to tackle other major challenges.

The main longer-term challenge will be to create the conditions for sustained rapid growth driven by innovation, investment, and the accumulation of human capital. While the prices of oil and other commodities may again become favourable for Russia when the global recession ends, such tailwinds cannot be relied upon to achieve sustained growth. To begin with, there are some signs that Russia was increasingly running into supply constraints before the onset of the crisis, and this would probably be true again early on in the next growth phase. Also, commodity prices are likely to remain volatile, so that a growth model too closely tied to the price of oil would likely lead to repeated boom and bust cycles.

This chapter discusses recent economic performance and policies, including notably the onset of the economic crisis in late 2008 and the policy responses to date. It goes on to outline some of the main challenges facing policy makers. Creating the basis for a dynamic economy enjoying strong self-sustaining growth will require reforms across a broad front. Some of the key areas have been addressed in past *Economic Surveys* and reviews, notably innovation policies, administrative reform, healthcare, education, and reform of some key sectors still distorted by the legacy of the Soviet era. Attention to these areas remains warranted, and many past recommendations still apply. This *Survey* will address a two-pronged approach to achieve and sustain rapid trend growth:

- Establishing a sound macroeconomic policy framework, with fiscal sustainability and a monetary policy oriented to price stability as the main anchors;
- Promoting a growth-friendly microeconomic environment, with a banking system which both yields more intermediation of savings and investment and is less crisis-prone, while strengthening competition throughout the economy *via* streamlined state involvement and the easing of entry barriers *via* trade, investment, and antimonopoly policies.

OECD ECONOMIC SURVEYS: RUSSIAN FEDERATION – ISBN 978-92-64-05433-2 – © OECD 2009

The high growth rates of the past 10 years were boosted by temporary factors, as the severity of the current crisis has confirmed

The period 1999-2008 witnessed the most rapid sustained economic growth that Russia had ever experienced.[1] Real GDP advanced by an average of 7% a year and, given the gradual decline in the population, *per capita* growth was faster still (Figure 1.1). The Federal State Service for Statistics (Rosstat) measure of absolute poverty fell from 29% in 2000 to 13.4% in 2007. Initial estimates on relative poverty – measured in line with the OECD framework – indicate a smaller but still significant fall from 20% in 2000 to around 17% in 2007, although this still leaves Russia about 6 percentage points above the OECD average.[2]

Figure 1.1. **Real GDP growth**

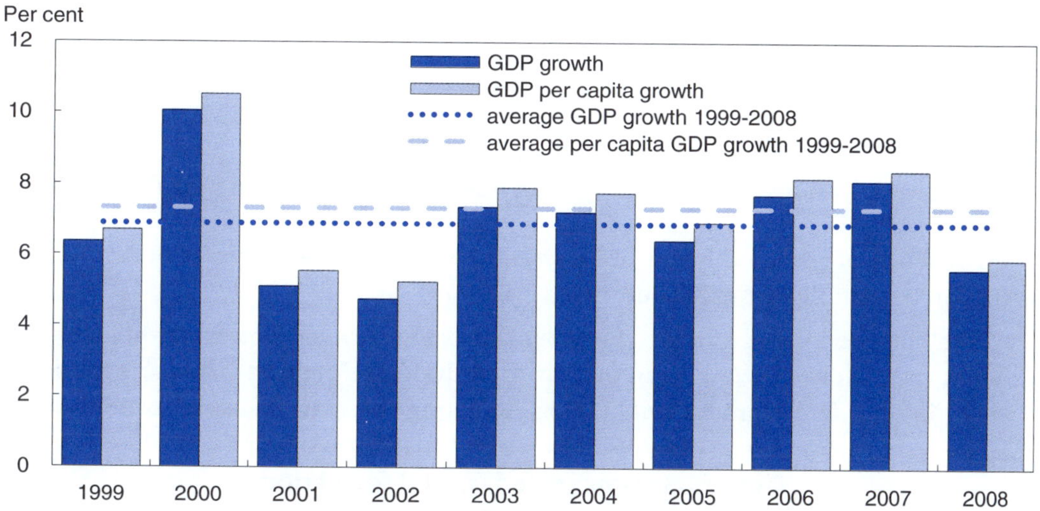

Source: OECD calculations based on Federal Service for State Statistics.

StatLink http://dx.doi.org/10.1787/648272852007

Part of this growth, of course, represented a recovery from the calamitous output performance of the 1990s. Only in 2006 did real *per capita* income reach the level attained at the end of the Soviet period. This rebound aspect of the period of strong growth was important, because the long slump of the early transition period left Russia with substantial spare capital and labour (Figure 1.2).[3] On the labour side, unemployment claimant rates were never high, but the estimated ILO-consistent measure shows the accumulation of substantial slack by the late-1990s, and this may even underestimate true unemployment as the underutilisation of labour resources at that time to some extent showed up as underemployment (one corollary of which was a high level of non-payments, including non-payment of wages).

The existence of idle resources made for relatively easy growth in the years following the 1998 crisis. In particular, the low level of capacity utilisation following the long decline of the early transition years facilitated the achievement of rapid output growth without high investment rates. Indeed, while investment did increase as a proportion of GDP over the past decade, it remained at relatively modest levels by comparison with other countries, especially those also experiencing strong growth (Figure 1.3).[4] Foreign direct investment was particularly anaemic, at least until the big inflows associated with electricity sector privatisation in 2007 and 2008 (Figure 1.4). There are also doubts about the

Figure 1.2. **Utilisation of labour and capital**

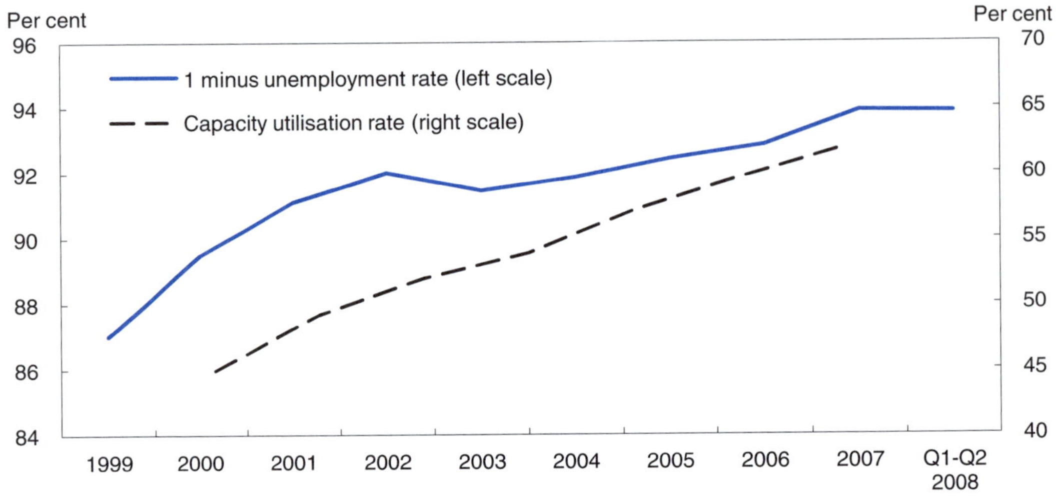

Source: OECD calculations based on Federal Service for State Statistics.

StatLink http://dx.doi.org/10.1787/648284047723

nature of much of recorded inward FDI, since much of it comes from entities in known havens for Russian flight capital, such as Cyprus.

Given only moderate growth of the capital stock and an even slower rate of increase of labour inputs, most of the strong output growth of the past decade corresponds to increases in total factor productivity (TFP).[5] Adjusting the growth decomposition for the

Figure 1.3. **Gross fixed capital formation**

As a percentage of GDP

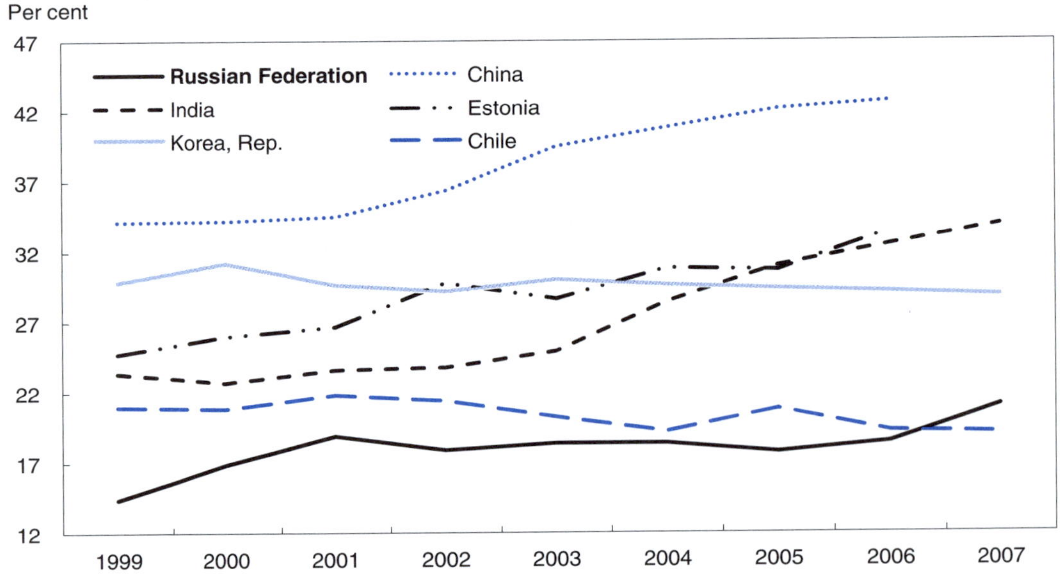

Source: World Bank, WDI database.

StatLink http://dx.doi.org/10.1787/648321030114

Figure 1.4. **FDI inflows as a percentage of GDP, average 1999-2007**

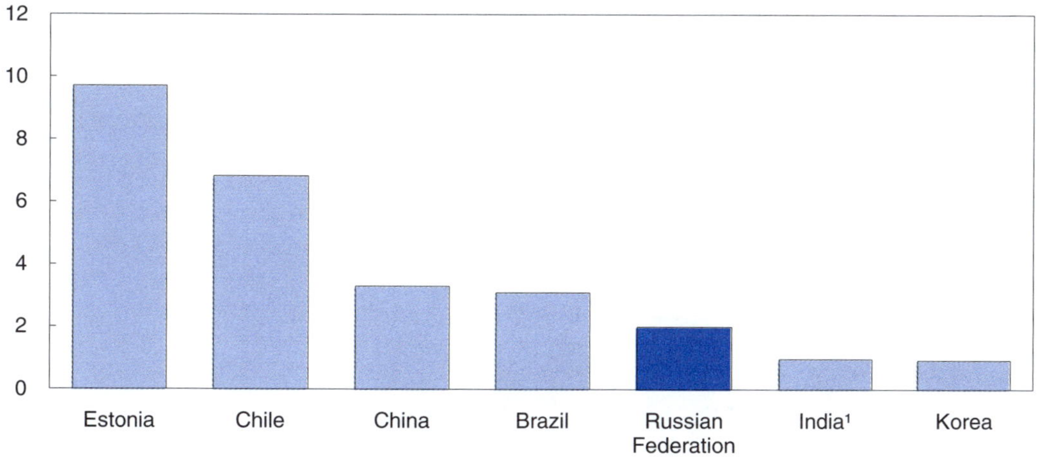

1. For India, 1999-2006.

Source: OECD calculations based on IMF, IFS database.

StatLink http://dx.doi.org/10.1787/648326411775

rate of capacity utilisation (*e.g.* Oomes and Dynnivoka, 2006) changes the picture only slightly, still leaving the bulk of output growth as being derived from TFP.

Part of the growth acceleration can be attributed to policies

The high rates of TFP growth can be partly explained by the conduct of economic policies. To begin with, the last ten years saw much greater macroeconomic stability than previously. Following the 1998 crisis, inflation fell steadily from 1999 through early 2007, before turning back up somewhat when food and other international commodity prices surged, largely in line with the experience in many other countries. Responding initially to the devaluation of the rouble in 1998 and later to the rise in export commodity prices, the current account was strong, with continuous surpluses averaging more than 10% of GDP between 1999 and 2008. In addition, the government ran a string of budget surpluses, paying down the bulk of external and domestic public debt (Figure 1.5). Russia's sovereign credit ratings were upgraded 7 times from 2000 before the onset of the latest crisis.[6] Not only was fiscal policy relatively prudent, but it was bolstered by a number of structural reforms, such as improvements in the budgeting process, including the introduction of multi-year budgeting.

Another significant cause of the strengthening of productivity growth was the improvement in the business environment, following a series of reforms, some of which were undertaken in the 1990s. Important areas included tax policy, banking and antimonopoly regulation, and bankruptcy legislation. In addition, the improvement in public finances and the long period of strong economic growth permitted major increases in funding for infrastructure, education, health, and research and development.

Improvements in the terms of trade were another positive growth factor

While policy actions played a role in the productivity growth turnaround after 1998, another important factor, especially in the last few years, was the sustained surge in commodity prices, and especially the price of oil. Russia's terms of trade improved by one half between 2003 and 2008, and as a result command GDP grew even more rapidly than output, averaging 11% a year (Figure 1.6).[7] The soaring purchasing power of

Figure 1.5. **Public debt**

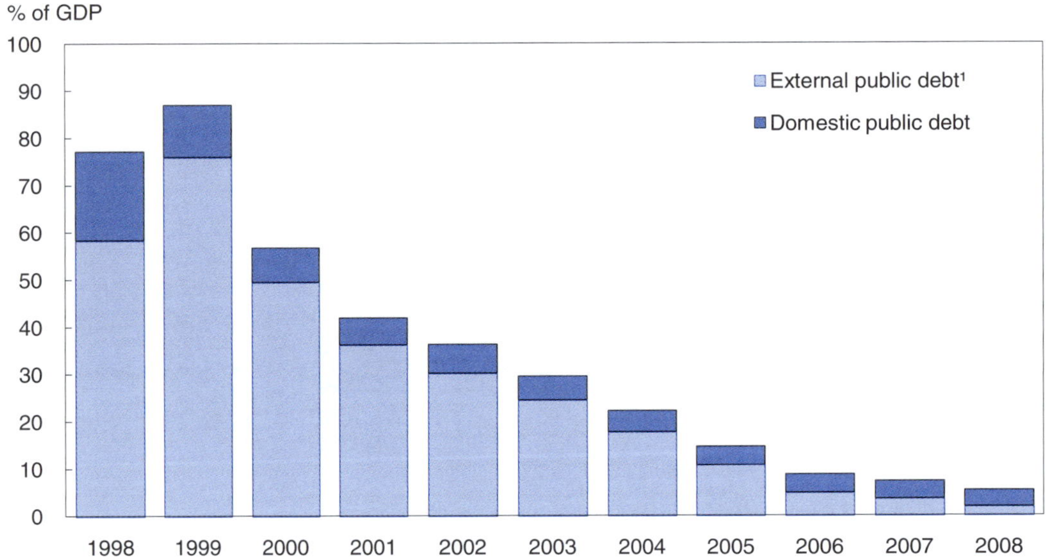

1. Liabilities of the general government and monetary authorities.

Source: OECD calculations based on Ministry of Finance of the Russian Federation and Central Bank of Russia.

StatLink http://dx.doi.org/10.1787/648350520038

commodity export goods was a key driver of domestic demand growth. This was visible in the regional distribution of growth: Moscow (site of the headquarters for most of the major commodity-producing corporations) and the resource-producing regions tended to have the highest growth rates during the period of strengthening commodity prices.

A development which was related to and reinforced the terms of trade improvement was the favourable global financial and macroeconomic environment which prevailed for most of the past decade. During that period, emerging market economies' access to international capital markets was on an uptrend, with falling advanced country interest rates and spreads on emerging market Eurobonds and rising capital inflows (Figure 1.7). For

Figure 1.6. **Command GDP**

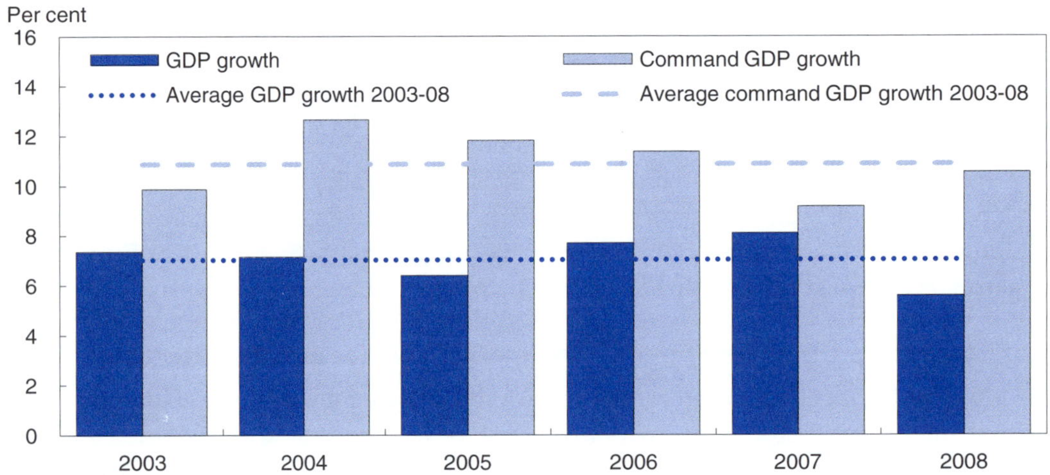

Source: OECD calculations based on Federal Service for State Statistics.

StatLink http://dx.doi.org/10.1787/648355624523

Figure 1.7. **Appetite for emerging market assets, 2000-07**

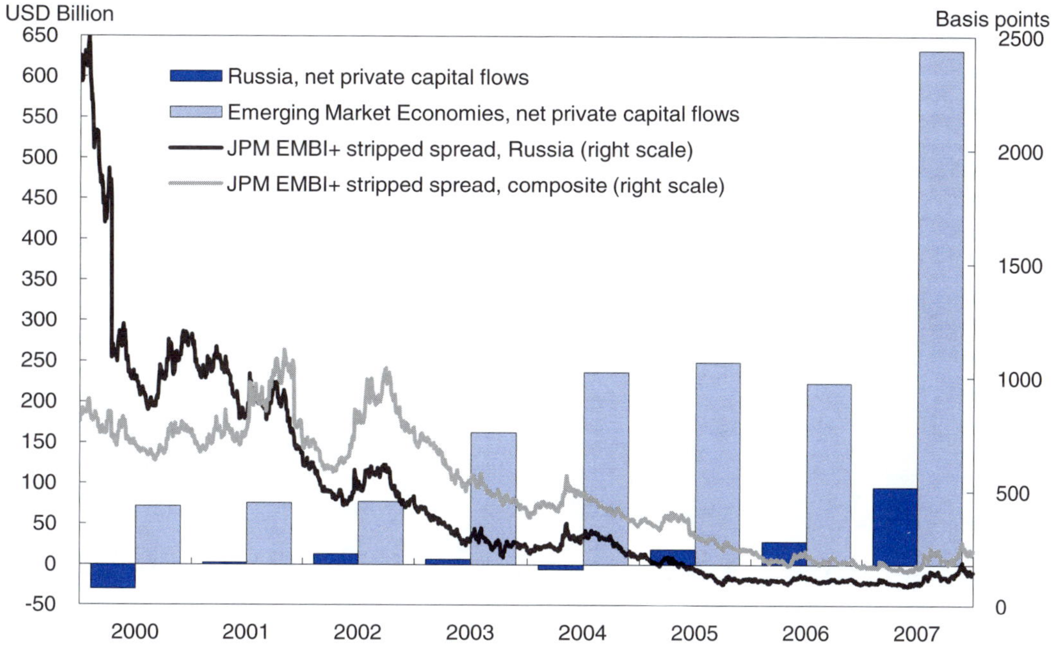

Source: Datastream, WEO October 2008.

StatLink http://dx.doi.org/10.1787/648376437344

Russia the fall in interest costs between 1999 and 2007 was considerable. Also, the strength of global economic growth during the past 5 years boosted demand for Russian exports.

The role in Russia's growth dynamics of improving terms of trade and increasingly favourable international capital market conditions was also reflected in the sectoral composition of growth. The most dynamic growth was registered in non-tradable sectors such as construction, finance, and wholesale and retail trade. Growth of tradable goods sectors overall lagged well behind, with especially slow growth in mining and agriculture. Although manufacturing was put under pressure by the sustained appreciation of the rouble in real effective terms, output growth in this sector was only slightly below the rate of overall GDP growth, reflecting in part the strong domestic demand for goods related to the real estate boom, such as construction materials and furniture.

The underdevelopment of the banking sector, which might otherwise have held back growth, proved not to be a binding constraint. Firms' strong cashflow allowed them to meet the bulk of their (relatively limited) investment needs out of retained earnings, rather than relying on loans from domestic banks (Figure 1.8). In addition, the favourable dynamics in international capital markets permitted Russian firms to borrow abroad, which they did to a significant and increasing degree, especially when nominal appreciation of the rouble against the dollar meant that the rouble cost of dollar loans averaged only about 1% between 2003 and mid-2007, and was often negative in nominal terms, while Russia's nominal GDP was growing at about 20% a year (Figure 1.9).[8]

The quality and resilience of growth were called into question well before the onset of the crisis

The importance of the terms of trade and a favourable international environment more generally for sustaining fast growth in recent years always raised questions about the

Figure 1.8. **Decomposition of financing of corporate investment**

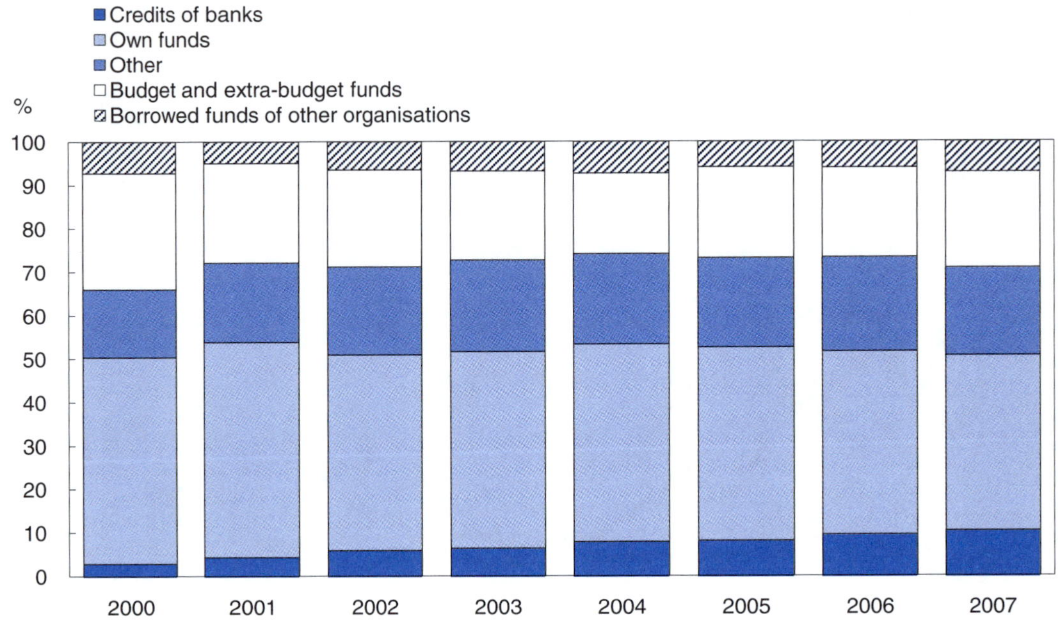

Source: Federal Service for State Statistics.

StatLink http://dx.doi.org/10.1787/648385488621

Figure 1.9. **Implied rouble cost of dollar borrowing**

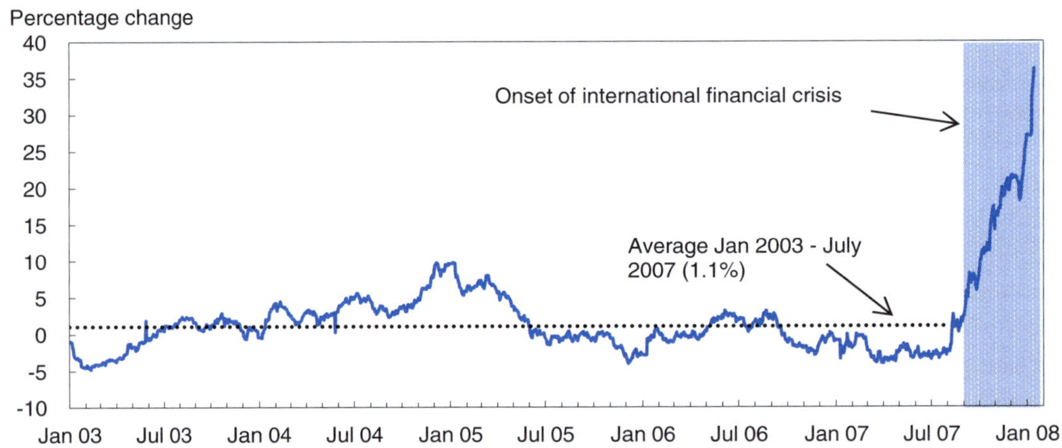

Source: Datastream, Central Bank of Russia, OECD calculations.

StatLink http://dx.doi.org/10.1787/648422232566

resilience of the expansion. By mid-2008, oil prices (and a number of other commodity prices) were at all-time records in real terms. Similarly, spreads on emerging market assets hit record lows in 2007, before the first wave of the global credit crunch struck. This combined with very low interest rates in the United States and (to a lesser extent) Europe meant that costs for Russian foreign currency borrowers were at unprecedentedly low levels. Meanwhile, world economic and trade growth was at or near its highest ever levels between 2005 and 2007. While calling turning points is always difficult, this extraordinarily favourable environment was unlikely to be sustained.

Moreover, by 2007 there were increasing signs of incipient imbalances and dangers. One such sign was the rapidly rising foreign borrowing by Russian banks and enterprises. Unlike a number of other eastern European countries, and some other emerging economies, the levels of foreign borrowing by Russian corporates did not look particularly dangerous, but the growth rates in 2006-07 were spectacular, giving rise to concerns about the increase in firms' foreign currency debt exposures (Figure 1.10).

Figure 1.10. **Long-term external debt of private sector borrowers as a percentage of GDP**

2007

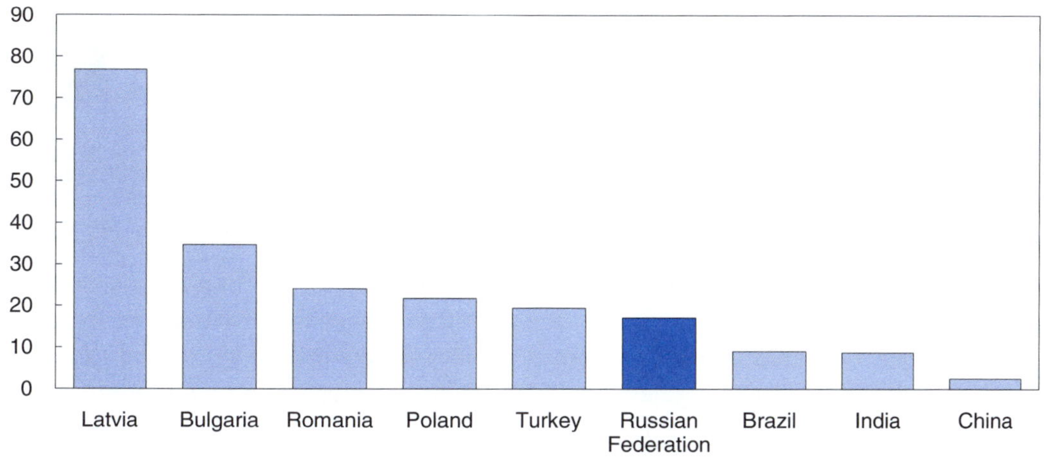

Source: OECD calculations based on World Bank GDF database.

StatLink http://dx.doi.org/10.1787/648454170476

The emergence of a real estate bubble in Moscow and St. Petersburg was another sign of growing imbalances. Although Russia is ranked only about 50th in *per capita* incomes, by 2008 Moscow had been identified as the most expensive city in the world for expatriate employees for the 3rd year in a row (Mercer 2008), due largely to runaway real estate prices.[9] Unsurprisingly, investment in construction and real estate boomed, although, as with foreign borrowing, the levels were not yet high in international terms.

Very high growth rates of bank lending, especially to households, constituted yet another factor warning of the increasing danger of financial imbalances. Bank lending to individuals grew at an average annual rate of 92% between 2003 and 2007, albeit from very low levels. Mortgage lending grew particularly rapidly, although again from a negligible base level by international standards. Taken together, these signals gave a worrying picture of the speed of increase of lending and asset prices. A sudden reversal was clearly becoming increasingly possible, although the still relatively modest levels of most indicators suggests that such a reversal was far from inevitable, and that the costs of such a reversal were still limited. The onset of the crisis in September 2008 was not an unavoidable consequence of financial excess in Russia. Rather, the financial turmoil and the plunge in oil prices represented a genuinely external shock, albeit one whose effects were accentuated by vulnerabilities in the Russian economy, including the emergence of asset price bubbles and unchecked debt accumulation by some sectors. One reflection of these growing imbalances was the deterioration of the non-oil trade balance, which clearly indicates the growing vulnerability of the current account to a downturn in oil prices (Figure 1.11).

Figure 1.11. **Non-oil-and-gas trade balance**

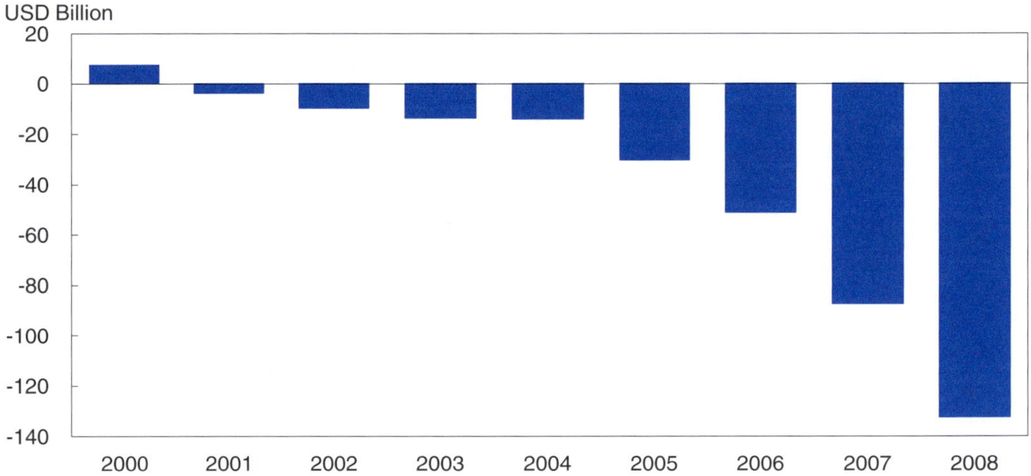

Source: OECD calculations based on Central Bank of Russia.

StatLink http://dx.doi.org/10.1787/648510108818

There were also growing questions about the quality of growth. Across a range of indicators of the business environment, Russia either stagnated or worsened in recent years. The country's ranking in international surveys of corruption, which had improved markedly from the late 1990s to the early years of this decade, began to deteriorate again. Progress towards the adoption of international accounting standards was relatively slow, and the perception of growing state involvement in business, especially in a number of key sectors designated as strategic by the authorities, was reinforced by the adoption of the law on strategic industries in 2008 (Box 5.3).[10] In addition, reform of the important gas sector stalled, and progress towards establishing a functioning market for agricultural land was slow.

The *2006 OECD Economic Survey* warned that pursuing the reforms needed to facilitate the transition to a period of sustained growth driven by investment and innovation was the main challenge facing policy-makers. For the most part, that challenge was not taken up while external conditions were favourable, and the chance to achieve an improvement in the quality of growth was missed. The growth model through mid-2008 therefore remained broadly the same as in the preceding few years: domestic demand growth continued to accelerate in response to improving terms of trade. This pattern was interrupted by the effects of the global financial crisis, especially after its sudden intensification in September 2008. The scale of the shock has meant that the Russian authorities do not now have the luxury of striving for a smooth transition from strong growth fuelled by improving terms of trade to strong growth supported by high levels of investment and innovation. Growth stopped dead and then reversed in the matter of a month or so, and, like much of the rest of the world, by late 2008 Russia found itself in the midst of a deep recession.

The main short-term challenge is minimising the extent of the economic downturn while safeguarding macroeconomic stability and fiscal sustainability

As recently as mid-2008 Russia's growth momentum was largely unchecked and the main near-term danger for Russia appeared to be the risk of overheating. From around that time, however, a series of (inter-related) shocks hit the Russian economy, all of which had the effect of weakening demand.

A number of adverse shocks have weakened demand

The deterioration in the international appetite for risk in general translated into worsened sentiment towards emerging market assets and resulted in a *de facto* interruption of access to international capital markets for most Russian borrowers. Although the upturn in borrowing spreads and the turnaround in net capital flows were seen across most emerging market economies (Figure 1.12), some Russia-specific factors contributed to the greater-than-average extent of the shift in Russia's case. These included well-reported cases of perceived government interference in business (*e.g.* in the dispute between the Russian and foreign shareholders of TNK-BP, and the metals and mining conglomerate Mechel) and the conflict with Georgia in August 2008. With Russian banks and enterprises having large external debt repayments to make in the second half of 2008, this interruption of access to international bank lending and bond markets was reflected in a big swing in net capital flows. Net private capital flows worsened by roughly USD 200 billion, or some 13% of GDP, between 2007 and 2008, with most of the deterioration occurring in the second half of 2008 (Table 1.1).

The steep decline in oil prices after the peak achieved in July 2008 was unprecedented: by December 2008 they had fallen by three quarters and despite a significant recovery so far this year, average prices in the first five months of 2009 were still only about half the average in 2008 (Figure 1.13). Gas prices only peaked in early 2009, but have been falling steeply in recent months, as most of Russia's export contracts are based on a price formula that links the gas price to the spot price of oil products with a lag of 6-9 months. Oil prices have an impact on the Russian economy that goes well beyond the contribution of the sector to GDP, especially given that price elasticities of supply are small. Oil and gas

Figure 1.12. **Worsening conditions on international capital markets for emerging markets**

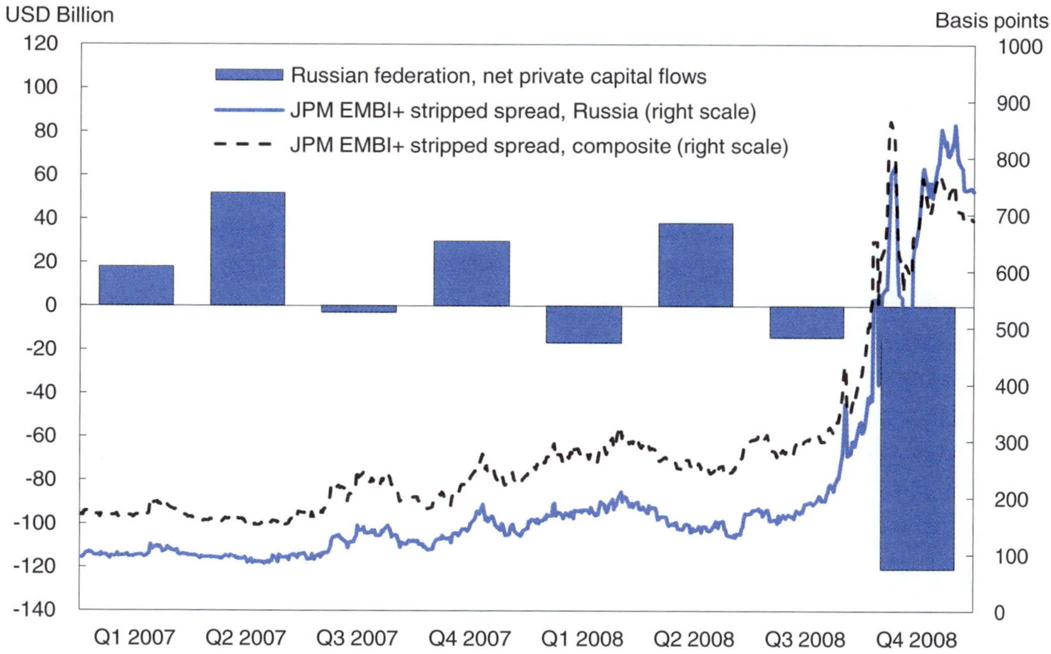

Source: Datastream and Central Bank of Russia.

StatLink http://dx.doi.org/10.1787/648532020825

Table 1.1. **Net private capital flows**

	2007				2008			
	Q1	Q2	Q3	Q4	Q1	Q2	Q3	Q4
Net private capital flows (USD billion)	13.9	54.5	–7.0	21.7	–23.1	41.1	–17.4	–139.1
Of which:								
Direct Investment	12.1	–10.0	0.3	6.9	4.0	6.5	5.4	–4.8
Portfolio investment	–4.8	4.8	–5.0	6.0	–3.6	6.1	–7.2	–7.5
Other (including errors and omissions)	6.7	59.8	–2.3	8.7	–23.5	28.3	–15.6	–129.5

Source: OECD calculations based on Central bank of Russia.

Figure 1.13. **Major intra-year declines in oil prices**

Brent oil price, maximum decline within year

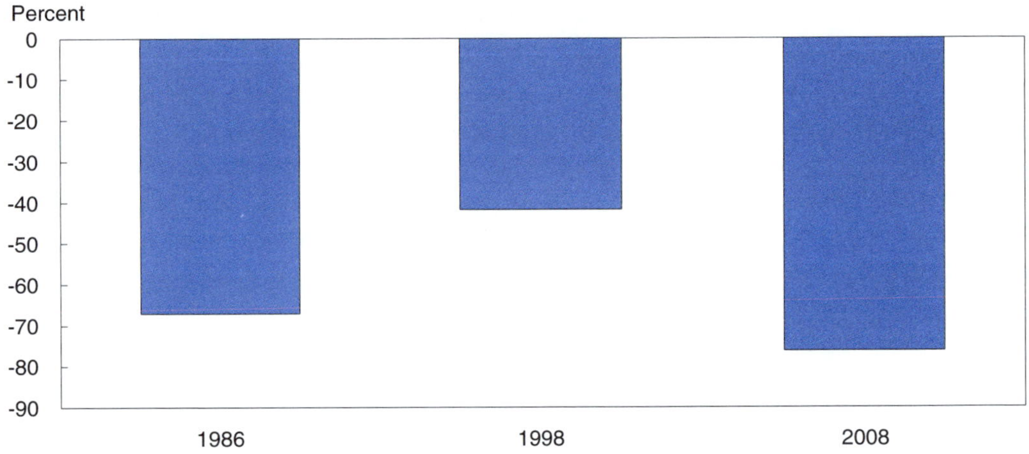

Source: OECD calculations based on Datastream.

StatLink http://dx.doi.org/10.1787/648544635812

represent about two thirds of Russia's exports, and generate roughly half of government revenue. Moreover, this sector was a major source of domestic demand growth during the period of rising energy prices.

Falling oil prices were part of a broader retreat of commodity prices. Other export commodities whose prices followed a similar pattern to oil included base and precious metals, coal, and lumber (Figure 1.14). Together, these non-oil and non-gas commodities account for roughly 15% of exports.

The deceleration of bank lending, which began in mid-2007, also depressed domestic demand. Annual bank lending growth had already slowed significantly through June 2008, before the global financial crisis began in earnest. This largely reflected a sharp slowdown in lending growth on the part of some medium-sized banks which had borrowed abroad to fund consumer loans, mortgage and real estate loans, but which found their access to foreign capital drying up as a result of the international credit crunch. By October 2008, however, bank lending was falling, and it continued to do so in seasonally adjusted terms throughout the final quarter of the year. This reflected not only a further worsening of international borrowing conditions, but also the seizing up of the domestic interbank market in September 2008 and, increasingly, a reassessment by Russian banks of credit risk as the onset of recession became apparent.

Figure 1.14. **Non-oil commodity prices**

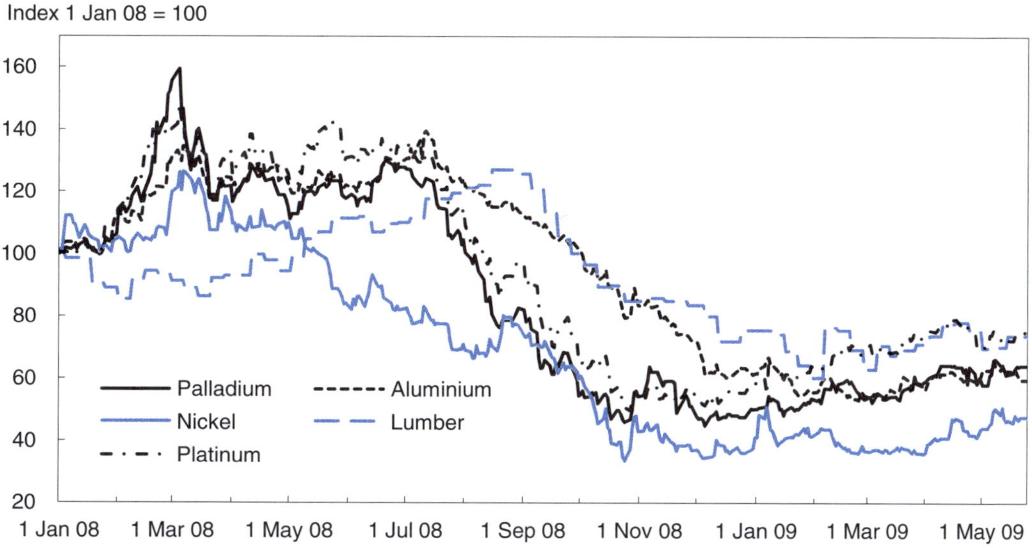

Source: OECD calculations based on Datastream.

StatLink http://dx.doi.org/10.1787/648632140322

Yet another demand-reducing shock was the collapse of the domestic stock market. To a large extent, this was not an independent shock, but was related to the oil price: the bulk of the earnings of the RTS comes from oil and gas companies, and the correlation of stock prices to the oil price is marked (Figure 1.15). Nonetheless, an aggravating factor appears to have been the need for highly-leveraged shareholders who were using stock holdings as collateral for loans to meet margin calls. This provoked more selling and created a vicious circle of falling prices and forced sales.

The last of the external shocks to hit the Russian economy in 2008 was the sudden drop in international demand. An initial sign of this was the sharp decline in industrial production in the Ukraine in October, largely as a result of a sudden collapse in global demand for metal products. Subsequently, similarly dramatic falls in exports to a number of Asian countries, including China, Japan, and Korea, were seen in November and December. Overall, the world economy experienced an exceptionally sharp drop in output and trade in the fourth quarter of 2008. This was reflected in Russia's trade flows, with exports and imports falling in seasonally adjusted terms between September and December (Figure 1.16).

The impact on growth was severe

The result of the succession of (interrelated) shocks was a startling deceleration in economic activity, greater than for most other major economies (Figure 1.17). Seasonally adjusted industrial production fell by over 10% in November alone, and by nearly 18% between September 2008 and January 2009. The manufacturing component of industrial production was particularly weak, declining by about 30% in the four months through January. A wide range of other monthly indicators confirmed the dramatic slowdown of economic activity beginning in November (Figure 1.18). The extent of the downturn in the last quarter of 2008 and the first quarter of 2009 ensures that real GDP growth in 2009 will

Figure 1.15. **The oil price and equity prices**

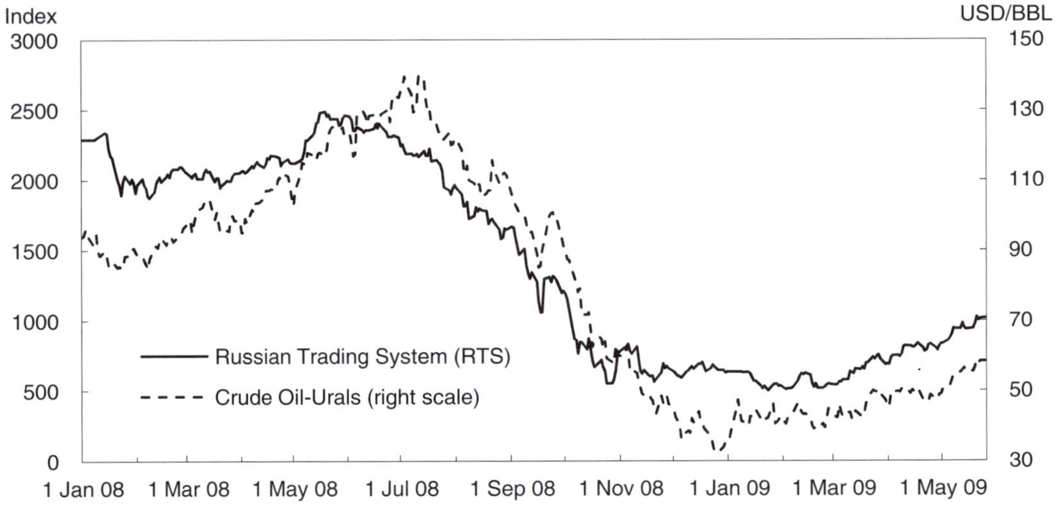

Source: Datastream.

StatLink http://dx.doi.org/10.1787/648665584183

Figure 1.16. **Merchandise exports and imports**

Seasonally adjusted, fob

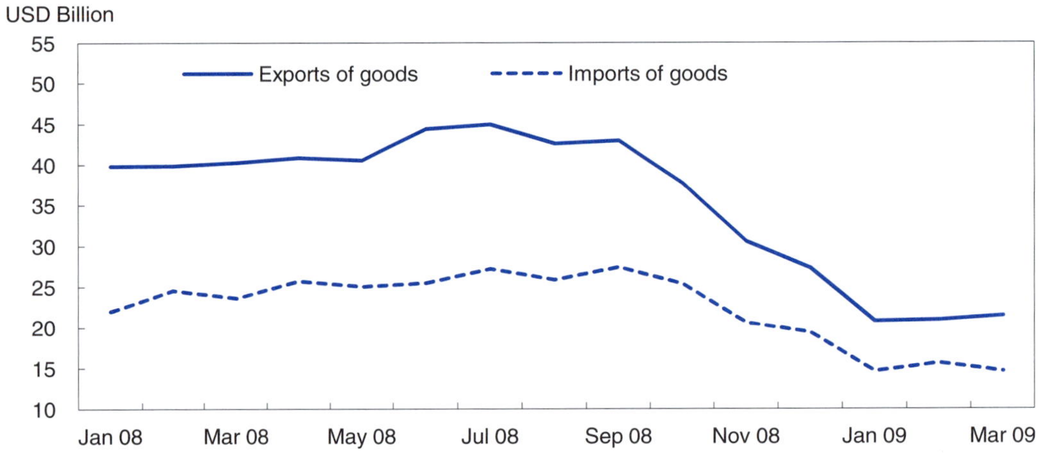

Source: OECD calculations based on Central Bank of Russia.

StatLink http://dx.doi.org/10.1787/648670377550

be sharply negative, although the rebound in oil prices, combined with substantial policy stimulus, should deliver some recovery in the second half of 2009 and 2010 (Box 1.1).

The reaction of the labour market signals structural changes in the economy

During the long downturn of the 1990s, culminating in the 1998 crisis, an important coping mechanism of Russian employers was to stop paying workers. However, the current crisis appears to signal a significant change in the environment for Russian employers. So far, wage arrears are increasing, but from a very low level. On the other hand employers are adjusting labour input to the level of activity more quickly than before. After reductions in job protection employers find it more attractive to terminate work contracts than to delay wage payments. Surveys report that fewer and fewer employers report legal obstacles to

Figure 1.17. **Change in seasonally adjusted quarterly GDP growth between Q3 and Q4 2008**

Percentage points

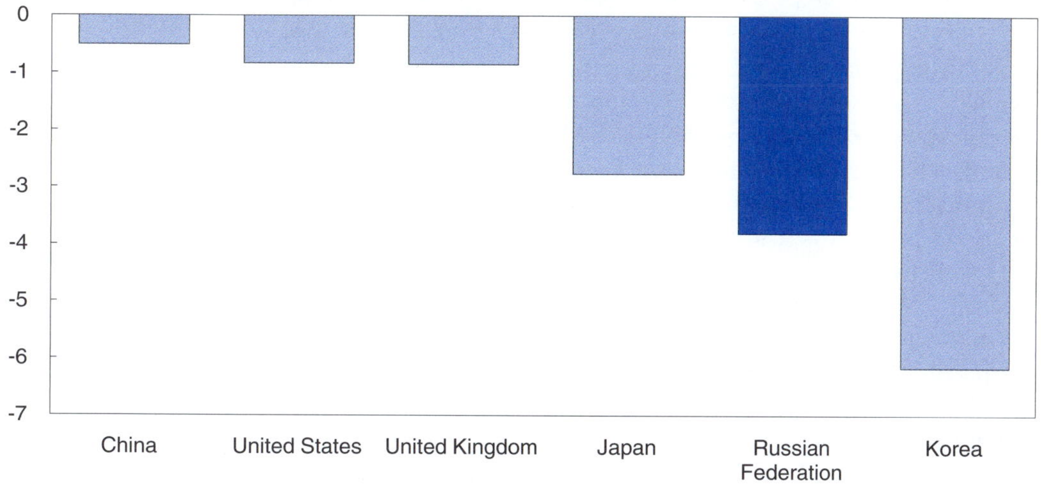

Source: OECD Quarterly National Accounts and Russian Ministry of Economic Development, and OECD estimates.

StatLink http://dx.doi.org/10.1787/648676751657

Figure 1.18. **Economic activity indicators**

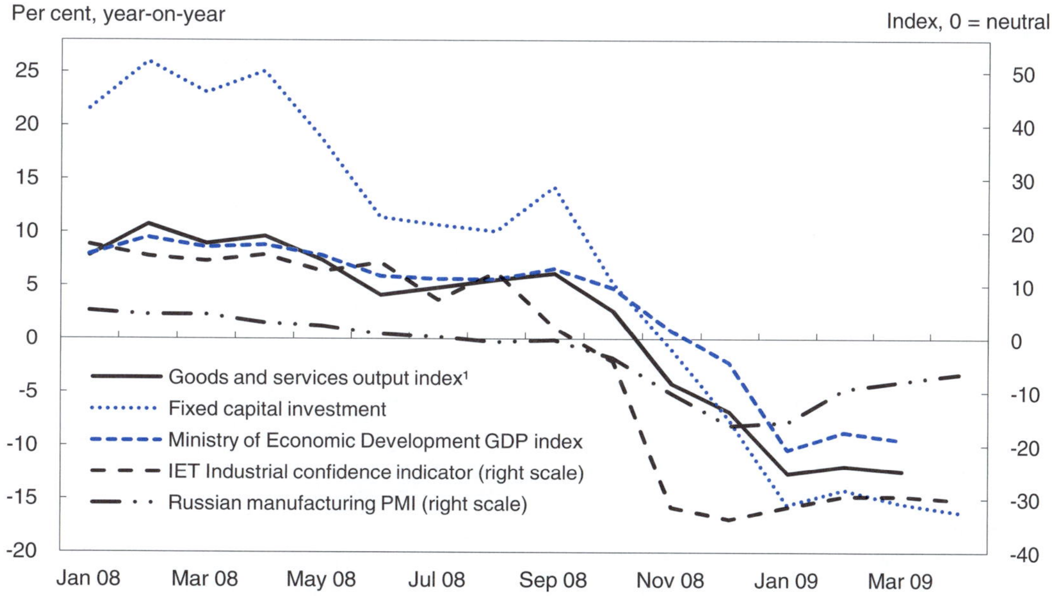

1. Estimated on the basis of data on change of physical volume of production in agriculture, mining and quarrying, manufacturing, electricity, gas and water supply, construction, transportation, wholesale and retail trade.

Source: Federal Service for State Statistics, Institute for the Economy in Transition, Ministry of Economic Development and VTB Europe.

terminating work contracts. The first waves of layoffs have already hit construction and financial services. Many companies are reported to have reduced the number of paid work hours. Open unemployment has risen sharply and the importance of non-standard (fixed term, short hours, on leave) labour contracts is increasing. In December 2008, 900 000 workers worked short hours or were on forced vacations.

Box 1.1. **Macroeconomic projections for 2009-10**

Russia is suffering a severe recession, but the rebound in commodity prices and the expected effects of policy stimulus point to some recovery through 2009 and into 2010.

Reflecting extreme weakness in the first few months of the year, growth for 2009 as a whole will be sharply negative, but output declines may end as early as the second quarter, and positive growth is expected to continue through 2010. The recent surge in oil prices changes the near-term outlook for the Russian economy significantly. Stronger current account inflows help maintain international reserves and the value of the rouble, which tends to improve sentiment towards rouble assets. Less negative (and perhaps again positive) net private capital flows lessen one major source of weakness in domestic demand, raising the probability of a resumption of growth. International capital market conditions are less important than oil prices, but nevertheless affect domestic demand. To the extent that a recovery in risk appetites allows emerging-market private-sector debt to be rolled over rather than repaid, Russian enterprises will have more resources for domestic expenditures.

The delays in implementing fiscal stimulus contributed to the depth of the downturn, but fiscal measures should now help to stabilise output. It was not until April 2009 that anti-crisis fiscal measures were approved by the Duma, and the federal budget was broadly in balance in the first quarter, despite declining revenue. As deficit spending comes through in the rest of 2009, fiscal policy should be more supportive of demand. Interest rates were raised in late 2008 to help defend the rouble, which contributed to a tightening of monetary conditions. With the rouble strengthening against the dollar-euro basket since early-February, the central bank reduced interest rates in April and May, and more rate cuts should be possible as inflation and capital outflows subside.

Inflation in early 2009 was subject to conflicting forces, with pass-through of the depreciation of the rouble and large administrative price increases being offset by the falling money supply, lower producer prices and weak demand conditions. The main administrative price increases for the year have now taken place, however, and the rouble has appreciated against the basket since early February, so inflation is expected to trend down, falling to single digits this year and declining further in 2010 (Table 1.2).

Table 1.2 **Macroeconomic indicators**

	2006	2007	2008	2009	2010
Real GDP growth	7.7	8.1	5.6	–6.8	3.7
Inflation	9.0	11.9	13.3	8.0	6.5
Fiscal balance (per cent of GDP)[1]	8.4	6.0	4.8	–6.0	–4.0
Current account balance (per cent of GDP)	9.5	5.9	6.1	3.3	2.9

1. Consolidated budget.

Source: Data for 2006-08 are from national sources. Data for 2009-10 are OECD estimates and projections.

Exports and imports will both begin to grow again during 2009, and the current account will probably remain in surplus, with stable or rising reserves (Table 1.3).

Risks have become less skewed to the downside, and are now fairly evenly balanced. Bad bank loans are likely to carry on rising, which may require the injection of further public capital into the banking system to sustain the provision of credit. If the global recession is

Box 1.1. **Macroeconomic projections for 2009-10** *(cont.)*

more severe than expected, oil prices could weaken sharply again, triggering further capital outflows and withdrawals of bank deposits and putting renewed pressure on the rouble. On the other hand, a continuation of recent more favourable trends in commodity prices and international financial conditions would likely result in a stronger pick-up in economic growth this year and next.

Table 1.3 **External indicators**

	2006	2007	2008	2009	2010
			USD billion		
Goods and services exports	335	394	523	343	383
Goods and services imports	209	283	368	263	297
Foreign balance	126	111	155	79	87
Invisibles, net	–31	–35	–52	–38	–45
Current account balance	94	76	102	41	41
			Percentage changes		
Goods and services export volumes	7.3	6.3	0.5	–5.6	3.7
Goods and services import volumes	21.3	26.5	15.0	–20.0	10.0
Terms of trade	10.5	3.6	16.7	–22.5	5.4

Source: National sources and OECD projections.

The number of unemployed workers finding a job is falling dramatically. While in December 2007 73 700 unemployed workers found a job, this number fell to 7 300 in December 2008. The number of vacancies fell sharply from 1.5 million in August 2008 to less than 900 000 in December 2008. Furthermore, vacancies are becoming more of a skill mismatch phenomenon. While unemployed workers are predominantly unskilled or low-skilled, vacancies exist for skilled workers or workers with specialised skills. Regional and sectoral differences in economic performance are adding to mismatches between job searchers and vacancies.

The government did respond in late 2008 by increasing the level of unemployment benefits, although its level is still far below the average wage. On the other hand, the number of work permits for foreign workers, mainly from former Soviet Republics, has been cut in half. Open unemployment is rising rapidly, hitting 7.7 million (10.2%) in April 2009, and is expected to reach about 10 million within the next year. It will be important that the Russian government allocate sufficient funds and resources to deal with this challenge and to assist job seekers acquire the skills needed to find a new job. It is welcome that the government has already taken precautionary steps to allow for increased spending to support retraining and regional mobility, although it remains to be seen whether the allocated funds are enough.

The authorities' policy response was immediate and large-scale

The response of the Russian authorities to the onset of the crisis was unusually rapid and large. The government and central bank had substantial resources to hand to finance support for the financial sector, defend the rouble, and undertake expansionary fiscal policy. Initially it was thought that these measures would be more than adequate to address the consequences for Russia of the global financial crisis. Apart from the Reserve Fund, which was funded to the statutory maximum of 10% of GDP, there was the National Welfare Fund, which by late 2008 amounted to about 3% of GDP, and government deposits with the CBR. International reserves at the onset of the crisis were nearly USD 600 billion, greater than combined private and public external debt.

All together, quantifiable measures announced in the first months of the crisis amounted to about 13% of GDP.[11] Further measures have been announced subsequently, but the growing severity of the situation appears to be causing a reassessment of how aggressively to respond. The initial net capital outflows and financial sector difficulties appeared to be of a manageable size in relation to the authorities' accumulated resources. As the crisis progressed, however, it became increasingly clear that the shocks were of a previously unsuspected magnitude, and that available resources could end up being overcommitted. In sharp contrast to the prevailing view in September-October 2008, within a few months the prospect of maintaining positive economic growth in 2009 or preserving fiscal surpluses had disappeared. Accordingly, debate grew within the government and the central bank about how to proceed, with a growing appetite for restraint.

The first wave of announced measures was aimed at stabilising the banking system (see Box 4.4). In mid-September, as falling securities prices and a drying up of interbank lending began to cause serious liquidity shortages for some banks, the authorities moved quickly to ease the shortages. Reserve requirements were cut, central bank repo operations stepped up, and government deposits were switched from the central bank to commercial banks (on an auction basis). The central bank also expanded the list of eligible collateral for refinancing operations, and subsequently began to offer uncollateralised credits.[12]

Further measures were taken to bolster trust in banks, both on the part of the population and other banks. The ceilings on insured deposits under the deposit insurance scheme were raised substantially, and the central bank guaranteed inter-bank loans made by the largest banks to smaller banks. In addition, state enterprises were used to take over a number of ailing small to medium-sized banks.

Indeed, in one sense rouble liquidity may even have been over-abundant in the months following the onset of the crisis. In addition to absolute deposit withdrawals, another result of the financial crisis was the switching of rouble deposits to foreign currency (mainly US dollar) deposits (Figure 1.19). That forced banks to shrink their rouble assets and accumulate foreign currency assets in order to avoid serious currency mismatches on their balance sheets. Banks therefore increasingly needed not rouble liquidity but dollar liquidity. They made heavy use of the foreign currency deposit facility established by the Central Bank of Russia (CBR). Beyond that, to a large extent the extensive rouble liquidity provided to the market was sold back to the CBR for foreign currency.

That process kept pressure on the rouble, as markets saw the CBR's international reserves dwindling rapidly.[13] The authorities were determined to avoid a sudden depreciation of the rouble, fearing that this would destabilize expectations further, and thus, in the face of the strong demand for dollars, engineered a sequence of step depreciations of the rouble against the dollar/euro basket. That policy, however, raised expectations of further rouble depreciation, encouraging dollarisation.[14]

Moreover, while the policy may have limited deleveraging, it did not succeed in preventing altogether. With rouble deposits falling, banks' rouble loan book had to be reduced, while banks needed to build up foreign currency assets to balance customers' rising foreign currency

Figure 1.19. **Foreign exchange individuals deposits**

As a share of total individuals deposits

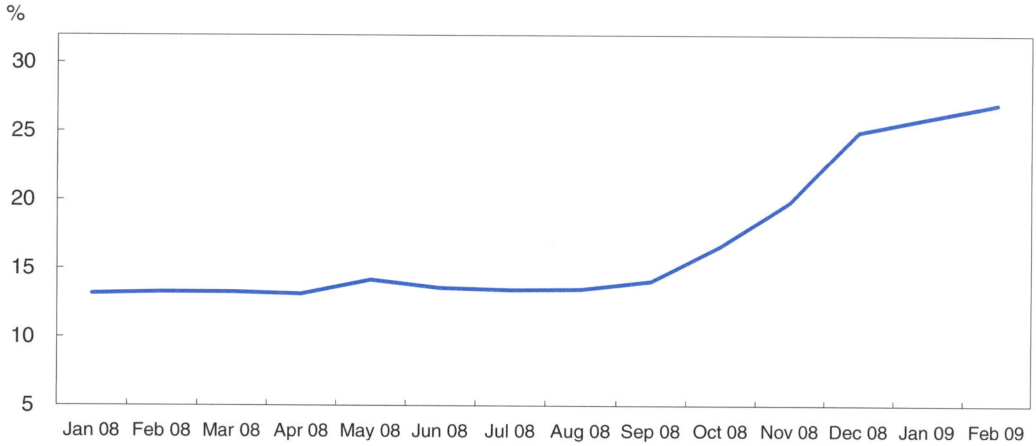

Source: OECD calculations based on Central Bank of Russia.

StatLink http://dx.doi.org/10.1787/648688882103

deposits, but did not want to expand their dollar lending, because of worries about credit risk in an environment of sharply slowing growth and a weakening rouble. As a result, in the fourth quarter of 2008 overall lending began to fall, notwithstanding the pressure of the authorities on banks to maintain lending (and the fact that the largest banks are state-owned).

Beyond measures aimed at the banking sector, the government also quickly announced plans to support domestic demand and to cushion the effects of the crisis on hard-hit sectors. One concern was for enterprises exposed to foreign currency debt, as the rouble came under pressure as a result of falling oil prices. Accordingly, USD 50 billion of the central bank's international reserves were made available to the state corporation Vnesheconombank (VEB) for lending to banks and enterprises with foreign currency debt service obligations.[15] At the same time, as already noted, large-scale foreign exchange intervention was used to resist the downward pressure on the rouble. The authorities viewed this as a justifiable measure to give exposed banks and enterprises a breathing space to accumulate sufficient dollar liquidity to meet debt service obligations. Although the central bank began to allow increasingly frequent small step depreciations of the exchange rate against the dollar-euro basket, which ultimately resulted in a 28% decline in the rouble against the basket, it nonetheless spent about a quarter of its reserves between September 2008 and January 2009 defending the rouble.[16]

The Duma approved the three-year budget for 2009-11 in November 2008, even though by that time it was clear that the growth and commodity price outlook had changed radically. The government's approach was to get the budget adopted as drafted (pre-crisis) and then submit amendments in the first quarter of 2009 to reflect the new situation. Given approved expenditures for 2009, the change in oil prices alone was enough to push the overall balance into deficit, but the government had also been preparing to add discretionary stimulus, as well as to commit large amounts to maintaining the solvency of the banking system. Pending the planned revisions to the 2009-11 budget, some *ad hoc* measures relating to 2009 were taken in late 2008. Notably, corporate profit tax was cut from 24% to 20% as of 2009, and unemployment insurance benefits were increased.

Echoing the approach in some advanced countries, Russia also began to design plans for providing budgetary support for non-bank enterprises. Several hundred large enterprises were designated eligible for support, though as of early 2009 no budgetary resources had been allocated for this purpose, and the modalities were not yet clear.

Key challenges in managing the crisis

The best strategy for Russia in tackling the economic crisis depends on the assessment of the size and duration of the global demand shock, the future path of oil prices, and the size of fiscal multipliers. Nonetheless, in principle measures should be chosen to maximise the immediate demand effect of any stimulus; to minimize distortions; to protect macroeconomic stability and fiscal sustainability *via* a clear exit strategy from stimulus measures; and, where possible, to yield longer-term efficiency gains while achieving short-term demand management goals. Designing a response that best conforms to these principles, including dealing with possible trade-offs between them, is the overarching near-term policy challenge.

Overlaid on the generally applicable principles for responding to a major adverse demand shock are certain Russia-specific factors. For example, Russia already exhibits a high degree of state involvement in the economy (see below, and Chapter 5), which both feeds and is fed by endemic corruption, deficiencies in corporate governance, and blurred lines between the private and public sectors. These features raise the risks attached to ratcheting up state ownership or command-and-control regulation to address the crisis.

Support financial stability

The effectiveness of demand-support measures will be weakened to the extent that the financial system is not functioning smoothly, which implies that measures to maintain the functioning of the banking system will be a particularly important challenge. It is not clear, however, that the main problem of the banking system is now, if indeed it ever was, excessively tight liquidity. In only a few banks have liquidity shortages seemed to have provoked deleveraging and these banks are relatively minor, none accounting for as much as 1% of total banking assets. At the level of the system as a whole there are few signs that liquidity constraints were ever severe. The period of mid- to late September 2008 is the main possible exception to this general point, as the global financial turmoil interrupted access to international capital markets and provoked significant deposit withdrawals by a population scarred by past banking crises (Figure 1.20).

Bank solvency is the main issue in this respect

Although there was little evidence by early 2009 of falls in bank capital, it nonetheless seems likely that to sustain positive lending growth this year bank solvency will need to be addressed. In particular, banks will need: *i)* sufficient capital to maintain capital adequacy ratios as non-performing loan rates on existing loans rise; and *ii)* reassurance about credit risks on new lending in an environment of negative real GDP growth both domestically and abroad. The challenge is to achieve this while minimising moral hazard and the cost to taxpayers.

As to bolstering capital adequacy, the preference of the government and the CBR so far has been to provide subordinated loans to boost banks' regulatory capital.[17] Subordinated loans have mainly gone to the largest state-owned banks (including the quasi-bank state corporation VEB, which is one of the largest lenders but does not have a banking license

Figure 1.20. **Bank liquidity**

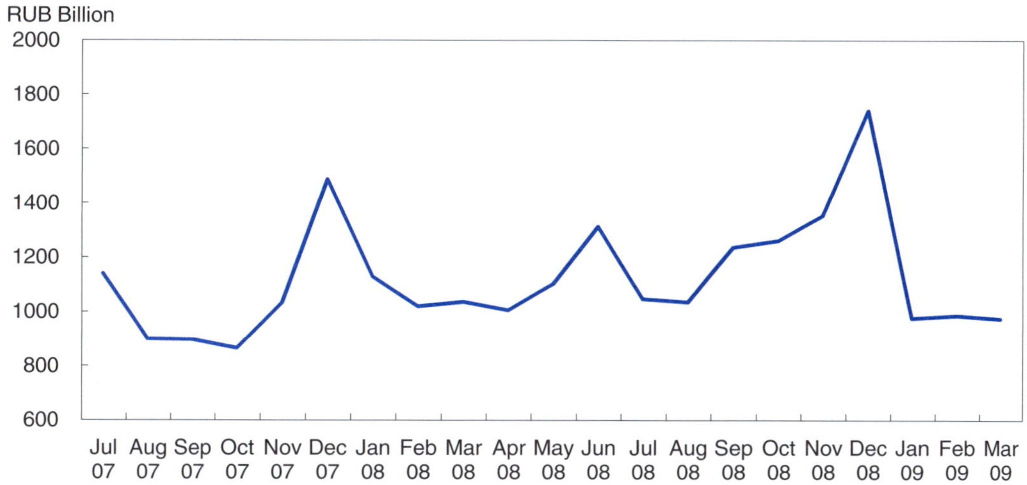

1. Cash in vaults, credit institutions' correspondent accounts in the Bank of Russia and bank deposits with the Bank of Russia.

Source: OECD calculations based on Central Bank of Russia.

StatLink http://dx.doi.org/10.1787/648708562382

and which is not subject to supervision by the central bank). Alternative approaches could include providing equity, government guarantees of loans, and the purchase of bad assets at favourable prices (possibly involving the creation of a "bad bank" to manage/dispose of bad assets). Normally, the main disadvantage of subordinated loans is that government does not get a say in management in return for its assistance, but in Russia the largest banks are already in state hands. Another disadvantage, which is shared by some other means of boosting bank capital, is that it will tend to impede needed consolidation. In that respect, an advantage of providing capital in the form of equity is that the government would be in a position to engineer the merger of some large banks, advancing consolidation (an example of a long term efficiency-enhancing goal consistent with short-term macroeconomic stabilization) before preparing for privatization in order to reduce the already large state share in total banking system assets.[18]

Concerning the problem of addressing rising credit risks, the authorities have already announced state support for bank loans to other banks and non-banks alike. In late 2008 lending by the largest banks to smaller banks was guaranteed by the CBR, and a government decree in February 2009 provided for guarantees of 50% of loans extended by Russian banks to enterprises in 2009 for core operations or investment for a duration of between 6 months and 5 years.[19] It is still too early to gauge the effectiveness of these measures in sustaining lending, but such guarantees, even if time-limited, clearly increase moral hazard.

Beyond these measures, addressing fears about credit risk on new lending may mean in part increasing confidence that the rouble will not suffer a renewed slide. The period in late 2008 and January 2009 when the authorities responded to a sharp deterioration of both the current and capital accounts of the balance of payments by pre-announcing a strategy of small step-wise depreciations had two negative effects on banks' willingness and ability to lend.[20] First, with further rouble depreciation in prospect, lending in foreign currency to domestic borrowers was less attractive, while rouble liquidity was drained as households and enterprises switched deposits from roubles to foreign currency, or withdrew deposits altogether – given banks' need to limit currency mismatches on the balance sheet, this impacted on their capacity for rouble lending. Second, with the real exchange rate moving less than seemed to be signalled by fundamentals, there was an increasing concern about overvaluation of the rouble and the profitability of the tradables sector (especially for commodity producers, given the big fall in international prices). The late January move to a wide intervention band, at a level that the market appeared to find credible given key exogenous factors such as the level of oil prices, succeeded in getting out of that negative dynamic, making the exchange rate more of a two-way bet. Subsequently, the strong recovery of oil prices has further strengthened confidence in the rouble, which by end-May had appreciated by about 10% versus the dollar-euro basket from its low point in early February (Figure 1.21). At prevailing oil prices, Russia's current account is likely to remain in surplus in 2009, further improving the country's already solid net foreign asset position. Moreover, despite the sizeable rebound so far in 2009, futures markets continue to indicate an expectation that oil prices will rise over the next year, which also helps to underpin confidence in the stability of the exchange rate. Although the authorities have signalled their willingness to adjust the band in the event of adverse moves in fundamentals, the danger remains that if commodity prices experience a renewed slump the CBR will again be impelled to defend levels of the exchange rate widely seen as implying overvaluation of the rouble, as was the case in late 2008. This episode highlighted the dangers of a monetary policy in which the main operational target is the exchange rate.

Figure 1.21. **Official exchange rate against dollar-euro basket**

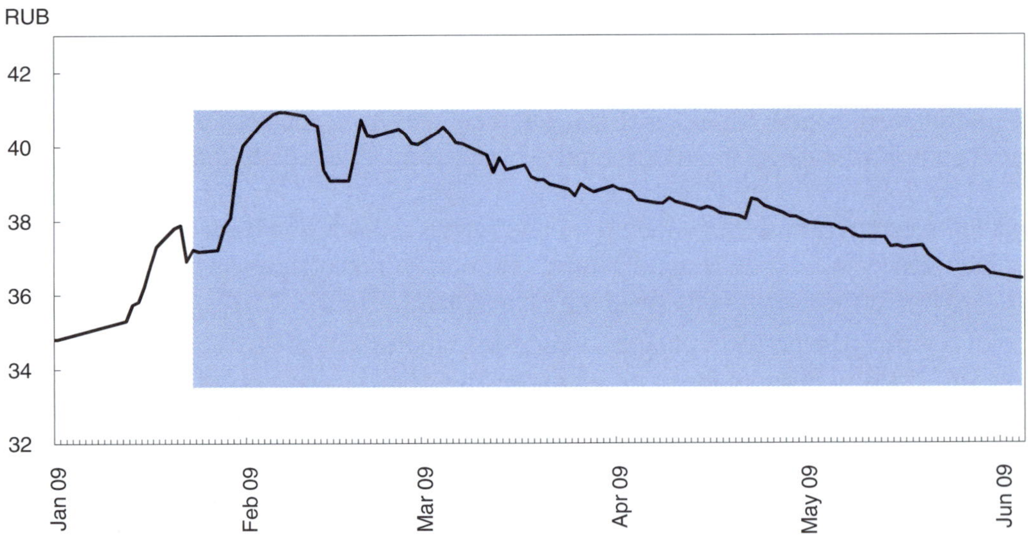

Source: OECD calculations based on Central Bank of Russia.

StatLink http://dx.doi.org/10.1787/648714082633

Putting more emphasis on price stability would also help guarding against deflationary pressures

Russia's central bank law charges the CBR both with achieving price stability and with maintaining stability of the currency. In practice, the CBR has articulated annual inflation objectives while using the nominal exchange rate as the operational target, with the path for the nominal rate being chosen to limit real appreciation of the rouble, given assumptions about domestic and foreign inflation. This has resulted in a potential conflict between the inflation and the exchange rate objectives. During much of the past decade, balance of payments surpluses were large, exceeding the authorities' capacity for sterilising the central bank's interventions. As a result, the money supply grew very rapidly, and inflation ceilings were regularly exceeded, although until 2007 this was not considered too worrisome, as inflation remained on a downtrend. Concern over the upturn in inflation from mid-2007 onward led the central bank to begin to give greater weight to controlling inflation. Exchange rate intervention bands were widened in late May 2008 to allow additional rouble appreciation, reserve requirements were tightened, and policy interest rates were raised on several occasions between mid-2007 and mid-2008. From September 2008, however, weight shifted back to maintaining exchange rate stability, now by defending the rouble against pressures for depreciation, while at the same time monetary policy was subordinated to the goal of supporting the banking system, which meant above all the provision of ample liquidity.

As it turned out, simultaneously defending the rouble and providing liquidity for the banking system were conflicting goals, as rouble liquidity fed demand for foreign currency and put more pressure on the rouble. But just as the exchange rate-oriented policy in a time of balance of payments strength meant unduly rapid money supply growth, in the face of large balance of payments deficits (owing to strong capital account outflows while the current account surplus weakened in line with oil prices) money supply growth turned negative. This has raised the possibility that inflation could fall faster than expected and perhaps even further than the authorities would like, especially given the fall in international food and energy prices. Modelling Russian inflation econometrically (see Annex 3.A2) indicates that money supply growth, producer price inflation and changes in the exchange rate are the most significant predictors of future inflation. The sharp falls in M2 and producer prices that occurred in the second half of 2008 and early 2009 suggested a fall in inflation from the spring of 2009, with the possibility of negative month-on-month inflation by the summer, notwithstanding the large depreciation of the rouble against the dollar-euro basket until February. In addition, although output measures were not found to be significant over the sample period (1999-2008), there are theoretical reasons to believe that inflation should be influenced by the output gap, which has turned sharply negative. As against that, to the extent that recourse to the Reserve Fund results in the fiscal deficit being monetised, money supply growth should recover during the rest of 2009, and the rebound in commodity prices will put renewed upward pressure on producer prices. In any event, whether the main risk turns out to be a resurgence of inflation driven by a new bout of rouble weakness or a slide into deflation as a result of monetary contraction and weak aggregate demand, making monetary policy more responsive to domestic inflation remains the main challenge for the central bank over time.

Reorienting monetary policy to achieving inflation objectives does not mean that limiting real appreciation was a wrong-headed objective during the period of oil price strength, or that the level of the real exchange rate should be a matter of indifference to the authorities. It does mean, however, that achieving such objectives will largely fall to fiscal policy, especially as regards the mechanisms for taxing and saving oil windfalls.

The challenge for fiscal policy is to support demand effectively with minimum risk to sustainability

As in other countries, since the onset of the crisis there has been a debate in Russia as to the role for fiscal stimulus in the current situation. On one side, there are fears about jeopardizing hard-won credibility concerning the sustainability of the fiscal position and about limited efficacy of fiscal policy in supporting demand (low or even negative fiscal multipliers). On the other hand, there are strong pressures on the government to ease economic dislocation for firms and households. As regards the fiscal multiplier, current conditions are at least relatively favourable to the efficacy of expansionary policy, since the proportion of credit-constrained agents (both regional governments and households) should be high. And a strong case can be made for mitigating the social cost of unemployment. The main short-term challenge for fiscal policy is to maximise the multiplier while managing moral hazard and risks to long-term fiscal sustainability.

There is a fairly broad consensus that a recession calls for fiscal stimulus measures which are "triple t": timely, targeted, and temporary. Timeliness can argue against infrastructure spending, which generally takes a good deal of time to plan and implement. Targeting involves maximising the fiscal multiplier, which tends to suggest increases in expenditure, possibly in the form of transfers to credit-constrained households or lower levels of government, rather than tax cuts. To the extent that infrastructure spending can be accelerated quickly, it should also be favoured, since there is evidence from elsewhere that the fiscal multiplier is highest for such spending.[21] The imperative to provide temporary stimulus militates against measures that are hard to reverse, such as raising entitlements or cutting taxes; on the other hand, one-off transfers or tax rebates are often cited as good examples.

Another challenge is to find measures which are useful for achieving longer-term goals as well as boosting demand in the short run. The reduction in the corporate profit tax was well-considered from this point of view, as such taxes have been found to be the least growth-friendly (OECD, 2009), although the likelihood is that it will have only a limited demand impact in the crisis, as many firms will not be paying the tax at all, and the impact of reduced tax bills on firms with positive profits is likely to be muted in such an unfavourable demand climate. Other long-term objectives that could be considered in designing a stimulus package include raising energy efficiency and improving the environment.

Maintaining fiscal sustainability appears to be less of an issue in Russia than in many OECD economies, given low levels of gross public debt and substantial public financial assets. Nonetheless, a federal deficit of about 6% of GDP is expected for 2009, and it is not yet clear how long deficits will last. A failure to rein in such deficits would mean an explosive debt path. Meanwhile, Russia faces unusually negative demographic trends, with a sharp rise in the dependency ratio in prospect in coming years. It also has serious environmental degradation problems which could entail major fiscal costs in the future. It is therefore important for Russia, as for many other crisis-hit countries, to set its stimulus efforts in a medium-term context that credibly charts out a return to a sustainable public debt path.

In April 2009 a number of amendments to the current-year budget were adopted (Box 1.2), which meet the main short-term fiscal policy challenges to varying degrees. New anti-crisis measures, amounting to some 3.4% of GDP, were all on the expenditure side, with the majority of extra spending constituting transfers to households, regions, and the Pension Fund.[22] On the other hand, other expenditures, including on public investment, were reduced, leaving overall spending higher by only 1.6% of the new projected value of 2009 GDP. In addition, new measures were skewed towards those which distort prices (such as the interest rate subsidies), hinder competition (*e.g.* support for large enterprises), and/or have a protectionist element (*e.g.* support for domestic auto manufacturers *via* subsidies and state orders). The sub-optimal composition of stimulus measures is likely both to limit their effectiveness in supporting demand and exert a drag on economic

Box 1.2. **Amendments to the 2009 federal budget**

Amendments to the 2009 budget to address the economic crisis were adopted in April. All underlying fundamentals for 2009, including the oil rice, GDP, the exchange rate and inflation were revised (see Table 1.4). Revenues were projected to be about 40% lower in nominal terms, or 4.6 percentage points of GDP compared to the previously approved figures, mainly because of much lower oil and gas prices. The budget amendments raise nominal expenditure by RUB 667 billion relative to the original 2009 budget, which amounts to an increase of 6.4% of GDP given a sharp downward revision of output. As a result, the revised projection for the budget balance is a deficit of 7.4% of GDP, a swing of 11 percentage points of GDP compared to the original budget. A further 0.6% of GDP is planned to be spent *via* the National Welfare Fund (NWF).

Table 1.4 **Amendments to the federal budget for 2009**

	2008 (outcome)	Budget 2009 (adopted November 2008)	Budget 2009 (amended April 2009)	Change from 2008 to amended 2009 budget	Change from original 2009 budget
In billions of roubles					
Revenues	9 274	10 927	6 714	–2 560	–4 213
Oil and gas revenues	4 389	4 693	2 057	–2 332	–2 636
Non-oil-and-gas revenues	4 885	6 235	4 656	–229	–1 579
Expenditure	7 567	9 025	9 692	2 125	667
Balance	1 708	1 902	–2 978	–4 686	–4 880
Non-oil-and-gas balance	–2 682	–2 790	–5 036	–2 354	–2 246
In per cent of GDP					
Revenues	22.3	21.2	16.6	–5.7	–4.6
Oil and gas revenues	10.5	9.1	5.1	–5.5	–4
Non-oil-and-gas revenues	11.8	12.1	11.5	–0.2	–0.6
Expenditure	18.2	17.5	24.0	5.8	6.4
Balance	4.1	3.7	–7.4	–11.5	–11.1
Non-oil-and-gas balance	–6.4	–5.4	–12.5	–6.0	–7.1
Memorandum items					
GDP, in billions of roubles	41 668	51 475	40 420	–1 120	–11 055
Real GDP, % change	5.6	6.7	–2.2	–7.8	–8.9
Urals oil price, USD/barrel	94	95	41	–53	–54
Inflation, per cent, end-year	13.3	7.5-8.5	13	4.5-5.5	–0.3
Exchange rate, RUB/USD, annual average	24.8	24.7	35.1	10.3	10.4

The amendments were based on the government's anti-crisis programme, a document outlining a broad set of fiscal and non-fiscal measures in response to the economic crisis. The overall 2009 "anti-crisis package" is estimated at 7.5% of GDP, of which 6.4% of GDP have fiscal implications for the federal budget.

Anti-crisis measures on the revenue side (the reduction in the corporate profit tax rate, the easing of rules on depreciation, and the simplification of taxation of small and medium-sized enterprises) were already adopted in December 2008. Their cost to the federal budget in 2009 was put at around 1.2% of GDP. On the expenditure side, the April amendments introduce "anti-crisis" measures of 3.4% of GDP while simultaneously reducing spending on other items, notably public investment. Adding other crisis-related items which are not classified as government expenditure, including using assets of the NWF to support the banking system, loans to the regions and extension of government guarantees would increase the gross amount of anti-crisis outlays to 5.1% of GDP. In terms of "above-the-line" commitments, the anti-crisis spending stimulus includes:

Box 1.2. **Amendments to the 2009 federal budget** *(cont.)*

Increase in social expenditure (1.3% of projected 2009 GDP):

- increase of various social benefits;
- increase in unemployment benefits and financing of employment-promotion activities;
- larger transfer to the Pension Fund to compensate for a deficit arising from increased pensions.

Support for selected sectors and enterprises (0.7% of GDP):

- increase in government subsidies;
- subsidising interest rates for various enterprises and households;
- additional support to the car industry, including purchase of domestic cars for use by federal and regional authorities.

Support for regions (0.4% of GDP).

Support for the banking system (0.7% of GDP).

Unallocated contingency (0.3% of GDP).

Amendments to the *Budget* Code were also adopted to provide the necessary legal basis for the revisions to the budget. In the event of a fall in projected non-oil and gas revenue of more than 15%, the government henceforth has the right to ask the Duma to suspend three-year budget planning. This right has been exercised to eliminate the out-years from the 2009-11 budget. The coming into force of a binding overall 1% deficit target and a 4.7% non-oil deficit target was pushed back from 2011 to 2013. Also, the government has acquired the right to use the Reserve Fund to cover deficits without amending the budget. In 2009, it intends to finance most of the budget deficit by using the Reserve Fund's assets.

efficiency in the longer term. As regards the duration of the stimulus, some measures, such as increases in social benefits, were permanent, while others, such as interest rate subsidies and state orders of domestically produced cars, were temporary.

Beyond the current crisis, Russian Federation faces a number of longer-term challenges

While the depth and duration of the current downturn is still unknown, the crisis will pass and economic growth will resume and Russia will be faced with the challenge of putting in place a healthier model for sustained catch-up growth, one based on innovation, investment, and the accumulation of human capital, rather than one relying on rising commodity prices.

Oil will continue to have a strong influence on the economy, and needs to be skilfully managed

The temptation to coast, allowing improving terms of trade to drive growth, may at times be strong. Indeed, it is not unlikely that a new strong oil price upswing will set in, again boosting Russia's real GDP growth *via* rapid increases in domestic demand. Current oil futures prices indicate a considerable recovery from recent lows within 2009, and the International Energy Agency's latest *World Energy Outlook* (IEA, 2008) projected a rise in the oil price to USD 110 per barrel in real terms (2007 dollars) by 2020. The factors driving rising oil prices during the period 2003-08 – in particular, strong growth in China and India, and high marginal costs of new production – are expected to return as the world economy picks up again.

Skilful management of Russian's natural resources, and in particular its oil and gas wealth, will remain important. Russia is the second largest producer of oil in the world and the largest producer of natural gas, and it commands considerable reserves. A perennial and major challenge for policy makers is to ensure that the Russian population gets the maximum benefit from that wealth without being overly dependent on it. Successful oil and gas wealth management has several components. Taxation and the regulatory regime should be designed to ensure that exploration and production are responsive to oil price fluctuations. Despite the multi-year surge in prices, from 2005 onward Russian oil companies barely managed to replace declining production from old fields. Indeed, in 2008, when prices were at all-time highs both as regards the intra-year peak and the average annual level, production and exports declined. This suggests an inefficient time-profile of production. Some reasons may be technical, but the poor supply response to an unprecedented rise in prices over a period of a few years is probably at least partly the result of disruptive state interference in the oil and gas sector and a suboptimal foreign direct investment regime. The increasing barriers to foreign participation in the Russian oil and gas sector are particularly unhelpful for the development of new fields in inaccessible parts of the country (*i.e.* all big new identified fields), as foreign know-how may be critical to the efficient development of such reserves.

At the same time, a high proportion of pure rents arising from price windfalls should be taxed and saved, to insulate the non-oil economy from oil price fluctuations.[23] The inter-sectoral reallocation of resources that is induced by swings in the real exchange rate driven by commodity price oscillations imposes costs of shifting resources from uncompetitive uses to profitable employment (the essence of the Dutch disease phenomenon). However, poor performance of commodity-dependent economies appears to be an empirical regularity that may have various other causes. These include forgoing positive externalities generated by more dynamic sectors, such as manufacturing or information technology; negative effects on labour supply from the positive income effects of natural resource wealth; the inducement of low-efficiency public investment, as grandiose projects are launched during oil price upswings and abandoned during downswings; and the deleterious effects of rent-seeking (Gelb, 1988; Sachs and Warner, 1995). In addition, measured economic growth in an economy largely based on the extraction of non-renewable resources is exaggerated relative to other economies not reliant on such activities, since converting non-renewable resources into financial wealth involves little if any true wealth creation, while the unaccounted environmental costs of such resource extraction are probably higher than for most other activities. These considerations argue for macroeconomic policies that resist Dutch Disease and resource curse effects. In Russia's case, despite a well-educated population and impressive technological achievements in some areas, the structure of the economy and of exports indicates a relatively low degree of sophistication, which suggests that avoiding the resource curse could yield considerable benefits.

In that respect, a possible lesson to be learned from the latest oil price cycle is that the public savings of oil revenue windfalls, though substantial, was insufficient. The widening non-oil deficit in the last years of the expansion reduced the fiscal sterilisation of balance of payments inflows and put upward pressure on inflation and the real exchange rate, while the scale of the current downturn threatens to exhaust the accumulated resources in the Reserve Fund and the National Welfare Fund in as little as two years. The Budget Code, which provided for a maximum transfer of 3.7% of GDP per year from the oil funds to the budget beginning in 2011, would imply substantially more conservatism than prevailed in recent years (the oil transfer reached 5.5% of GDP in 2008), but has been amended in conjunction with the 2009 budget amendments to push back the entry into force of the 3.7% limit until 2013. This may well prove to be necessary given the budgetary impact of the current recession, but it could equally turn out to have been a premature abandonment of the limits, one which risks signalling a willingness to relax the constraints even before they bind. Henceforth, considerable importance should be attached to demonstrating the government's determination to ensure that a sufficient proportion of incremental oil revenues is saved.

As ever, capable implementation of macroeconomic policies is key

More generally, prudent macroeconomic policies, in which management of petroleum resources plays a critical role, are essential for the success of an overall strategy for rapid convergence to OECD income levels.

With regard to monetary policy, a key challenge will be to decide on the speed and modalities of the shift to inflation targeting, a shift that has already been signalled by the central bank. Monetary policy should as soon as possible be freed of the task of trying to resist excessive real appreciation of the rouble when the balance of payments is strong, and should be progressively oriented to the goal of price stability. The exchange rate-oriented regime was clearly fuelling some imbalances during the cyclical upswing, as monetary policy was effectively being determined by interest rates in the US and the euro zone, which were too low for Russian conditions. As a result, real interest rates in Russia were negative from 2002 onward, which added impetus to the credit boom and encouraged inefficient investment (notably in Moscow and St. Petersburg real estate). Smoothing real exchange rate fluctuations driven by swings in commodity prices is a valid policy goal, but it should be achieved *via* fiscal policy, which needs to ensure taxation and saving (ideally abroad) of the bulk of commodity price windfalls. This would ensure that fiscal policy sterilises a large part of the current account inflows that come with strong commodity export prices.

The other immediate task for fiscal policy as the economy emerges from recession will be to provide credible assurance regarding long-term fiscal sustainability. The fiscal stimulus provided to respond to the economic contraction should be explicitly cast in a medium-term framework, based on plausible assumptions, that provides for a rapid reduction in the non-oil deficit and permits the rebuilding of the Reserve and National Welfare Funds, assuming oil prices do not fall further in the medium term. In this respect it would be helpful to return quickly rolling three-year budgets and the Budget Code limits for the non-oil deficit. This would help provide a margin for dealing with long-term fiscal pressures such as the ageing of the population and the associated rise in the dependency ratio as well as the likely future costs of cleaning up environmental degradation, which has occurred in the past.

Russian government revenues rely to a large extent on indirect taxes and corporate income taxes, while there is relatively little revenue coming from personal income tax and even less from property taxes. The introduction of a flat income tax rate reduced the progressivity of the tax system considerably, inhibiting its capacity to contribute to efforts to tackle the still high incidence of poverty. Resource extraction taxes do play an important role, but could be fine-tuned to capture resource rents more efficiently, and there is scope to expand the use of environmental taxes (Chapter 2).

Comprehensive reform in a range of areas would boost long-term potential substantially

The current government has often articulated a recognition of the need for broad-ranging reforms to advance the development of a market-oriented economy. However, there is little sign of follow-through as yet, and long-term planning has understandably been derailed to some extent by the need to respond to the economic crisis.[24]

Notwithstanding the considerable progress made by past governments, substantial scope remains for reforms in a range of areas. For example, education performance is mediocre, the healthcare system is deficient in a number of respects, innovation policy does not get the most from Russia's potential, administrative reform is needed to improve the efficiency of the public service, and some important prices, notably for natural gas, remain distorted, making the economy more energy-intensive than it should be.[25]

A key problem is that Russia continues to be perceived as a country where the rule of law is not applied vigorously and even-handedly. International surveys of corruption indicate that Russia has been stagnating or going backward in this area in recent years. For example, in September 2008 Transparency International (TI) ranked Russia 147 out of 180 countries, a deterioration relative to 2007, and TI's 2009 Global Corruption Barometer indicated that the proportion of Russians acknowledging having paid bribes in the preceding 12 months increased from 17% in 2007 to 31% in 2008. Improving public governance is a major challenge that has been acknowledged by the current and previous Presidents, but significant improvements have so far proved elusive.[26]

An important long-term challenge is to address Russia's especially unfavourable demographic trends. This overarching problem will require determined action in a number of areas: social policies effectively targeted at reducing preventable mortality and improving health and productivity; labour market policies which facilitate immigration and foster labour market flexibility; and pension reform to provide for adequate old-age incomes while ensuring sustainability of the system.

Yet another area where Russia faces major long-term challenges concerns the environment.[27] The legacy of the Soviet era, with its emphasis on heavy industry, is a prevalence of environmental hazards which pose risks to health and safety. In addition, Russia is an energy-intensive economy, with considerable scope for improving efficiency which would both increase national income and reduce Russia's contribution to environmental degradation, notably as regards greenhouse gas emissions.

Some of these areas have been taken up in past *Surveys*, and many of the conclusions and recommendations remain pertinent.[28] This *Survey* focusses, however, on two challenges for creating framework conditions conducive to rapid, sustained, and broad-based growth: strengthening the performance of the banking sector, and improving product market regulation to provide for a greater role for competition. These two areas are complementary and inter-connected. To begin with, banking itself is one area where stronger competition would be beneficial – indeed, it is an apparent paradox that the banking sector would benefit both from more competition and more consolidation. Also, a banking system that does a better job of financing small and medium-sized enterprises would help boost competition, innovation, and productivity in the economy.

The banking sector could contribute to stronger potential growth, and could be made less crisis-prone

Banking is an area where major reforms have been undertaken in the last decade, and tangible benefits have been seen. Combined with the long period of strong economic growth up to mid-2008, the banking system has become increasingly deep, competitive, and robust. Nonetheless, it is clear both that there remains scope for the Russian financial sector to contribute more to long-run growth, and that the system remains too prone to crises. In that sense, well beyond the current crisis-management stage, there are many things to do.

Despite substantial improvements in the quality and efficiency of banking regulation, two major challenges in this area still face policy makers. First, there remains a significant gap between prudential supervision in Russia and international best practice. Second, the current crisis has shown that even the current state of the art is deficient in important respects. Notably, international rules have given too little weight to macro-prudential considerations, and have under-emphasised the importance of liquidity relative to capital. Russia therefore needs to continue to reinforce its existing approach to (micro)prudential supervision, while both contributing to international efforts to design a new approach, and perhaps moving ahead of the development of an international consensus to make its own supervision more systemic. Russia can ill afford further systemic banking crises.

Another major issue to be addressed in the long term is the role of state-owned banks. Such banks already accounted for about 40% of banking system assets before the crisis, and may well emerge from it with a significantly larger share. Already, some failing banks have been taken over by state-owned entities, and further mergers and acquisitions are likely as loan losses rise. Meanwhile, new state-owned institutions have been created in recent years, and the government has injected substantial capital into a number of the banks it controls. Evidence from other countries suggests that state-owned banks are relatively inefficient, despite often benefitting from advantages conveyed by the state. While state banks in Russia have brought benefits from greater stability during crisis periods, this is not the only option for achieving a stable banking system. Some advanced countries with wholly private banks (*e.g.* Canada) have so far seen little impact on bank solvency from the global financial crisis, and there is no evident reason why well-designed regulation cannot yield a banking system dominated by private banks which is stable as well as competitive and efficient.

The role of the state banks, along with the issue of the number of banks in Russia, is connected to the challenge of increasing bank competition. The Russian banking system appears to be characterised by both an unusually large number of banks, and by a relatively low degree of competition (though the latter varies by region and market segment). Part of the explanation for this apparent paradox is that the great majority of the roughly 1 100 banks active in the country are very small. State-owned Sberbank, the largest bank in the system, accounts for a greater share of assets than the 1 000 smallest banks. Accordingly, the long tail of small banks adds little if anything to competitive pressure, while taxing the supervisory resources of the central bank and adding to Russian banks' reputation as pocket banks and/or vehicles for money laundering, which has a negative effect on public confidence in banks in general. Many of the small banks are below any plausible minimum efficient scale, and their smaller size also tends to make them more concentrated both on the deposit and lending sides. Thus, more rapid consolidation of the sector would be beneficial to the stability and efficiency of the banking system. While the ongoing recession will help in this respect, facilitating the evolution of a system with fewer, larger banks which compete with each other is another strategic challenge.

More competitive product markets would boost innovation and productivity growth

Past *Surveys* have remarked on Russia's relatively low levels of product market competition, entrenched corruption, and high levels of state involvement in the economy. In the current *Survey*, the OECD's indicator of product market regulation is computed for Russia, enabling it to be benchmarked against OECD economies and a number of other non-member economies for which the exercise has been conducted.

This exercise confirms that Russia faces major challenges to improve the level of competition in the economy. Overall, Russia's product market regulation is found to be more restrictive than all other countries for which the PMR indicator has been calculated. There are several reasons for this finding, including pervasive state control, higher than average barriers to entrepreneurship, excessive administrative burdens on start-ups, variable quality of regulation of network industries, and relatively high barriers to international trade and foreign direct investment.

This suggests that Russia faces several broad challenges in order to improve the functioning of product markets. One is to reduce political interference in the operation of state-owned enterprises (SOEs) and private firms. This is likely to mean improving corporate governance of SOEs, revitalising privatisation, narrowing the list of firms and sectors designated strategic, and reducing the use of command and control regulation and direct intervention. Another challenge is to reduce barriers to entrepreneurship and increase competition. To this end, competition law must be applied without exemptions (including for public corporations), administrative reform should be pursued to reduce red tape, and barriers to entry in network sectors should be reduced. Finally, the trade and foreign investment regimes should be liberalised.

Notes

1. According to Maddison (2006), average annual real *per capita* GDP growth in the former Soviet Union was 1.8% between 1913 and 1950 and 3.4% between 1950 and 1973, with no ten-year period matching the rates of growth seen in Russia between 1999 and 2008.
2. A comprehensive assessment of Russia's social and labour market developments will be provided in the forthcoming *OECD Labour Market and Social Policy Review*.
3. Figure 1.8 in the *2006 OECD Economic Survey of the Russian Federation* (OECD, 2006) shows the considerable contribution of re-activated spare capacity for economic growth in the post-1998 boom year. Of course, much of the capital stock inherited from the Soviet Union was ill-adapted to a market economy, and thus had little value.
4. The failure of investment to increase as a share of GDP was to some extent a function of deflators: investment volumes increased by 12% a year from 1999 through 2008, considerably faster than overall GDP, but the relatively slow increase of the investment deflator left the investment-to-GDP ratio little changed.
5. Russia's population began falling in 1993, but the working age population continued increasing until 2006. Given also the absorption of unemployed and inactive individuals during the long boom that began in 1999, employment grew by 0.7% a year through 2007.
6. See Table 2.3.
7. Command GDP is a measure of real income defined as follows: command GDP = TDDV + XGSV*(PXGS/PMGS)-MGSV, where TDDV is real domestic demand, XGSV and MGSV are, respectively, export and import volumes, and PXGS and PMGS are the export and import deflators.

8. The rouble cost of dollar borrowing is here just calculated as the *ex post* cost in roubles over one year of debt at the yield-to-maturity of the Russian government 2010 Eurobond. Clearly, this a lower bound on such costs for private sector borrowers, since they also faced a significant spread over sovereign rates.
9. St. Petersburg also ranked among the most expensive cities in the world, at 18th place, down from 12th in 2007.
10. The 2003 attack on Yukos, at that time the largest Russian oil company, which culminated in the imprisonment of its Chief Executive Officer and the takeover of the company by state-owned Rosneft, was the most prominent example of this tendency, but there have been dozens of less high-profile cases of growing state involvement in the oil and gas industry and certain other sectors.
11. This estimate refers to total measures announced between September and December 2008: lowering of reserve requirements, support for financial markets, shifting of deposits to commercial banks, consolidated loans to banks, expansion of deposit insurance, and tax cuts.
12. Not all measures were used to the maximum extent of the announced scale, at least in the fourth quarter of 2008.
13. The fall in reserves was exaggerated by the move in the euro/US dollar exchange rate between early August 2008, when dollar reserves peaked at nearly USD 600 billion, and end-January 2009, by which time reserves had fallen to USD 387 billion. With about half of reserves held in euros (with a small amount also in sterling), valuation effects accounted for significant part of the USD 209 billion decline in the dollar value.
14. There were anecdotal reports of firms falling behind on wage payments and/or defaulting on rouble loans and incurring penalties in order to maintain long dollar positions, so profitable was that trade in their view.
15. In the event, only about USD 12 billion of the amounts allocated for this purpose were taken up.
16. The decline in the stock of reserves was somewhat larger than this, approximately 1/3, with the difference arising from valuation effects – see footnote 13.
17. The second largest bank, VTB, has also announced that it will be issuing equity (to be taken up by government), and the largest bank, Sberbank, could do likewise (with the CBR maintaining its controlling stake).
18. The large share of banking sector assets accounted for by state-owned banks does, in the current circumstances, represent an advantage of sorts *vis-à-vis* most OECD economies, since the systemic banks are already state-owned. Whether and how to bail out troubled banks has been a difficult question in many OECD countries, with a reluctance to take over major banks, but at the same time a recognition that taxpayers should get some control of banks in return for bailing them out.
19. A separate decree provides for guarantees to loans to the defence sector.
20. Of course, there are also arguments in favour of resisting pressures on the exchange rate. First, market-determined exchange rates sometimes substantially overshoot fundamentals. Oil prices were still above USD 100 per barrel when the CBR initially began intervening in defence of the rouble, while capital outflows looked to be driven in part by temporary factors. Also, especially for commodity dependent economies like Russia, fundamentals themselves may be very volatile. Russia effectively resisted some of the appreciation that would have been implied by the long rise of oil prices from 2004 through mid-2008, and the subsequent evolution of oil prices suggests that this was not without foundation. Most importantly, in the case in question, the authorities appear to have feared that excessively large jumps in the exchange rate would lead to a vicious circle of dollarization, deleveraging, negative growth, capital outflows, and more depreciation. Whether such a risk outweighs the costs of making the exchange rate a one-way bet is an empirical question, and one which cannot be definitively answered without knowing the counterfactual.
21. See Spilimbergo *et al.* (2008). There is no available Russia-specific econometric evidence on the efficacy of different forms of government expenditure, however, and some caution is in order in applying the findings from advanced countries to emerging economies like Russia, where there may be a greater tendency for wasteful spending.
22. Revenue measures amounting to approximately 1.2% of 2009 GDP had already been adopted in late 2008.
23. That is, Dutch disease effects, when prices are rising. As in the current crisis, it can make sense to run down accumulated reserves when oil prices fall to offset in part the negative demand effects coming through deteriorating terms of trade.

24. This seems to be the case for the economic growth strategy "Russia 2020", which was intended to provide a roadmap for Russia to embark on a growth path, which is determined by innovation, investment and human capital.

25. As regards educational performance, Russia's mean scores in the 2006 PISA tests (OECD, 2007) ranked 39th of 57 countries in reading (with only one OECD country having a lower average), 32nd of 56 in mathematics (6 OECD countries with lower scores), and 35th of 56 in science (with 5 lower-performing OECD countries).

26. The 2009 Transparency International Global Corruption Barometer continued to report a much larger number of Russians reporting that official anti-corruption efforts were ineffective (52%) compared to those calling them effective (22%). Chapter 5 discusses the Russian government's most recent anti-corruption measures, which largely came into effect after this survey.

27. A number of major environmental challenges were set out in an *Environmental Performance Review* of the Russian Federation conducted in 1999 (OECD, 1999). The main problems remain, and in some cases have become even more acute over the past decade.

28. For example, the previous *Economic Survey for Russia* (OECD, 2006) addressed administrative reform, innovation policy, and healthcare, while in 2002 the gas and electricity sectors were analysed (OECD, 2002), with gas sector reform again addressed in 2004 (OECD, 2004).

Bibliography

Gelb, A. (1988), *Oil windfalls: Blessing or curse?* Oxford University Press, for the World Bank, New York, NJ.

IEA (2006), *World Energy Outlook*, OECD/IEA, Paris.

Maddison, A. (2006), *The World Economy: Historical Statistics*, OECD, Paris.

Mercer (2008), *Mercer 2008 Cost of Living Survey*, available at *www.mercer.com/costofliving*.

OECD (2006), *OECD Economic Surveys: Russian Federation* , OECD, Paris.

OECD (2004), *OECD Economic Surveys: Russian Federation* , OECD, Paris.

OECD (2002), *OECD Economic Surveys: Russian Federation* , OECD, Paris.

OECD (2007), *PISA 2006*, OECD, Paris.

OECD (1999), *Environmental Performance Reviews: Russian Federation*, OECD, Paris.

OECD (2009), *Economic Policy Reforms: Going for Growth*, Chapter 5: "Taxation and Economic Growth", OECD, Paris.

Oomes, N. and O. Dynnikova (2006), "The Utilization-Adjusted Output Gap: Is the Russian Economy Overheating?", *IMF Working Papers*, No. 06/68, IMF, Washington, DC.

Sachs, J. and A. Warner (1995), "Natural Resource Abundance and Economic Growth", *National Bureau of Economic Research Working Papers*, No. 5398, NBER, Cambridge, MA.

Spilimbergo, A. *et al* (2008), "Fiscal Policy for the Crisis", *IMF Staff Position Notes*, SPN/08/01, 29 December 2008.

ISBN 978-92-64-05433-2
OECD Economic Surveys: Russian Federation

Chapter 2

Ensuring growth-friendly fiscal policy in both the short and the long term

Until late 2008 the main fiscal policy challenge for Russia was to decide what proportion of abundant oil revenues to save and which assets to accumulate. The onset of the crisis transformed that situation, giving rise to large deficits and bringing questions of fiscal sustainability back into play. The main short-term fiscal policy challenge is to gauge the optimal amount and form of fiscal stimulus as well as the right scale and modalities of public support for the banking system, while safeguarding fiscal sustainability. Over the longer term, fiscal policy has an important contribution to make to raising potential growth rates. Taxation of natural resource wealth will remain a critical issue in this respect, and scope exists for the government to appropriate economic rents more efficiently and consistently across sectors while protecting incentives for exploration and development. Reforms in this and other areas can make the overall tax system more growth-friendly without worsening equity.

The fiscal situation in Russia was transformed virtually overnight by the onset of the global economic crisis. The problems of plenty – how to invest rising public assets, which taxes to cut first, how to resist political pressures for inefficient spending increases – faded as fast as the Russian summer when the crisis hit in September 2008. The new challenges became how to use the government's considerable resources to maintain the functioning of the banking system and support aggregate demand without compromising long-term sustainability, in the face of a dramatic decline in revenues. Initially, sustainability did not appear to be a major concern, given Russia's negative net debt position and the string of large surpluses since 2000, but as the depth of the downturn became increasingly clear, it was soon obvious that Russia would be facing a very large deficit in 2009, with the likelihood of further sizeable deficits to come. As in most OECD countries, the Russian government is now faced with the problem of how most effectively to provide fiscal stimulus in the near term while safeguarding sustainability in the context of some unfavourable long-term trends. This chapter discusses these challenges and makes a number of recommendations concerning how to respond to the crisis. It also indicates some longer-term fiscal policy orientations to raise potential growth in the longer term. The recommendations are selective, focussing mainly on tax policies, which should not be taken to suggest that there are few improvements to be made on the expenditure side. Indeed, past *Economic Surveys* and other OECD reviews have provided considerable advice concerning public expenditures in areas such as health, innovation, education, and public administration (OECD 2006, 2004, 2000 and 1998).

A golden decade of fiscal policy ended with the onset of the economic crisis

Fiscal conservatism was established after the 1998 crisis, and only gradually eroded

Creating and maintaining a strong budgetary position was a key plank of the government's macroeconomic policies during the period of strong economic growth from 1999 through mid-2008. The 1998 crisis, and the prolonged period of fiscal weakness that preceded it, withered any remaining political appetite for deficits. Together with other macroeconomic weaknesses, fiscal indiscipline had brought default on government debts, widespread non-payment of wages and other obligations, rampant dollarisation, and an erosion of federal control in the regions, raising the spectre of disintegration of the federation. Thus, despite the economic downturn that followed the financial crisis in August 1998, strong measures were put in place to limit the deficit in 1999, and in 2000 the first in a long string of surpluses emerged, as growth surged and oil prices rose by 66%, causing fiscal revenues to overshoot targets by wide margins. At the federal level budget surpluses continued through 2008, averaging over 4% of GDP, with a peak of 7.5% in 2005 (Table 2.1). As a result, gross public debt shrank steadily, reaching very low levels by end-2008 (Figure 2.1).[1]

Strong surpluses over the past decade were in part the product of conservative assumptions, especially about oil and gas prices (Figure 2.2). Whereas actual prices were on an

Table 2.1. **Federal budget outcomes**

As a percentage of GDP

	2005	2006	2007	2008
Revenues	23.7	23.4	23.6	22.3
Oil revenues	8.7	9.5	7.7	9.3
Non-oil revenues	15.0	13.9	15.8	13.0
Expenditures	16.3	15.9	18.1	18.2
Overall balance	7.5	7.4	5.4	4.1
Non-oil balance	–1.3	–2.1	–2.3	–5.2

Source: Ministry of Finance of the Russian Federation.

Figure 2.1. **Primary balance and debt**

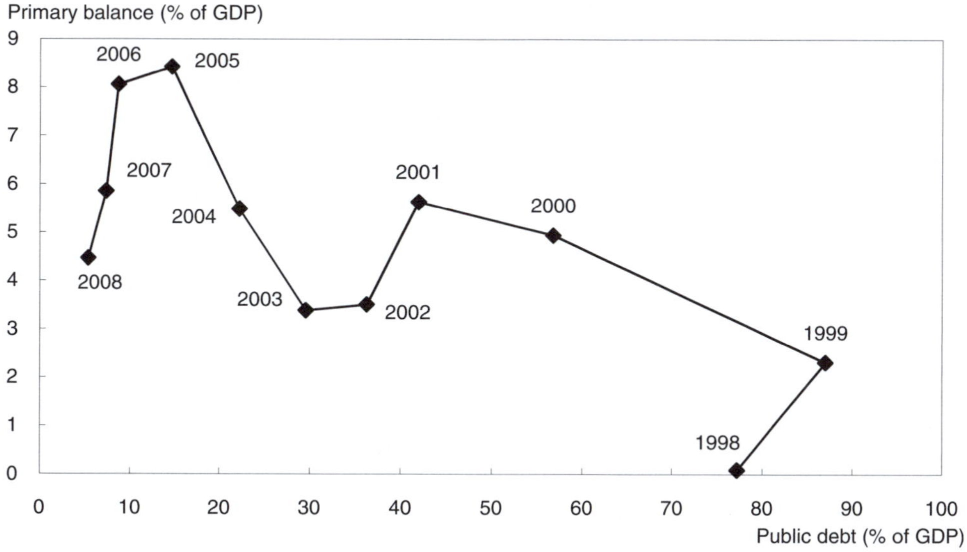

Source: Federal Service for State Statistics, Central Bank of Russia and Ministry of Finance of the Russian Federation.

StatLink http://dx.doi.org/10.1787/648746445614

Figure 2.2. **Budgeted and actual average annual oil prices**[1]

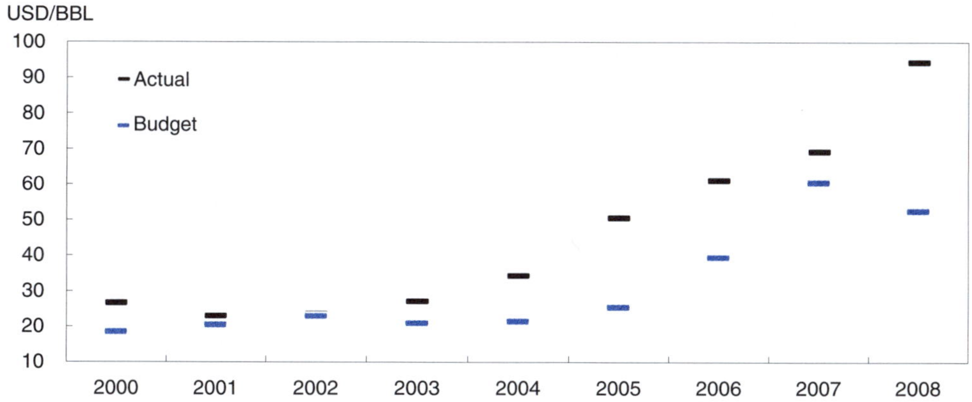

1. Price of Urals assumed in Federal Budget and actual outturn.

Source: Economic Expert Group.

upward trend beginning in 2003, the budget generally assumed declines back toward long-term historic averages. Largely as a result, revenues generally exceeded budget assumptions by a substantial margin during the period 2000-08.

It is impossible to identify precisely the extent to which the rise in oil prices after 1999 represented an exceptional windfall. Taking the average real price of oil during the preceding 20 years, however, suggests that Russia had windfall export revenues of about 10% of GDP per year during the period 2004-08, of which the amount accruing to the public sector was about 7% of GDP per year, and the amount saved by the government around 4% of GDP. From 2005 onwards, the saving of excess oil revenues was institutionalised *via* the creation of the Oil Stabilisation Fund, which in 2008 was expanded to collect natural gas revenues as well and split into two separate funds. Initially, the cut-off price used for triggering savings in the Oil Stabilisation Fund was USD 27 per barrel, which is indicative of government thinking at the time concerning what constitutes windfall revenues.

Expenditures also overshot initial budget figures, *via* a series of within-year supplemental budgets, but the spending overshoots were kept within the excess revenue, so that the overall balance generally exceeded the budget plan by a large margin. Over the period of surpluses, more than half of excess revenues were saved. This restraint in spending incremental oil and gas revenues is notable even in comparison with most other oil-exporting countries.

Saving oil revenue windfalls was an incomplete buffer against Dutch Disease pressures

Although a large part of Russia's oil price windfall revenues were captured by the state, and although most budgetary oil windfall revenues were saved, the rouble nonetheless appreciated substantially in real effective terms, and import growth was extremely rapid. Of course, not all of excess revenue was saved, so it was not to be expected that fiscal policy would completely insulate the economy from exchange rate pressures arising from successive improvements in the terms of trade. The non-oil budget deficit was allowed to expand gradually, with a large part of the deterioration coming in 2007-08. As a result, the non-oil deficit increased by about 3½ per cent of GDP in 4 years.

One reason why some excess revenue was increasingly allowed to be reflected in higher expenditure is doubtless that assessments of the permanent oil price were revised upward in the light of market developments. As noted above, oil prices surprised to the upside almost every year from 2000 to 2008, and consensus estimates of long-term prices moved up sharply over this period. Most analysis of the oil market saw the factors behind the oil price surge as primarily permanent in nature: limited supply combined with strong secular demand growth in emerging economies like China and India. Beyond this understandable reassessment of long-term commodity prices, the more rapid expansion of non-oil deficits in 2007-08 also reflected a pre-election loosening of fiscal policy. Finally, oil was not the only Russian export commodity whose price surged after 2003. Tax revenues from natural gas, base and precious metals, coal, and forest products all rose strongly as well, but unlike oil, there was no institutional mechanism to save this excess revenue, except in the case of gas from 2008 onward.

The rise in the real effective exchange rate was, however, greater for Russia than for any other comparable oil-exporting country during the period of rising oil prices (Figure 2.3), while Russia saved a comparatively large proportion of windfall revenues. Given that public

Figure 2.3. **REER for the Russian Federation and other oil exporters**

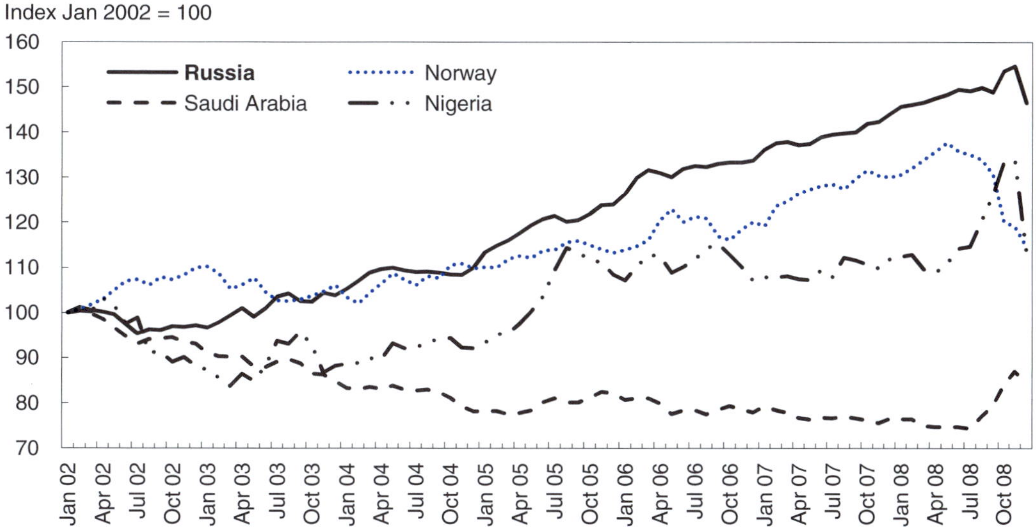

Source: JP Morgan.

saving is the standard prescription for insulating commodity-exporting economies from swings in the terms of trade, the question therefore arises as to why real appreciation of the rouble was so substantial. A number of answers suggest themselves.

One reason is the size of the real depreciation of the rouble in the wake of the 1998 crisis. Between July 1998 and January 1999 the rouble depreciated by nearly 50% in real effective terms. While much of this probably represented an unwinding of previous overvaluation, part of it was likely an overshooting (as suggested, for instance, by the swing in the current account balance from near zero in 1998 to a surplus of 18% of GDP in 2000. A portion of the rebound after 1999 can correspondingly be attributed to a reversal of that overshooting.

Relatedly, in the immediate aftermath of the 1998 crisis Russia had a GDP *per capita* of only around USD 1 000. As such, it was to be expected that convergence towards the income levels of advanced countries would be associated with real appreciation of the rouble, *via* Balassa-Samuelson effects: productivity catch-up in traded goods, whose prices are fixed in world markets, is reflected in a falling relative price of tradables, which is to say a rising real exchange rate (see OECD, 2006, Box 2.2). A similar trend real appreciation has been seen in most other European transition economies, none of which are oil exporters (Figure 2.4).

Third, it is a striking fact that the public saving corresponding to unspent oil and gas revenues was much more than offset (especially in the last few years) by falling private savings (Table 2.2).

A corollary is that while the public sector's net foreign assets rose by nearly USD 500 billion between 2000 and 2007, the net foreign liabilities of the private sector over the same period increased by substantially more.[2] The foreign borrowing by the private sector was an increasingly important source of the upward pressure on the rouble: in 2007 net private capital inflows exceeded the current account surplus for the first time. While the standard Ricardian equivalence argument offers one rationale for the opposite movements in public and private savings, the theoretical conditions for full equivalence are quite restrictive, and in practice the degree of offset is generally observed to be much less than unity, whereas in Russia it was about 1.5 over the period 2000-07. In any event, other forces

Figure 2.4. **REER trend for European transition economies**

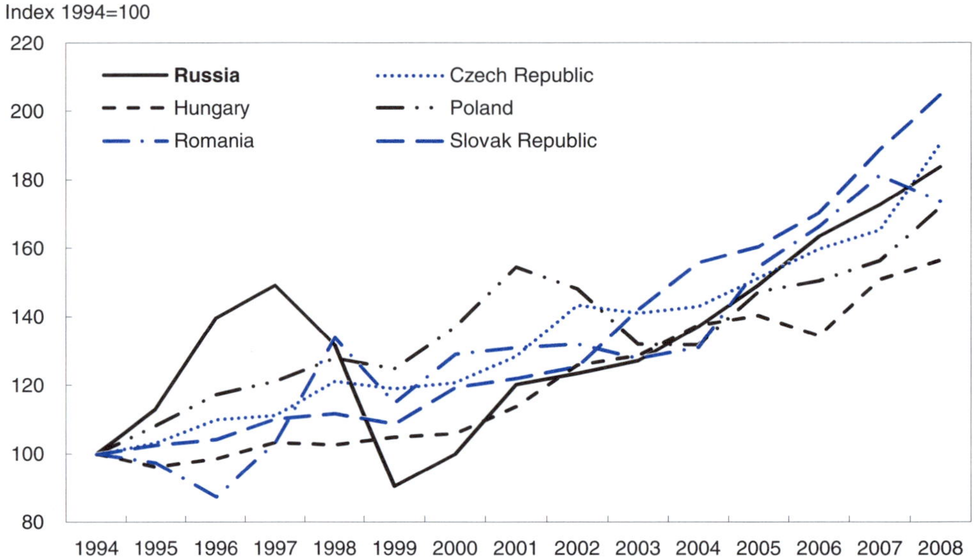

Source: IMF, IFS database.

StatLink http://dx.doi.org/10.1787/648747272280

Table 2.2. **Savings and investment**

As a percentage of GDP

	2000	2001	2002	2003	2004	2005	2006	2007	2008
National savings	34.9	30.0	26.4	26.6	28.4	28.8	28.1	27.0	28.0
Public	1.9	3.0	0.9	1.3	4.5	8.1	8.4	6.0	4.8
Private	33.0	27.0	25.5	25.3	24.0	20.7	19.7	21.0	23.2
Gross fixed capital formation	16.9	18.9	17.9	18.4	18.4	17.7	18.5	21.1	21.9
Current account balance	18.0	11.1	8.4	8.2	10.1	11.1	9.6	6.0	6.1

Source: OECD calculations based on Federal Service for State Statistics and Central Bank of Russia.

were probably more important in explaining falling private saving in Russia in the last few years. Major factors included:

- *The falling cost and increasing availability of access to international capital markets.* Borrowing spreads for virtually all emerging markets fell to record low levels (Figure 2.5), while lending flows increased strongly. The benign global macroeconomic environment was in turn one reason for this improvement in access, and Russia's own macroeconomic fundamentals were better than most. Indeed, the radical turnaround in fiscal sustainability after the 1998 crisis changed perceptions of Russia's macroeconomic stability and made it easier for Russian corporate borrowers to access international bond, equity, and syndicated loan markets. Sovereign credit ratings typically constitute an effective ceiling for ratings on other borrowers, and the strong improvement in Russia's sovereign rating, which reached investment grade in 2003, facilitated a re-rating of non-sovereign Russian entities (Table 2.3).
- *The decision to make the rouble convertible in July 2006.* This decision was mostly symbolic, as by that time there was little in the way of remaining capital account restrictions. Nonetheless, some obstacles to portfolio inflows were removed, and the symbolism may

Figure 2.5. **EMBI+ spreads**

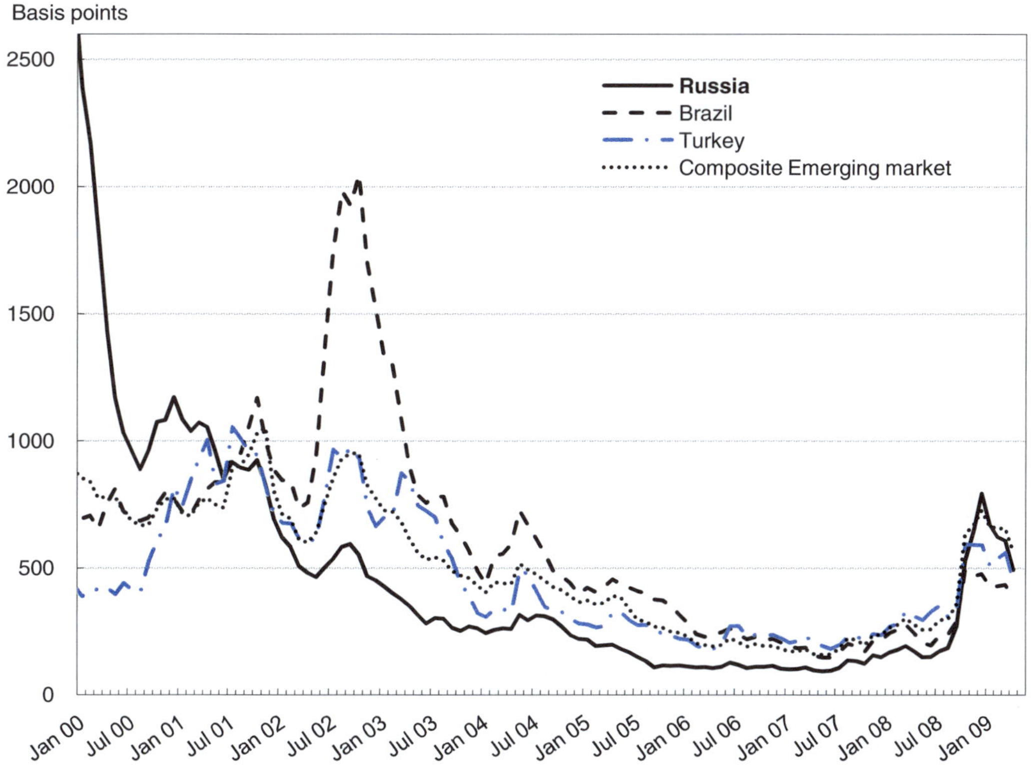

Source: Datastream.

StatLink http://dx.doi.org/10.1787/648777678207

Table 2.3. **Russian sovereign ratings**

End-year rating	Standard & Poor's	Fitch	Moody's
	Credit rating	Issuer default rating	Government bond
	Foreign currency, long term/Outlook		
1998	CCC-/Negative	CCC/n.a.	B3/Negative
1999	SD/NM[1]	CCC/n.a.	B3/Negative
2000	B-/Stable	B/Stable	B3/Stable
2001	B+/Stable	B+/Stable	Ba3/Stable
2002	BB/Stable	BB-/Positive	Ba2/Stable
2003	BB/Stable	BB+/Stable	Baa3/Stable
2004	BB+/Stable	BBB-/Stable	Baa3/Positive
2005	BBB/Stable	BBB/Stable	Baa2/Stable
2006	BBB+/Stable	BBB+/Stable	Baa2/Stable
2007	BBB+/Stable	BBB+/Stable	Baa2/Stable
2008	BBB/Negative	BBB+/Negative	Baa1/Stable

1. Selective default/not meaningful.

Source: Standard & Poor's, Fitch ratings, and Moody's Investors Service.

have had some effect on sentiment, as the move did coincide with a surge in net capital inflows, which reached their peak in the first half of 2007.

- *The improving financial situation for the private sector.* Not all of commodity price windfalls were taxed away, and profits of commodity exporters in particular soared. This was another factor easing the borrowing constraint on major Russian corporates in the extraction industries. Strong economic growth also drove rapid increases in profits in domestically-oriented industries such as banking, construction, and telecommunications.

Tax structure, budgeting rules, and fiscal institutions were improved

Over the last ten years Russia has taken a number of steps to improve the quality of fiscal policy-making and implementation. These include:

- the gathering of virtually all government activities on a single Treasury account in 1999, which, together with the elimination of most extra-budgetary funds, did much to improve the coherence and transparency of the budget;[3]
- revisions to the Budget Code in 2003 and 2004 which created the Oil Stabilisation Fund and imposed fiscal rules on sub-federal levels of government; and
- a further reworking of the Budget Code in 2007 to provide for:
  - A move, beginning in 2008, to 3-year budgets (a feature unmatched in the OECD);
  - the creation in 2008 of a National Welfare Fund to accompany the Reserve Fund, which took over the role of the Oil Stabilisation Fund; and
  - the establishment of ceilings on the overall budget deficit of 1% of GDP and on transfers of oil revenues to the budget of 3.7% of GDP, both starting in 2011.

Despite the real advances represented by these and other changes, it must be observed that improvements in the framework were not sufficient to ensure predictable outcomes. In practice, rules have often been observed in the breach: for example, annual budgets were regularly amended to permit additional expenditure; three-year budgets were suspended one year after their introduction; rules for the investment of assets in the Reserve Fund and the National Welfare Fund were loosened; and in April 2009 the Budget Code was amended again to postpone the application of the limit overall deficits from 2011 to 2013.

Assessing the fiscal response to the crisis

Actions already taken

As noted in Chapter 1, the Russian authorities responded quickly and on a large scale to the onset of the global crisis, and that response included a number of fiscal measures (Box 2.1). The main initial emphasis was on supporting the banking system and financial markets, given that these were the hardest-hit areas at the outset. Thus the government moved deposits from the central bank to commercial banks (on an auction basis), amended the 2008 budget to allow for purchases of equities by the state corporation Vnesheconombank (VEB), and boosted the capital of major government-owned banks.

Quite quickly thereafter, however, the crisis spread through the real economy, and the approach was broadened. As regards fiscal instruments, the government cut the corporate profit tax rate from 24% to 20% and announced its willingness to support enterprises *via* guarantees, although the amounts, timetable and modalities were not immediately made clear. While the 2009-11 three-year budget was adopted in November 2008 as drafted (pre-crisis), the government began working on revisions to reflect the new economic situation and provide for more of a fiscal stimulus. Numerous scenarios for amendments were considered, with some within government favouring expenditure cutbacks to limit the deficit, and others pushing for additional spending and deficits up to 10% of GDP. A compromise between these approaches was reached, with the budget amendments

Box 2.1. **Initial fiscal anti-crisis measures**

- Allocation of funds to VEB for supporting securities markets.
- Capital injections into VEB, Deposit Insurance Agency, and Mortgage Agency.
- Provision of subordinated loans to banks to match capital raising efforts by shareholders.
- Switching deposits from CBR to commercial banks.
- Reduction in the rate of corporation tax.
- Easing of rules on depreciation.
- Further simplification of taxes for small and medium-sized enterprises.
- Adjustment of the basis for calculating the oil export tax, to allow for faster reductions in price downturns.
- Increase in unemployment insurance benefits.
- Increase in regional transfers.
- Guarantees of 50% of loans extended by Russian banks to enterprises in 2009 for core operations or investment for a duration of between 6 months and 5 years (government decree in February 2009).
- Price preferences for domestic suppliers in public procurement.

adopted in April leaving spending little changed from the original budget and a projected deficit in 2009 of 7.4% of GDP, based on an average price for Urals grade oil of USD 41 per barrel (see Box 1.2).

Automatic stabilisers

Much of the change in the budget balance between 2008 and 2009 is due to the effect on tax revenues of lower commodity prices and real GDP; automatic stabilisers in Russia operate mainly on the revenue side. With oil prices budgeted to average around half of the outcome for 2008, the government expects oil revenue to be approximately 5 percentage points of GDP lower in 2009. Added to this will be reductions in natural gas and metals-related revenues, and further losses on general corporate profit tax (excluding the reduction in the rate), VAT, and personal income tax. All in all, revenues are projected to be lower by nearly 6 percentage points of GDP. Automatic expenditure increases are negligible in comparison, being mainly limited to extra unemployment benefit payments, which should amount to only a fraction of a percent of GDP, notwithstanding the expected upsurge in unemployment claims. Despite the increase in benefit rates for 2009, replacement rates in Russia are very low, and many unemployed workers do not even bother claiming benefits.

Discretionary stimulus

Beyond such automatic stabilisers, there are the questions of how much discretionary stimulus to provide, and in what form. *As to the question of how much, there are several reasons for Russia to be bold, at least in the current year. First*, in common with many other countries, Russia is facing an exceptional adverse shock to aggregate demand, and the functioning of the financial system remains under threat. *Second*, the exchange rate orientation of monetary policy affords limited scope to use interest rates or quantitative easing to stimulate demand – although the wider target band adopted in January 2009 does provide more room for manoeuvre than before, which has been exploited via a series of interest rate reductions in recent months as confidence in the rouble has strengthened – which leaves fiscal policy as the main available instrument. *Third*, there is some reason to expect fiscal multipliers to be higher than normal in current conditions, with an unusually large proportion of credit-constrained agents (households, enterprises, and sub-federal governments). *Fourth*, the accumulation of fiscal reserves in previous years means that the government's room for manoeuvre is relatively great, notwithstanding the enormous scale of the shock to revenues. And *fifth*, greater discretionary stimulus is warranted where automatic stabilisers are weak, which, outside the oil sector, they are in Russia.

As against these arguments for fiscal expansion, to the extent that the crisis in Russia is driven by the deterioration in the terms of trade, it can be questioned whether trying to offset the impact of that deterioration on demand is warranted. If Russia were merely facing a new much lower permanent oil price than previously foreseen, then the country's permanent income would be correspondingly lower and consumption should be curtailed, while the real exchange rate should adjust to shift resources to the non-oil tradables sector. This is not a sufficient argument for passivity, however. To begin with, it is not clear that the low oil prices seen in late 2008 and early 2009 represented the best assumption about their long-term level. The oil price has already roughly doubled relative to its trough levels, and futures prices indicate some further rise over the next two years. In addition, most long-term assessments (*e.g.* IEA, 2008; Kjarstad and Jonsson, 2008) indicate limited global supply increase while strong economic growth in emerging economies drives continued trend growth in demand. In any event, adjustment to sharply lower terms of trade necessarily takes time, and there is a case for smoothing the costs of such adjustment, especially when the exogenous shock is large and the risk of serious social disruption in the event of a deep slump is non-negligible.

Apart from the size of the anti-crisis fiscal package, its composition also matters for the final effect on demand, as well as on efficiency and equity. As noted in Chapter 1, the conventional wisdom on fiscal stimulus measures in a recession are that they should be timely, targeted and temporary (*e.g.* OECD, 2008b). New programmes or infrastructure projects that take time to implement are not ideal from the point of view of timeliness, although there is not necessarily a disadvantage for "shovel ready" infrastructure spending, such as accelerating implementation of existing projects. Since the multiplier (the key consideration in targeting) for such spending is generally found to be higher than for other measures, *infrastructure spending, especially when it can be quickly implemented, should have a place in Russia's stimulus package*. More generally, maximising the multiplier effect on aggregate demand militates in favour of expenditure measures rather than general tax cuts, since in a recession private agents will tend to save much of any tax relief. Apart from public investment, *transfers to credit-constrained households or lower levels of government would be likely to have a relatively strong effect on aggregate demand*. The imperative to provide temporary stimulus argues against measures that are hard to reverse, such as raising entitlements or cutting taxes. *Easily reversed measures that could be considered include one-off transfers or tax rebates.*

To the extent possible, consistent with the need to deliver quick and effective demand stimulus, the government should use measures which are useful for achieving longer-term goals as well. A key long-term goal is a high rate of potential growth – the government's economic programme through 2020 calls for average annual real GDP growth of more than 6% over that horizon. From this point of view the reduction in the corporate profit tax rate was well-considered, as such taxes have been found to be the least growth-friendly in the long term (OECD, 2009). As noted above, however, tax reductions tend to be less effective in boosting demand in recessions. In the case of the corporate profits tax, many firms will not be paying the tax at all, and the impact of reduced tax bills on firms with positive profits is likely to be muted in the current unfavourable demand climate. Overall, this cut was probably of little value as an anti-crisis measure, although it should be maintained on account of its long-term benefits.

Another tax measure that has been debated for some time in Russia is a reduction in VAT rates. A limited-time VAT cut could meet the criteria of being timely and temporary, and might also be reasonably well targeted insofar as a cut in a regressive tax would benefit poor and liquidity-constrained households disproportionately. Such a measure would cut against long-term efficiency, however, as the VAT is a relatively non-distortionary and growth-friendly form of taxation. Moreover, it may be hard to make such a cut credibly temporary, as the political pressure not to put the rate back up would be intense.

Other long-term objectives that could be considered in designing a stimulus package include improving energy efficiency and protecting the environment. For example, subsidies or tax incentives could be provided to induce the replacement of older more polluting cars with newer models having lower emissions and greater fuel economy. As a measure to support the struggling domestic car industry this would have been preferable to the November 2008 increase of tariffs on second-hand imported cars, as the latter distorts relative prices and sends negative signals to trading partners while having no obvious environmental benefit.

Supporting the financial sector

Beyond stimulus measures *per se*, fiscal action is also key to maintaining the functioning of the banks. Some of the fiscal commitments associated with supporting the financial system are best seen as exchanges of assets rather than expenditures, and do not directly add to aggregate demand.[4] Their effect, however, may be at least as critical. If the banking system experiences major loan losses, as it did at the time of the 1998 recession, its existing capital would be largely wiped out, which could impose a damaging degree of deleveraging on the economy. The challenge for the government is on the one hand to provide enough assistance to allow the core of the banking system to maintain capital adequacy and to give banks a sufficient incentive to make new loans despite the increase in credit risk, while on the other hand containing moral hazard and the cost to taxpayers.

In some respects, Russia is in a relatively favourable position as regards the policy options for supporting the banks in the current context. First, the sector is smaller in relation to the size of the economy than in OECD countries, which means both the economic impact of bank failures and the cost of bail-outs are relatively limited. Second, the largest banks are already state-owned, so the issue of whether, when, and how to nationalise for the most part does not arise. Ownership of the biggest banks also gives the Russian authorities an unusually high degree of leverage to ensure that lending is sustained, although it also increases the danger of misallocated resources, such as directed lending to state-owned enterprises.[5]

These favourable factors suggest that *Russia should err on the side of limiting blanket support to banks and bailing out failing banks*. Attention should be focussed instead on closing and liquidating or selling such banks, and ensuring speedy payout of depositors to maintain public confidence in the system. This would facilitate bank consolidation, which is in the long-term interests of the sector (see Chapter 4), while limiting fiscal costs and moral hazard. Actions with a fiscal dimension may already have gone too far in the direction of aggravating moral hazard and costs to the public purse: subordinated loans at favourable rates have been extended to a number of banks, and the government has already guaranteed 50% of bank loans to enterprises in 2009 for core operations.

Banks of systemic importance should be kept functioning in one way or another, whether by provisions of emergency liquidity, arranged mergers, public injections of capital, and/or selective guarantees. There are few such banks, however, probably none beyond the largest 20 banks by assets. The government and central bank have already taken steps to bolster the state-owned banks, so remaining policy responses should be focussed on ensuring the viability of the other very large banks. Many of these are foreign-owned, which hitherto has been seen as a sign of strength, since it was assumed that the foreign parents were willing and able to come to the rescue of their subsidiaries in case of need. This has been put in question with the difficulties experienced by major banks in the West, however, and already there have been indications that in some cases liquidity has been funnelled back to the parent bank from the subsidiaries.

The exit strategy

Safeguarding fiscal sustainability is less of an issue in Russia than in many OECD economies. The public sector has low levels of gross debt and negative net debt, given the accumulation of financial assets in recent years (Figure 2.6). Nonetheless, the outlook for sustainability is sensitive to oil prices in particular. The federal government non-oil deficit was already running at about 6% of GDP in 2008, while oil revenues are expected to amount to only 5% of GDP in 2009. Even taking into account the exceptional effects of the crisis on the 2009 budget, at current oil prices the government would be facing overall deficits indefinitely in the absence of corrective action. With the federal deficit expected to be as

Figure 2.6. **Net public debt in OECD and Russian Federation, 2008**

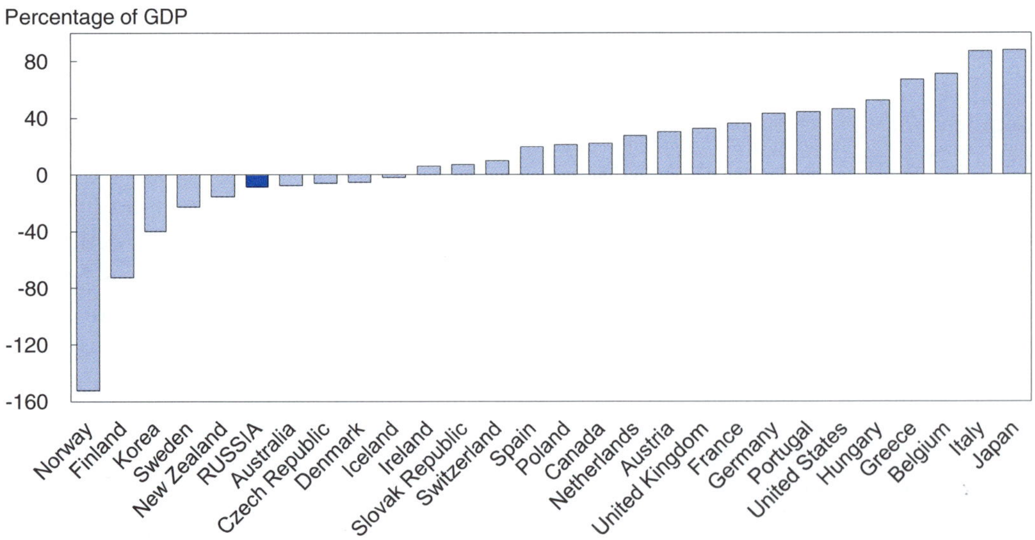

Source: OECD Economic Outlook 84 database, Federal Service for State Statistics, Central Bank of Russia and Ministry of Finance, OECD estimates.

StatLink http://dx.doi.org/10.1787/648845820234

much as 8% of GDP in the current year, while GDP contracts, Russia could quickly find itself on an unsustainable debt path. This risk is heightened by unfavourable long-term factors, notably an ageing and declining population and environmental degradation problems. These factors call for prudent public saving behaviour as Russia emerges from the crisis. Public statements by the President, Prime Minister and Finance Minister suggest that this is understood at the highest levels, and that there is no wish to fritter away the positive legacy of fiscal prudence built up over the past decade.

As in other crisis-hit countries, therefore, it will be important for Russia to set its stimulus efforts in a medium-term context and credibly chart a return to a sustainable debt path. The existence of the three-year budgeting mechanism and the fiscal rule embedded in the Budget Code offer useful instruments to this end. As noted earlier, however, Russia has a track record of circumventing fiscal policy commitments, which weakens credibility of future commitments. Although amendments to annual budgets, the first three-year budgets (for 2008-10 and 2009-11), and the Budget Code have generally been adequately justified by circumstances, greater weight could be placed on abiding by the established rules. The temporary suspension of three-year budgeting and the easing of the constraint imposed by the Budget Code on deficits from 2011 may be a case in point. Eliminating the out-years of the three year budget for 2011 are a case in point. *Despite the considerable uncertainty regarding oil prices and economic growth, the government should now set out a credible vision for how deficits will be reduced after 2009. Credibility would be enhanced by taking hard decisions to limit budgetary assistance to individual sectors and enterprises this year.*

Actions to be avoided

Indeed, succumbing to pressures to provide costly subsidies and guarantees, especially outside the financial system, is one of the main fiscal policy dangers to be avoided in the crisis. The banking sector is a special case, given the crucial role of the financial system for the functioning of the economy, but even here, as argued above, support can be selective. As to aid for enterprises in other sectors, apart from the risks for fiscal sustainability, intervening to keep incumbent firms alive will tend only to suppress competition and aggravate the extensive involvement of the state in goods and services markets, which is a key reason for the finding that Russia's product markets are highly restrictive (Chapter 5). As already noted, a number of commitments have already been announced. *The government should try to limit the uptake and cost of guarantees, and resist pressures to expand them further. To the extent that assistance is offered to enterprises it would be preferable to tilt it towards small and medium-sized firms, which are relatively underdeveloped in Russia, rather than large incumbents.*

The other siren call that should be resisted in the current downturn is protectionism. Such measures are of course distortionary and welfare-reducing at the global level, but they are also likely to prove self-defeating, by provoking retaliation from trading partners. Moreover, they may complicate Russia's already tortuous negotiations for accession to the World Trade Organisation (WTO). WTO accession would bring many benefits, which would easily outweigh any costs to the Russian economy of competitive pressures on the domestic automobile industry from imported second-hand cars.

Deficit financing

In the context of large deficits, questions of financing constraints arise, especially given the sharp reduction in capital flows to emerging markets since mid-2008. In Russia's case, with the Reserve Fund amounting for more than 10% of projected 2009 GDP, it could more than cover the expected deficit, allowing the government to dispense with any issuance of debt. Nonetheless, there are two good reasons not to rely exclusively on the Reserve Fund. First, even though the form of financing makes no difference as regards net liabilities, it would probably aid confidence to maintain a sizeable Reserve Fund than to deplete it in little more than a year. Second, issuing government bonds would help to develop domestic bond markets, which have suffered from the relative shortage of government paper in recent years. Government bonds provide a risk-free benchmark for private sector issues which facilitates the deepening of financial markets. *The government should therefore finance a significant part of the 2009 deficit via the issuance of domestic bonds.*

Finetuning the treatment of oil and gas

The two basic questions concerning the fiscal treatment of the private extraction of exhaustible natural resources are how much to tax and what to do with those tax revenues.

Oil and gas taxation

The standard theoretical answer to the first question is that economic rents should be taxed away rather than accruing to oil company shareholders.[6] Private companies extracting non-renewable natural resources should be able to earn a normal return on capital, but no more: the population at large, as owners of the natural resource, should get the benefits of economic rents derived from such activity.

Thus, if there were certainty on what constitutes rent, and on the future path of oil prices, theory would suggest a marginal tax rate of 100% above some threshold representing the normal return on capital. Other considerations militate in favour of a fiscal regime that even goes beyond taxing away pure economic rents from oil extraction, owing to negative externalities associated with this activity. Such externalities could include negative environmental effects, as well as foregone benefits from an economic structure more oriented towards activities which generate innovation and productivity growth (Sachs and Warner, 1995). Other things being equal, such negative externalities would justify not only capturing all pure rents but also using a higher tax rate below the threshold at which pure rents begin to accrue.

In practice, while most oil-producing countries with private producers do set tax rates on oil extraction above the normal corporate profit tax rate, none attempt to tax away all economic rent, and higher tax rates are rarely justified in terms of economic diversification or environmental considerations. The incomplete taxation of rents probably reflects above all the recognition that oil exploration and development is risky, and if the tax regime does not leave sufficient inducement to take such risks, extraction activity will be inefficiently low. In addition, as the marginal tax rate approaches 100%, the incentive to find ways to avoid the tax burden become very strong, which may induce Laffer curve effects.

In a number of oil-producing countries (*e.g.* Saudi Arabia, Mexico, Brazil, Venezuela) most or all of the oil extraction sector is owned by the state. This facilitates the public appropriation of rents and does away with the tricky problem of deciding when the firm undertaking the exploration and development is earning supra-normal profits. At the same time it has the familiar disadvantage of having the public sector running commercial enterprises: a tendency for rent-seeking, inefficiency, soft budget constraints, and a lack of responsiveness to market signals.

Russia taxes oil extraction *via* three instruments. The mineral extraction tax (MET) applies at a rate of 22% on all oil income in excess of an oil price of USD 15 per barrel. Export taxes (roughly two thirds of Russian oil is exported) apply at a rate that is adjusted monthly according to the realised average oil price in the previous month. Oil companies also pay the standard corporate income tax, the rate of which was cut from 24% to 20% in December 2008. The combined effect of these taxes gives rise to a marginal rate in the region of 85% for oil produced from a mature field when oil prices are above USD 25 per barrel. This is one of the highest marginal rates among major oil producers, with Norway's 78% combined regular and petroleum specific corporate income tax rates being the closest comparator.[7]

The high marginal tax rate no doubt played some role in the limited supply response to higher oil prices from 2003 onward (Figure 2.7). In particular, the limited profit element of overall oil taxation may have unduly discouraged risky exploration and development. Most new oilfields in Russia are in relatively remote and inaccessible areas, which increases the difficulty and cost of developing them. The government has for some time been reviewing its oil sector taxation, and in 2008 made a number of adjustments to the MET, to ease the tax burden on depleted fields and to make it more attractive to explore for oil in eastern Siberia and on the continental shelf in the Arctic. The inducements take the form of tax holidays rather than a higher threshold for the application of the MET, which is at best an approximation to the taxation of rents.

Other countries with substantial private involvement in the extraction of oil generally have a system of regular corporate profit tax plus royalties to capture some part of economic rents. In Canada, royalties, which vary across provinces and territories, range up to about 40%, which is applied in addition to federal and (where applicable) provincial corporate income taxes, once projects have covered costs and are generating net income. Australia has a similar system. Norway applies a special corporate income tax rate of 50% on top of the regular rate of 28%, although it has also used other fees and state participation in the development of oil resources which resulted in a higher share of rents

Figure 2.7. **Production of oil and gas condensate**

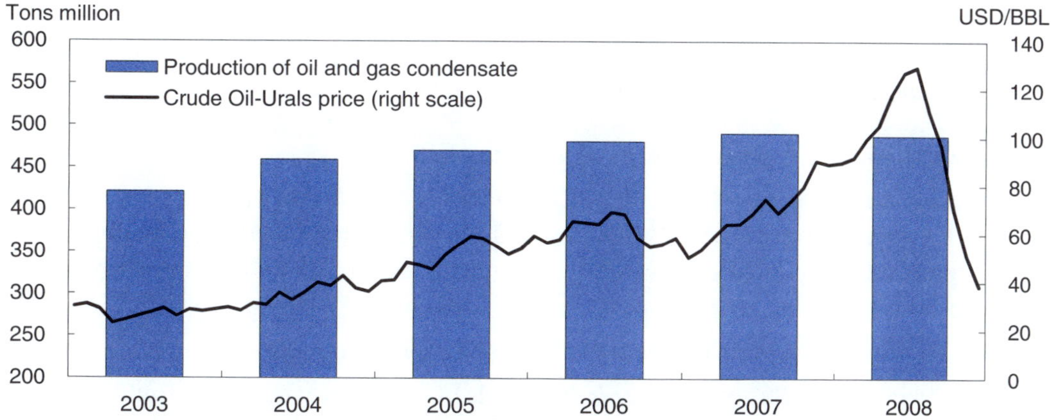

Source: State Statistics Service.

StatLink http://dx.doi.org/10.1787/648854166647

being captured.[8] The United Kingdom formerly also applied an oil-specific Petroleum Revenue Tax at a higher rate than for normal corporate profits, although from 1993 new projects faced only the normal corporate profit tax. In all these cases, oil-specific taxation takes into account the different cost structures of different oil fields and/or distinguishes between new and existing oil fields, in order not to unduly discourage exploration and development in high-cost and/or high-risk fields.

Export taxes are both the largest burden on oil companies in Russia and the least efficient fiscal instrument. Although graduated, with higher rates at higher oil prices, export taxes only roughly approximate to the taxation of oil rents. At the same time, their application distorts the price of domestic oil, which is depressed by the tax. The principal advantage of export taxes is their ease of administration and the fact that they cannot be circumvented by transfer pricing schemes. These advantages are shared by the MET however, and the latter is less distortionary. *In the context of a reform of oil and gas taxation to achieve a more precise and consistent capture of economic rents, export taxes should be removed.*

One issue that arises in taxing profits, not only in Russia, is transfer pricing. Russian companies have used notional prices for sales to subsidiaries offshore or in special zones in order to minimise their tax obligations. In part as a result of such behaviour, a previous elimination of export taxes on oil resulted in a major shortfall of revenue, and such taxes were restored, along with the introduction of the MET. The Russian legislation to limit transfer pricing to avoid taxes is relatively lax (Ahrend and Tompson, 2006) and could be strengthened, in line with approaches used in OECD countries and the OECD Model Tax Convention.

Oil and other non-renewable natural resource sectors should be taxed in broadly the same manner. Currently, natural gas has a somewhat lighter tax burden, with lower MET and export tax rates. Gurvich *et al.* (2008) estimate that about 83% of oil rents in Russia were captured by the state in 2006-07, while for gas the figure was just over 50%. Other exhaustible resources, like coal, are not subject to export taxes. For gas the situation is complicated by the regulation of domestic prices, which leads to a system of cross subsidies between exports and domestic sales. *Despite rapid increases in domestic gas prices in recent years, the subsidisation of gas for domestic users continues to give rise to the greatest remaining price distortion in the Russian economy, and should be eliminated speedily. When that is done, taxation of gas and oil should be broadly harmonised, with the elimination of export taxes in both cases.* There can be other considerations leading to differences in optimal tax rates, such as environmental damage or energy security, but such considerations are not plausibly consistent with the existing discrepancies in taxation across natural resource sectors.

Allocating the resources taxed from oil and gas activities

Although the question of the optimal tax rate on the extraction of non-renewable resources like oil and gas is not straightforward, the problem of allocating those revenues is perhaps even more difficult. Broadly, there are three options, all of which have pros and cons:

- spend the proceeds from the capture of economic rents from oil;
- use the taxation of oil rents to have lower levels of other tax rates than would otherwise be possible; and/or
- save the oil revenue, acquiring financial assets either in Russia or abroad – indeed, a more basic division of options is between saving rents and spending them, whether *via* higher public expenditures or lower taxes.

As regards the first option, Russia clearly has both deficiencies in infrastructure and pressing social needs. Considerations of prudence, diversification, and perhaps also intergenerational equity argue against spending all income from natural resource extraction, however. Other oil-producing countries have shown the dangers of allowing public investment to surge when oil prices are high. The result can be massive waste if projects have to be left unfinished when prices recede and access to capital markets dries up. Desired investment may also exceed absorptive capacity when resource rents are large, reducing the efficiency of such spending. The question of intergenerational equity arises because the exhaustible resource can be considered to belong to both current and future generations. As against that, if real *per capita* GDP is rising through time, it can be argued that equity is actually worsened by saving some resource rents to provide a stream of income for future generations. The main rationale for saving a substantial part of the economic rents captured from the extraction of oil and other non-renewable resources for a middle-income country like Russia is to avoid falling victim to the resource curse, whereby in recent decades resource-rich countries are found to have relatively poor long-term growth performance (Auty, 2001; Sachs and Warner, 1995). The main proposed mechanism for the operation of the resource curse is that the exploitation of natural resources results in real appreciation of the currency, displacing non-resource tradables (the Dutch Disease effect). Spending the revenues from oil extraction puts upward pressure on the exchange rate.

Having lower marginal tax rates than would be possible in the absence of natural resource rents is beneficial for economic efficiency and long-term growth. The main disadvantage of using captured resource rents in this way is similar to that for raising public expenditure: that savings of such rents will be inefficiently low, leading to excessive resource dependence and undue exposure to commodity price cycles.

There is no agreed principle for determining the optimal amount of saving from the accumulation of resource rents. One proposed rule of thumb, owing to Hartwick (1977), is to consume only the estimated permanent income from the stock of wealth. This is similar to, though somewhat less conservative than, the approach used by Norway, which transfers from its oil fund to the budget only the estimated permanent return on the fund. It is also broadly in line with the rule in Russia's Budget Code to allow only 3.7% of GDP of oil and gas revenues to be spent annually as from 2013.

If indeed a large proportion of the rents accruing to the public sector is saved, the further question arises of what form such saving should take. There is some reason to expect that returns on domestic investment should be higher on average than investment in advanced countries (a point that also applies to the option of spending on public investment), as Russia has considerable scope for catch-up growth in coming decades. Saving abroad, however, also has advantages, as it helps insulate the exchange rate and the domestic economy from swings in oil prices. The current crisis indeed highlights the utility of saving a large part of oil revenues in good times, and suggests that *public saving of oil rents during the next oil price upturn should be even greater than during the last cycle.*

In addition, the strategy of saving the surpluses abroad, accumulating foreign assets (or running down foreign liabilities) should be maintained. In this way, fiscal policy will provide greater support for resisting Dutch Disease effects and encouraging greater diversification, while allowing monetary policy to be devoted to price stability.

Scope for further tax reform to raise potential growth rates

As noted in Chapter 1, since 2000 Russia has carried out important tax reforms, which had the effect of broadening tax bases, reducing marginal rates, and simplifying the tax structure. These changes constituted possibly the single most important reform of the first Putin administration. Major measures included the introduction of a 13% flat-rate personal income tax, the mineral extraction tax, and the unified social tax (which finances the social security funds), the elimination of the various sales taxes, the lowering of the corporate profit tax rate together with the elimination of numerous tax breaks, and the reduction in the standard rate of VAT.

As a result of these reforms, compared to OECD countries the current tax structure shows a relatively high degree of reliance on indirect taxation *vis-à-vis* personal and corporate income taxes (Figure 2.8). This is in line with one of the main conclusions of the recent *OECD Taxation for Growth* (OECD, 2009) research, which finds VAT to be more growth-friendly than direct taxation, and corporate income tax in particular.

Figure 2.8. **Composition of tax revenues**

Percentage of total tax revenues, 2006

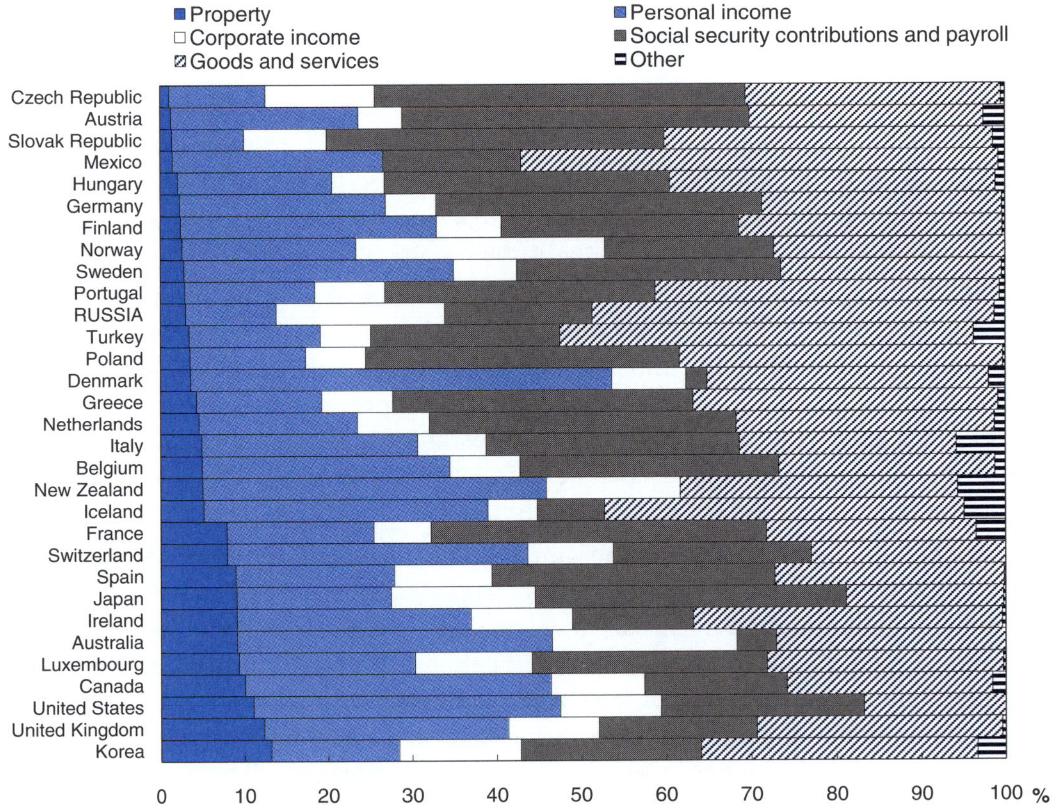

Note: For Mexico, personal income tax revenues include all taxes on income, including corporate income.

Source: OECD calculations based on OECD Revenue Statistics database and IMF, Government Financial Statistics database.

StatLink http://dx.doi.org/10.1787/648863278200

VAT appears to be more burdensome in the Russian context than in some other countries, however, as refunds are notoriously slow. This is what led business lobbies to press for VAT cuts even above cuts in corporate income tax, whose relationship to firms' bottom line is more obvious. VAT is applied at two rates, with some goods exempted altogether. *Efficiency could be served by increasing the harmonisation of rates in a revenue neutral way, which would allow for some reduction of the main rate of 18%, but the government should continue to resist the calls for revenue-reducing cuts in VAT rates.* Although the long-standing problems with refunds point to deficiencies in the administration of VAT, it appears to be fairly efficiently administered in Russia (Figure 2.9).

Figure 2.9. **VAT Revenue Ratio (VRR)**[1]

2005, index increasing in efficiency

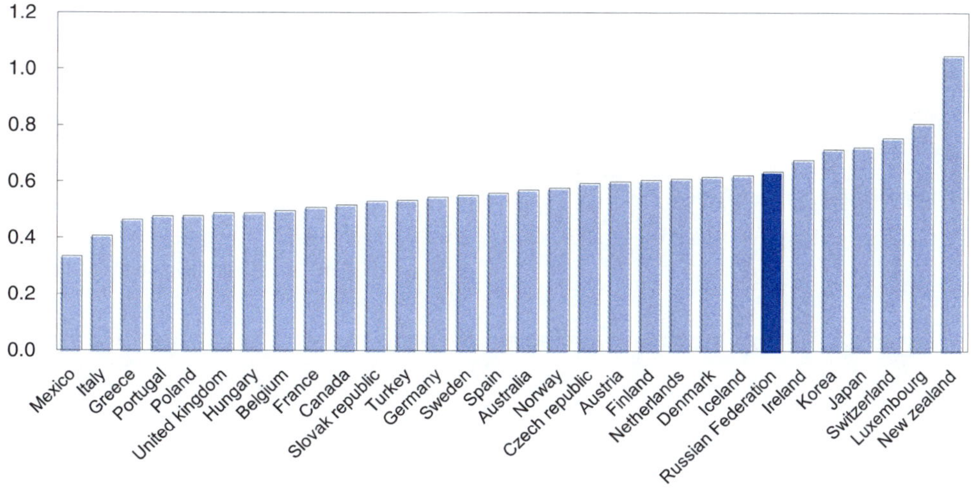

1. VAT Revenue Ratio = (VAT revenue)/([consumption – VAT revenue] x Standard VAT rate).

Source: OECD, Consumption Tax Trends 2008 and OECD estimates.

StatLink http://dx.doi.org/10.1787/648867253480

Some scope remains for further fine-tuning of the tax structure to promote long-term growth, despite the important reforms already implemented, and there also appear to be ways to increase the equity of the tax system without sacrificing efficiency. For example, as shown in Figure 2.8, Russia makes relatively light use of taxes on immovable property, which the OECD's *Taxation for Growth* work finds to be the most efficient tax instrument (OECD 2009). *Over the long term, the authorities should seek to raise the share of total tax revenues accounted for by property taxes.* Corporate profit tax is found to be the least growth-friendly form of taxation, and although Russia already taxes corporate income (not including resource rents) comparatively lightly (Figure 2.10), there may be scope for further reduction. For one thing, Russia applies a lower rate of personal income tax than any OECD country (Figure 2.11), with minimal progressivity – there is a single 13% rate, but with an exemption up to a threshold, which means the average rate rises slightly with income. A rebalancing of corporate and personal income taxes, providing for somewhat more progressivity in the latter, could probably improve both economic efficiency and equity.

As is well recognised by political leaders, Russia remains a highly energy- and emission-intensive economy. The World Bank estimates that the annual energy waste in Russia is equivalent to the annual primary energy consumption of France (World Bank, 2008). This problem has many aspects, including domestic energy pricing, access to gas pipelines (to make flaring of associated petroleum gas less attractive), and building standards, but

Figure 2.10. **Statutory corporate income tax rate**

2008

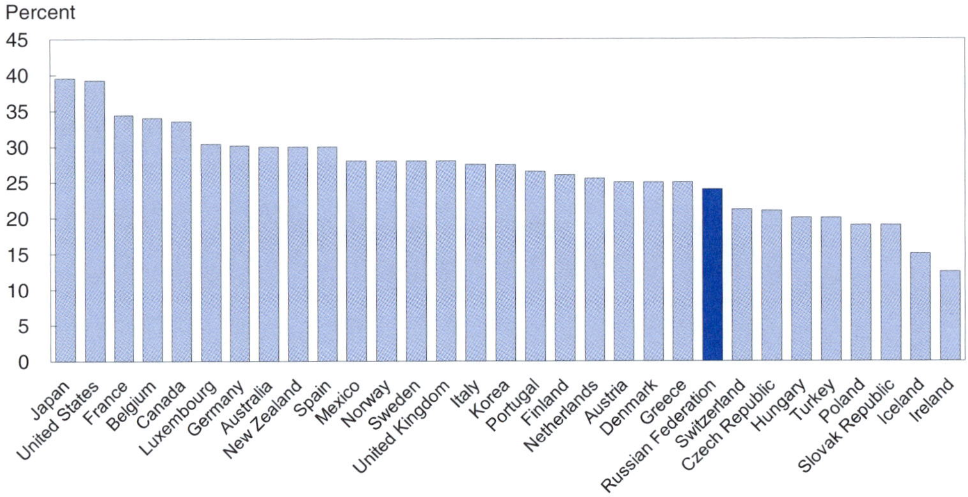

Source: OECD Tax Database (www.oecd.org/ctp/taxdatabase) and OECD estimates.

StatLink http://dx.doi.org/10.1787/650007646572

Figure 2.11. **Top statutory personal income tax rate on wage income**

2007

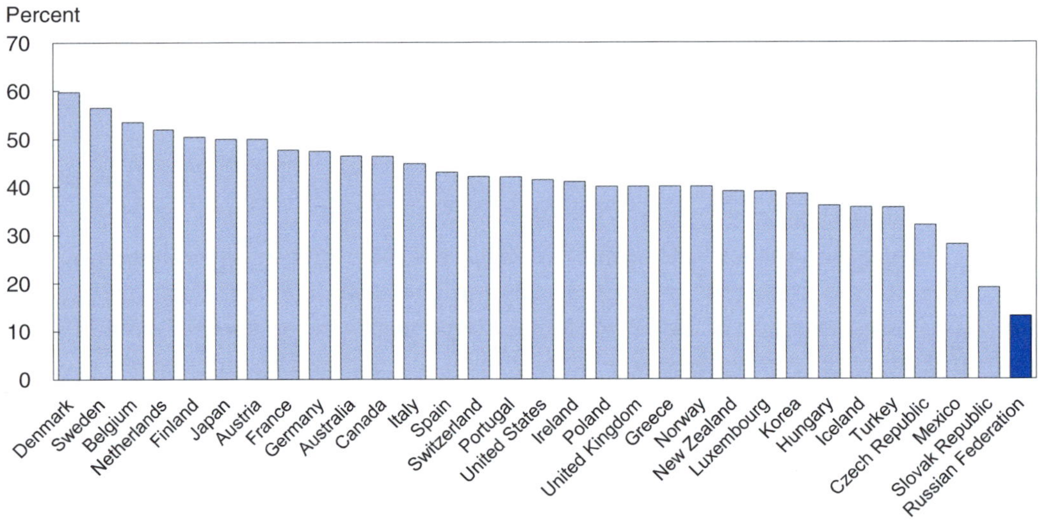

Source: OECD Tax Database (www.oecd.org/ctp/taxdatabase) and OECD estimates.

StatLink http://dx.doi.org/10.1787/650021448476

there is also a role for fiscal instruments. In particular, *Russia should move swiftly to put in place taxation or cap-and-trade systems for emissions of carbon and other pollutants.* Such instruments would assist with the goal of improving energy efficiency, which would boost national income, while addressing the externalities associated with emissions of greenhouse gases or other forms of pollution.

Other important reforms

As regards post-crisis fiscal policy, while the focus in this chapter has been on tax measures to enhance long-term growth, a number of other issues are of particular importance and warrant brief mention. First, despite the substantial progress made in reducing poverty during the decade of rapid growth after 1998, Russia continues to have relatively high poverty rates and extreme levels of income inequality compared to OECD countries. There is considerable scope to improve social safety nets.[9] As discussed in the previous *Economic Survey* (OECD, 2006), health outcomes also remain poor in several areas, suggesting a need both for increased public resources and substantial efficiency gains in the healthcare system.[10]

As is well recognised by the government, the ageing and shrinking of the population poses a threat to Russia's economic vigour and fiscal sustainability. The main aspect of the threat to fiscal sustainability is the prospective increase in dependency ratios and the impact on public expenditures, especially on pensions. One particularity in Russia is that

Box 2.2. **Fiscal policy recommendations**

Crisis-response measures

- Move quickly to provide aggressive fiscal stimulus to support aggregate demand. Measures which have the greatest demand impact – transfers to credit-constrained regions and individuals, plus quickly implementable infrastructure spending – should be given priority. Cutting tax rates, particularly if it cannot be done in an explicitly (and credibly) temporary manner, should be avoided.
- Use the three-year budgeting mechanism and the Budget Code to place fiscal stimulus in the context of a medium-term framework consistent with a sustainable debt path.
- Finance part of the deficit with domestic debt, to provide a risk-free benchmark and assist with financial market development.

Long-term issues

- Establish a tighter link between exhaustible natural resource taxation and economic rents, such as by applying the mineral extraction tax on a project basis, taking into account the cost structures in each field. Harmonise tax rates to achieve a better balance between the taxation of economic rents from oil and that from the extraction of other non-renewable natural resources, including natural gas.
- In the context of an overall reform of oil and gas taxation, eliminate export taxes on oil and gas.
- Improve the administration of VAT (in particular to address the problem of slow refunds), but refrain from cutting average VAT rates. Any harmonisation of the existing high and low rates should be at least revenue neutral.
- Explore the scope for expanding the use of property taxes, while further reducing corporate profit taxes and if possible social security contributions over time.
- Address the challenge of ageing-related public expenditures by providing for rising pensionable ages in line with increases in longevity.
- Expand the use of fiscal instruments to improve environmental outcomes. Measures to reduce greenhouse gas emissions would both contribute to international efforts to combat climate change and address Russia's excessive energy intensity.

standard retirement ages remain lower for women (55) than for men (60), even though life expectancy for men is substantially lower than for women. *Harmonising standard retirement ages for men and women, as has been done in most OECD countries, would be a first step to addressing the fiscal pressures from population ageing, and consideration should subsequently be given to raising retirement ages in line with increases in longevity.* Life expectancy at age 65 is currently over 11 years for men and almost 16 years for women, so a gradual increase from 60 over time appears reasonable. In addition, access to early pension schemes co-funded by employers and the Pension Fund should be tightened.

Trade liberalisation, after progressing well in the 1990s, has largely stalled since 2000. In addition to numerous bilateral frictions with individual trading partners, reductions in general tariff and non-tariff barriers have slowed, with selected cases of backtracking and the emergence of numerous bilateral disputes, where health or other standards were used as pretexts for protectionist measures. As noted in Chapter 5, imports are an important source of competitive pressure in product markets, and innovation and productivity growth would be spurred by renewed progress on trade liberalisation. Russia should not wait for WTO accession to move ahead with further reductions in the level and dispersion of applied tariffs, along with the progressive elimination of non-tariff barriers.

Notes

1. In 2007-08 the fall in gross public debt slowed, as the continuing primary surpluses were reflected mainly in an accumulation of public assets in the Oil Stabilisation Fund (in 2007) and the Reserve and National Welfare funds (2008).
2. The deterioration of the international investment position of the Russian Federation despite a string of large current account surpluses is due primarily to larger valuation changes on liabilities (non-residents' holdings of Russian securities and foreign direct investments) than assets (which are dominated by the central bank's holdings of low-risk advanced country government debt), as well as write-offs of the Russian government's claims on other countries (largely developing country debt).
3. A limited number of activities, mainly related to defence, remain outside the single Treasury account.
4. Such assets swaps may best be seen as expenditures when the asset being acquired has a lower value than the one being provided, but this is often hard to discern.
5. The largest bank is majority-owned by the central bank and the fifth largest bank by the Moscow city government. The other major state-owned banks are controlled by the federal government.
6. The extensive literature on the optimal fiscal treatment of resource rents includes Gunton (2004), Helliwell (1978), and Bradley *et al.* (1981).
7. Norway's tax regime provides for allowances which limit the tax base and imply that the effective rate is well below 78%.
8. Including the participation of the then state-owned oil company Statoil, during the 1970s the Norwegian government's share in the discounted cash flows from oil production was estimated to be in the region of 90% (Kemp and Crichton, 1979).
9. Social and employment policies are assessed by the OECD's Directorate for Employment, Labour and Social Affairs in a forthcoming review of employment and social policies.
10. See the forthcoming OECD review of healthcare policies currently being conducted by the Directorate for Social, Employment and Labour Affairs.

Bibliography

Ahrend, R. and W. Tompson (2006), "Realising the Oil Supply Potential of the CIS: the Impact of Institutions and Policies", *Economics Department Working Papers,* No. 484, OECD, Paris.

Auty, R.M. (2001), "The Political Economy of Resource-driven Growth", *European Economic Review*, Vol. 45, pp. 839-846.

Gunton, T. (2004), "Energy Rent and Public Policy: an Analysis of the Canadian Cool Industry", *Energy Policy*, Vol. 32, pp. 151-183.

Bradley, P., J. Helliwell and J. Livernios (1981), "Efficient Taxation of Resource Income, the Case of Copper Mining in British Columbia", *Resources Policy*, Vol. 7, pp.161-170.

Gurvich, E., E. Vakulenko and P. Krivenko (2008), "Циклические свойства бюджетной политики в нефтедобывающих странах", Энергоресурс Экономического Развития, (Cyclical Properties of Fiscal Policy in Oil Producing Countries", *Energy Economy Papers*).

Hartwick, J.M, (1977), "Intergenerational Equity and the Investing of Rents from Exhaustible Resources", *American Economic Review*, Vol. 67, pp. 972-974.

Helliwell, J. (1978), "Effects of Taxes and Royalties a Copper Mining Investment in British Columbia", *Resources Policy*, Vol. 4, pp. 35-44.

IEA (2008), *World Energy Outlook*, OECD/IEA, Paris.

Kjärstad, J. and F. Johnsson (2008), "Resources and the Future Supply of Oil", *Energy Policy*, Vol. 37, pp. 441-464.

Kemp, A.G. and D. Crichton (1979), "North Sea Oil Taxation in Norway", *Energy Economics*, Vol. 1, pp. 33-46.

OECD (1998), *Reviews of National Policies for Education: Russian Federation,* OECD, Paris.

OECD (2000), *Tertiary Education and Research in the Russian Federation*, OECD, Paris.

OECD (2004), *Economic Surveys: Russian Federation*, OECD, Paris.

OECD (2006), *Economic Surveys: Russian Federation*, OECD, Paris.

OECD (2008a), "Budgeting in Russia", *OECD Journal on Budgeting*, Vol. 8, No. 2.

OECD (2008b), *Economic Outlook*, No. 84, OECD, Paris.

OECD (2009), *Economic Policy Reforms: Going for Growth*, Chapter 5, "Taxation and Economic Growth", OECD, Paris.

Sachs, J. and A. Warner (1995), "Natural Resource Abundance and Economic Growth", *National Bureau of Economic Research Working Papers* No. 5398, NBER, Cambridge, MA.

Spilimbergo, A. *et al.* (2008), "Fiscal Policy for the Crisis", *IMF Staff Position Notes*, SPN/08/01, 29 December 2008.

Watkins, C. and B. Scarfe (1985), *Canadian Oil and Gas Taxation, Energy Journal.*

World Bank (2008), "Energy Efficiency in Russia", *World Finance Review,* World Bank, Washington, DC.

ISBN 978-92-64-05433-2
OECD Economic Surveys: Russian Federation

Chapter 3

Making exchange rate policy more flexible and monetary policy more effective

This chapter discusses the challenges for monetary and exchange rate policy in an environment of large terms terms-of-trade shocks and a volatile capital account. It first examines how effective the quasi-fixed exchange rate regime was in fostering disinflation during the upswing in oil prices (2002 to mid-2008), arguing that, while the upturn in inflation from mid-2007 can be attributed partly to the surge in international commodity prices during this period, underlying inflation remained high due to an excessively accommodative monetary policy stance. The chapter then reviews monetary and exchange rate policy after the onset of the global financial crisis, which triggered a large negative terms-of-trade shock and massive capital outflows. It acknowledges that the pre-announced gradual depreciation of the exchange rate was costly, but suggests that this policy can be seen – ex post – as a second-best policy in an environment of debt dollarisation. However, the first-best policy would have been not to offer such strong incentives for corporate borrowing in foreign currency in the years leading up to the crisis by allowing more exchange rate flexibility. The chapter suggests that not all conditions for adopting inflation targeting in Russia are yet in place, but that preparations should be accelerated.

The record of monetary policy during the years of rising commodity prices was mixed

Over the past decade, monetary policy has pursued two goals: to reduce inflation and limit the real appreciation of the rouble. The Central Bank of Russia (CBR) has had annual targets for the speed of disinflation since 1999, but traditionally also set an explicit ceiling for real appreciation of the rouble.[1] In terms of monetary policy instruments, intervention in the foreign exchange market has been the CBR's main tool for achieving those objectives. Therefore, Russia's monetary and exchange rate policy framework has often been referred to as a *de facto* nominal exchange rate peg (OECD, 2006). Given the strength of Russia's balance of payments during the ten years through mid-2008, the tight management of the nominal exchange rate has involved large interventions which have been only partially sterilised.

As a result of rapid money supply growth, headline inflation, while on a downward trend since 1999, was persistent and the CBR's inflation targets were frequently overshot (Figure 3.1). While accelerating price pressures during mid-2007 to late 2008 were to some

Figure 3.1. **Consumer price index inflation**

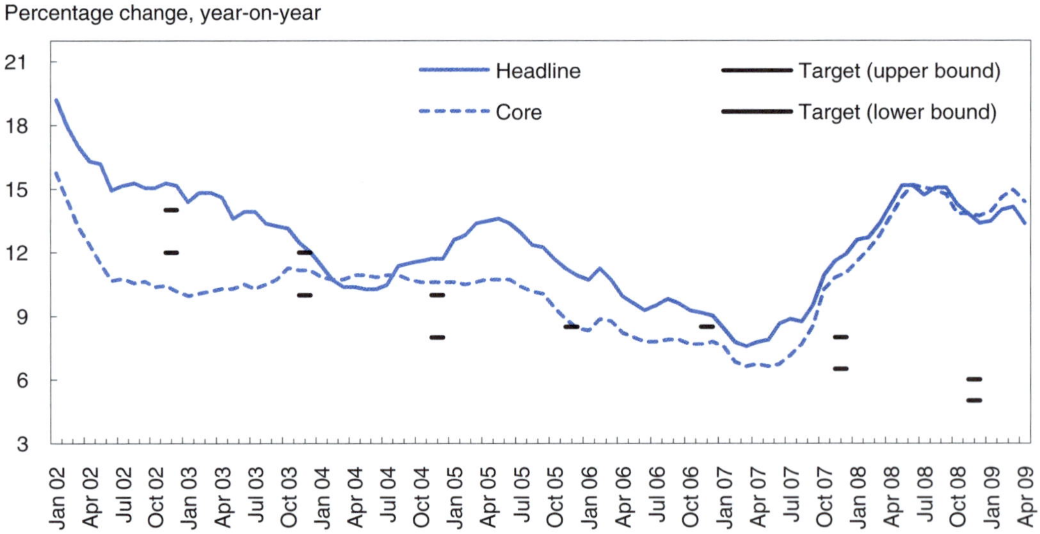

Source: Central Bank of Russia and OECD calculations.

StatLink http://dx.doi.org/10.1787/650072226374

extent due to the global rise in food prices, second round effects also started to materialize as the degree of underlying inflation had remained high (Box 3.1).

Past money supply growth has empirically been a robust determinant of consumer price inflation in Russia (see Annex 3.A2). However, rapid money supply growth did not

Box 3.1. **The impact of the 2007-08 surge in food prices on inflation**

The share of food items in Russia's consumer price index (CPI), currently around 40% has declined considerably (from more than 50%), but is still high when compared to other countries at similar levels of economic development (see Figure 3.10). From mid-2007 through late 2008 food price inflation in Russia accelerated sharply, peaking at an annual rate of around 20% in August 2008 (Figure 3.2, left-hand panel).[1]

Figure 3.2. **Inflation decomposition**

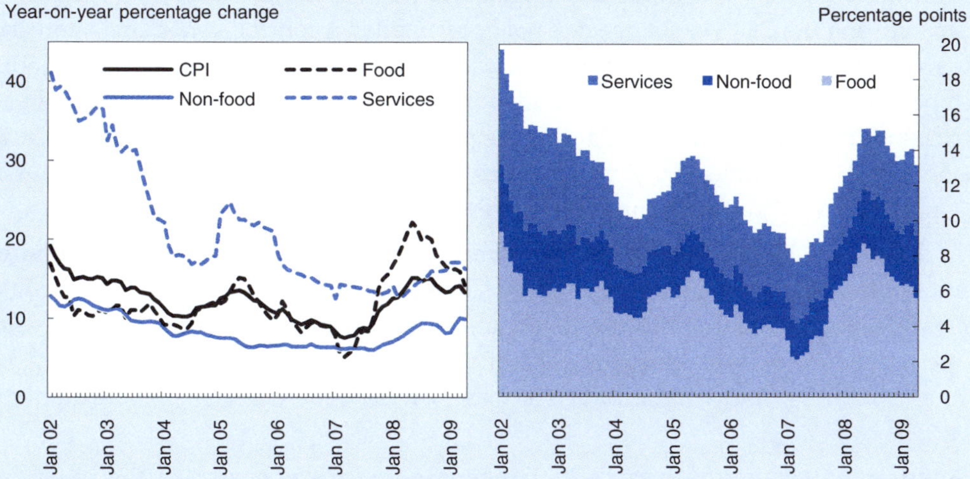

Source: Central Bank of Russia and OECD calculations.

StatLink http://dx.doi.org/10.1787/650087363154

The direct effects of the surge in food prices on Russia's headline inflation – which had been on a downward trend since 1999 – were substantial: CPI inflation re-accelerated into double-digit territory in October 2007. The contribution of food price to CPI inflation surged during 2008 to more than 50% (Figure 3.2 right-hand panel).

Russia's core inflation rate is not an adequate measure for assessing second-round effects, since it includes food prices with the exception of fruit and vegetable prices. Non-food and service price inflation also re-accelerated in early 2008, however, albeit much more gradually than food prices, which probably reflects a combination of second-round effects stemming from higher inflation expectations and excessive money supply growth, fiscal easing and macroeconomic overheating. This is supported d by econometric findings which tend to suggest that lagged money supply growth and producer price inflation are more robust empirical determinants of CPI inflation than past food price increases (see Annex 3.A2).

1. At the same time, administered domestic energy price increases have remained moderate. While an energy sub-component for Russia's CPI is not available, non-food prices excluding petroleum suggest that price increases in this area have been moderate.

fully translate into rising inflation as demand for roubles increased within a broader process of de-dollarisation. More elaborated tools of monetary analysis take into account changes in the equilibrium stock of money and compute "excess liquidity measures" as the difference between the actual money stock and an estimate of the equilibrium stock (see *e.g.* ECB, 2001). The CBR has started to compute such measures for the Russian economy, and, according to its measure of the "money gap", rapid money supply growth in Russia has often resulted in excess liquidity, in particular in 2001, 2004-05 and between 2007 and the first half of 2008 (CBR, 2008a).

By *de facto* importing the monetary policy stance of the Federal Reserve and, since 2005, a linear combination of the stance of the Federal Reserve and the European Central Bank[2], the CBR's monetary policy was generally too accommodative between 2002 and late 2008, with domestic real interest rates remaining negative throughout this period. Moreover, conditions were increasingly favourable for foreign borrowing as well. US interest rates were very low in historical terms, emerging market borrowing spreads were compressed, and the CBR's exchange rate policy resulted in a controlled nominal appreciation of the rouble against the US dollar. Thus Russian corporates increasingly borrowed abroad, which boosted domestic demand and added to inflationary pressures. Russia's monetary and exchange rate policy framework during the period of rising oil prices was a demonstration of the so-called "impossible trinity" which states that a country cannot have more than two of free capital flows, a fixed exchange rate and an independent monetary policy.[3]

As a result of cheap access to credit, monetary and exchange rate policy contributed to a credit boom. While rapid credit growth has been to some extent a reflection of desired financial deepening, and while the levels of credit were not yet such as to suggest an imminent need for deleveraging, the pace of credit expansion in the period leading up to the onset of the global financial crisis was nonetheless clearly unsustainable (see Figure 3.3).

Another implication of Russia's exchange rate policy has been that the rouble's real appreciation in response to the large positive terms-of-trade shock materialized mainly through a positive inflation differential *vis-à-vis* the average of Russia's trading partners instead of nominal appreciation.[4] While such reasoning has been interpreted as suggesting that the exchange rate regime is irrelevant for the transmission of terms-of-trade shocks to the real exchange rate, some have also argued that in pegged exchange rate regimes inflation may become persistent so that the real exchange rate during a positive terms-of-trade shock may overshoot its equilibrium value (Svensson, 1997).

Figure 3.3. **Real credit growth and real lending rate**

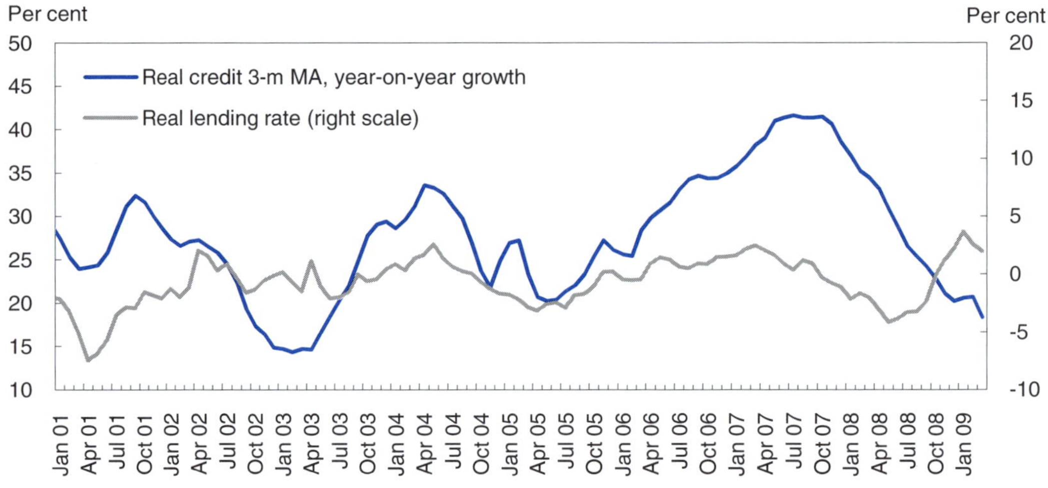

Source: Central Bank of Russia, Federal Service for State Statistics, OECD.

StatLink http://dx.doi.org/10.1787/650101120808

Statistical measures suggest that inflation in Russia is indeed relatively persistent. For example, the coefficient of one-month lagged inflation in a simple univariate inflation process in Russia is around 0.8 (see Figure 3.4), suggesting that the time needed to halve the magnitude of a unit shock to inflation in Russia is around 3 months.[5] This estimate compares, for example to half-lives of one to two and a half months in Central European countries and around one month for Turkey.[6] While univariate measures of inflation persistence are subject to a number of statistical and conceptual caveats, richer models for inflation also suggests that inflation in Russia has a high degree of persistence (see Annex 3.A2), possibly due to backward-looking price-setting behaviour (IMF, 2007).

Figure 3.4. **Univariate inflation process with trend** $\Pi = \alpha_t + \beta\Pi_{t-1} + \varepsilon_t$

Recursive coefficient estimates of β in Russia

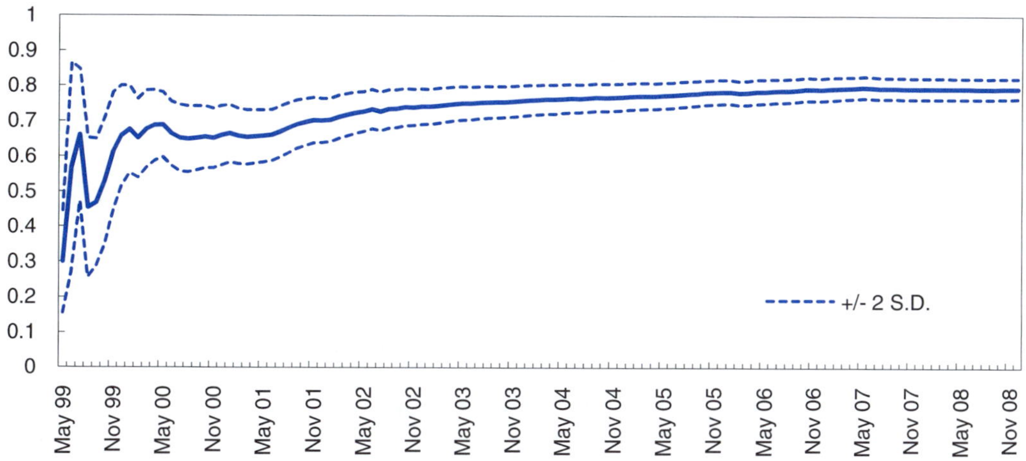

Note: The inflation rate p refers to monthly seasonally adjusted changes in core inflation.

Source: Central Bank of Russia and OECD calculations.

StatLink http://dx.doi.org/10.1787/650108538878

Notwithstanding the relatively high persistence of inflation, however, Russia's real exchange rate is unlikely to have overshot its equilibrium value during the upswing in oil prices, at least given the prevailing prices of oil and other Russian export commodities. Large current account surpluses throughout this period suggest instead that the rouble remained undervalued in real terms, given the strength of the prices of oil, natural gas, and metals. Moreover, some measures of Russia's external competiveness were preserved despite the quite rapid and sustained real appreciation of the currency (IMF, 2008).

Over the past few years, and in particular during the first half of 2008, the CBR intensified its efforts to allow for somewhat greater exchange rate flexibility and to counter inflationary pressures by using interest rate policy and reserve requirements. During conditions of excess liquidity in the banking system, the CBR's deposit rate had some impact on interbank money market rates, but its overnight credit rate remained largely irrelevant. However, increases in the CBR's deposit rate were too small to actually tighten credit conditions as large interventions until mid-2008 continued to fuel money supply growth and most real interest rates remained negative (see Figure 3.5). In view of the risk of further accelerating capital flows during the upswing in oil prices, excessively low interest rates are a natural implication of the CBR's exchange rate target and the "impossible trinity". At the same time, the CBR, with assistance from the International Monetary Fund,

Figure 3.5. **Nominal interest rates and inflation rate**

Per cent

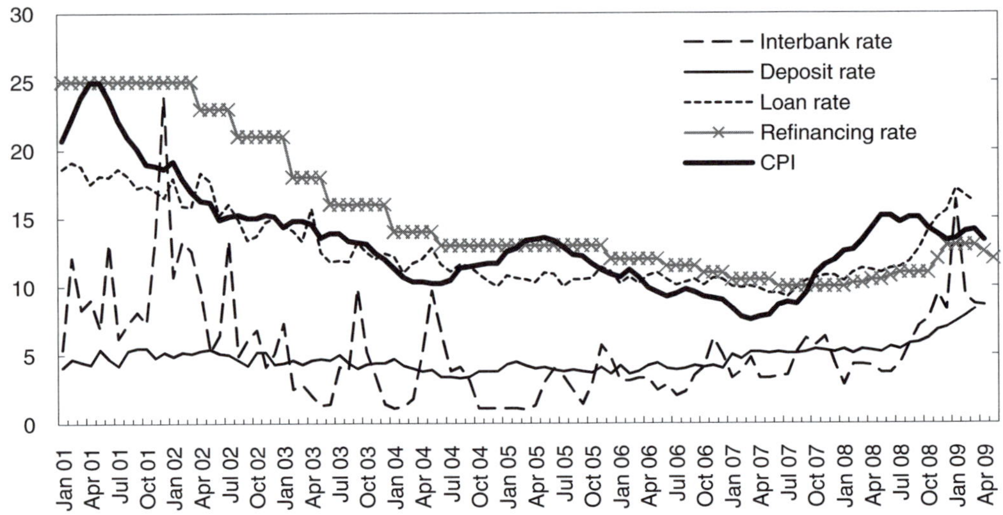

Source: Central Bank of Russia, Russian Federal Service for State Statistics.

StatLink http://dx.doi.org/10.1787/650115086480

has started to publish quarterly inflation reports in order to strengthen its commitment to price stability as a primary goal of monetary policy and to prepare the ground for the transition to formal inflation targeting.

The global recession and sharply falling commodity prices posed a severe policy challenge

Since August 2008, the rouble has been under depreciation pressure due to heightened political risk and a large adverse shift in Russia's terms of trade. Through stepwise depreciations the CBR allowed the rouble to fall by around 30% against the currency basket since early August 2008. The CBR declared that it intends to defend this new level of the exchange rate within a trading band of +/10% (see Figure 3.6). The credibility of CBR announcements to defend the new informal trading band using interest rate policy rather than interventions is questionable, as recent interest rate increases have been too small to compensate for persistent depreciation expectations.

The policy of allowing the exchange rate to adjust only in small steps has been costly. During the period of the stepwise depreciations the CBR lost more than USD 200 billion in foreign exchange reserves (around 36% of the end-July level). In addition, the strategy fuelled speculation against the rouble, given widespread market expectations of further depreciation. In fact, non-deliverable forwards market rates suggest that market participants have continued to factor in a sizable depreciation of the rouble against the dollar until the spring of 2009 (see Figure 3.7). The recent rebound in oil prices has probably been an important catalyst for the reduction in implied depreciation since February 2009.

In view of a high degree of foreign-currency borrowing in the corporate sector, however, the gradual depreciation of the rouble gave the corporate sector time to address some of its currency mismatches by acquiring foreign assets at more favourable rates than otherwise. A large one-off depreciation of the rouble, on the other hand, might have led –

Figure 3.6. **Official exchange rate against dollar-euro basket**

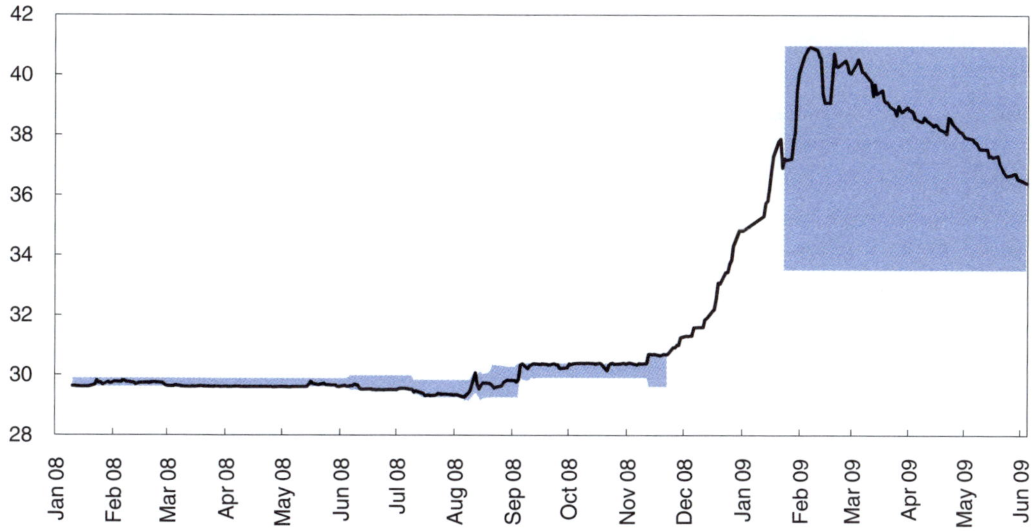

Source: OECD calculations based on Central Bank of Russia.

StatLink http://dx.doi.org/10.1787/650131652888

Figure 3.7. **Premium of NDF rate over RUB/USD spot rate (in %)**

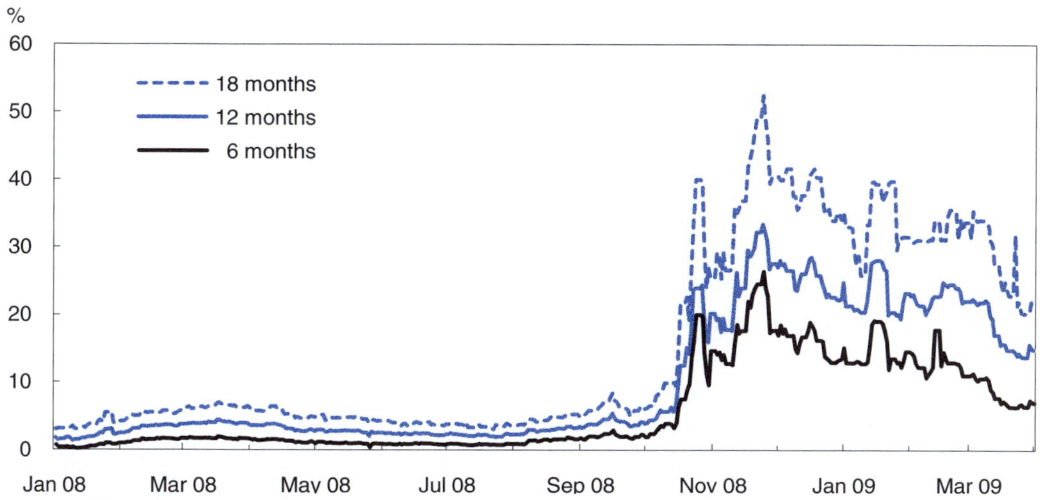

Source: OECD calculations.

StatLink http://dx.doi.org/10.1787/650148783706

in addition to a sharply increasing rouble-value of foreign-currency denominated corporate debt – to bank runs and an even broader re-dollarisation of the economy.

At the same time, despite the increasingly large and frequent step depreciations against the dollar-euro basket through mid-January, and the subsequent establishment of a new wider intervention band, the exchange rate moved comparatively little in nominal and real effective terms. This was because some currencies of key trading partners weakened even further against the dollar and the euro and because Russia's inflation differential *vis-à-vis* its trading partners remained positive (see Figure 3.8). Given the magnitude of the drop in the terms of trade in the initial months of the crisis, it is doubtful whether the extent of depreciation through early February was sufficient to keep the real exchange rate near its equilibrium level. Assuming that Russia's real effective exchange

Figure 3.8. **Oil price and Russian exchange rates**
Index July 2008 = 100

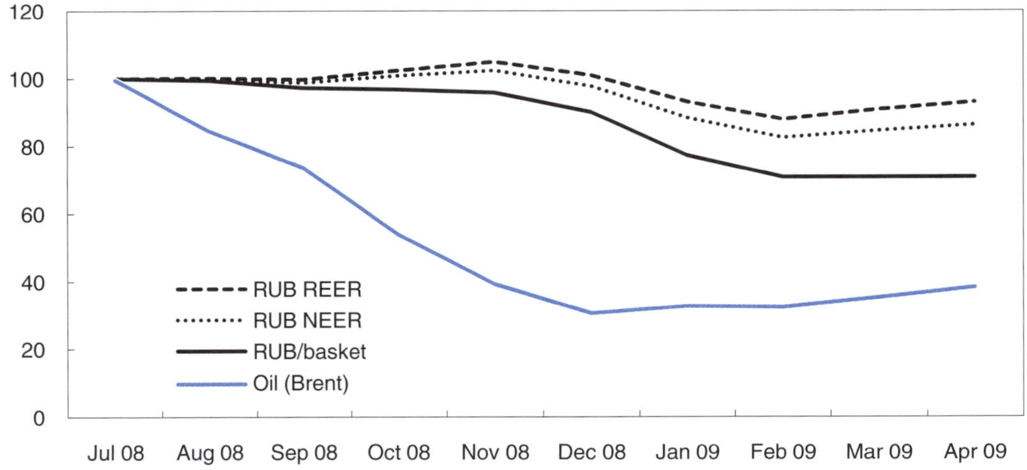

Source: OECD calculations.

StatLink http://dx.doi.org/10.1787/650153435154

rate was close to its equilibrium rate in the run-up to the crisis, as argued in IMF (2008), a larger adjustment of the real effective exchange rate (REER) appeared to be needed to offset the fall in oil and other export commodity prices. In the event, however, there has been a large rebound in oil prices in particular, which, notwithstanding some nominal appreciation since early-February suggests that the rouble is probably again close to its equilibrium value.

Preparations for inflation targeting should be accelerated

With the exchange rate already playing less of a nominal anchor role, the authorities' should accelerate preparations for a framework in which price stability is the primary goal of monetary policy. The CBR has already stated its intention to move to inflation targeting within the next few years, and has allowed for more exchange rate flexibility than in the past.

In general, the experience of other countries suggests that inflation targeting may work in Russia despite its emerging market status and its exposure to commodity price fluctuations and volatile capital flows (see Annex A.3.1). In fact, many of the traditional pre-conditions for inflation targeting (see Table 3.1) tend to be "endogenous", *i.e.* more likely to be fulfilled after inflation targeting has been introduced. For example, the independence of the central bank and its understanding of the monetary transmission process may be strengthened once inflation targeting has been introduced. In addition, despite the absence of other nominal anchors, it may still be optimal under inflation targeting to have a monetary policy response to an exchange rate shock. The same applies to terms-of-trade shocks and to sudden stops in capital inflows, provided that the nature of these shocks is fully understood (see Annex 3.A1).

Nevertheless, certain economic, financial and institutional requirements for successful inflation targeting should be addressed before fully-fledged inflation targeting is introduced in Russia.

- First, cross-country experience suggests that most successful transitions to inflation targeting have taken place after a considerable amount of disinflation (*i.e.* to single-digit levels) occurred already as double-digit inflation rates tend to be more volatile and thus more difficult to target (see Figure 3.9).
- Secondly, successful inflation targeting, as with any market-based monetary policy framework, requires the availability of a full range of monetary policy instruments and a

Figure 3.9. **Inflation and GDP *per capita* in countries which have introduced inflation targeting**

Source: IMF and OECD estimates.

StatLink http://dx.doi.org/10.1787/650155820773

functioning transmission mechanism of monetary policy. While the CBR has developed its own sterilisation tools (mainly Bank of Russia "OBR" bonds), it has used them only sparingly, most likely due to concerns over damage to the CBR's balance sheet arising from the interest rate differential between foreign reserve assets and OBRs. At the same time, at least until late-2008 the CBR's policy rates had only a limited impact on interbank rates. In addition, given a long succession of fiscal surpluses the government bond market has remained thin. At the same time, short-term interest rates are only loosely connected with long-term rates. Finally, the still relatively low level of bank intermediation in the Russian economy suggests that the transmission of monetary policy to the real economy is still limited.

- Thirdly, weaknesses in the banking system (see Chapter 4) may undermine the credibility of inflation targeting in Russia, since price stability might at some point come into conflict with financial stability considerations. Under inflation targeting both the banking system and the real sector would have to be able to withstand a monetary tightening cycle, something which has yet to be fully played out.
- Fourthly, the still large weight of food (see Figure 3.10) and administered prices in Russia's consumer price index may complicate inflation targeting.

While the CBR's measure of core inflation could be used instead of headline inflation as the operational target, it excludes only the most volatile food items. A further narrowing of the inflation measure would, within the trade-off between transparency and controllability, increasingly, run the risk of becoming both non-transparent and irrelevant for the purchasing power of consumers. In fact, while choosing a more controllable inflation target in general increases the credibility of the central bank, since inflation targets will be met more often, choosing too narrow a measure may also undermine the credibility of the authorities if headline inflation deviates significantly and persistently from the target rate.

Figure 3.10. **Weight of food prices in CPI versus income in selected countries, 2007**

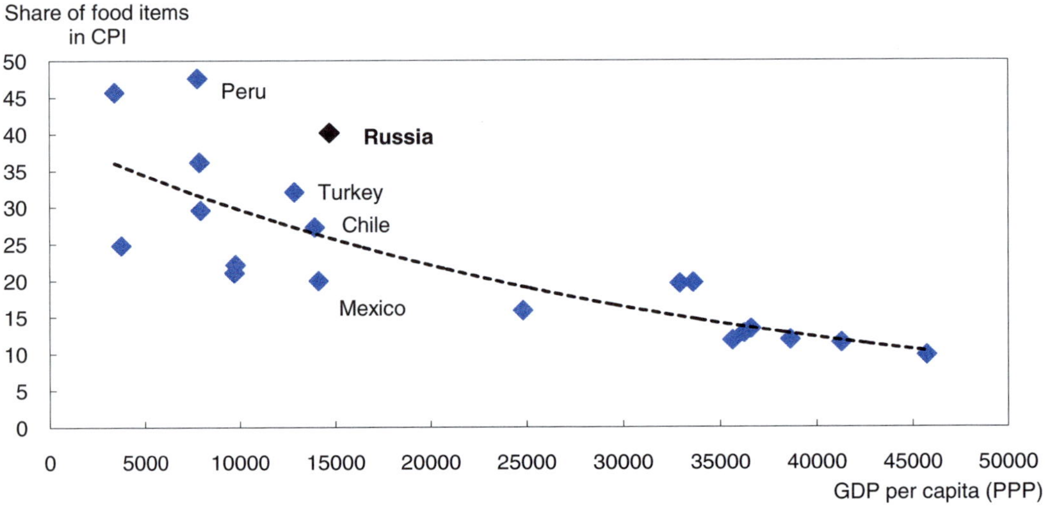

Note: The countries shown in this chart are: Australia, Brazil, Canada, Chile, Colombia, euro area, Indonesia, Japan, Korea, Mexico, Peru, Philippines, Russia, South Africa, Sweden, Switzerland, Thailand, Turkey, United Kingdom and the United States.

Source: IMF (WEO), ECB, OECD and national sources.

StatLink http://dx.doi.org/10.1787/650164152316

Table 3.1. **Main traditional preconditions for successful inflation targeting**

Strong fiscal position
Well-understood transmission mechanism between monetary instruments and inflation
Well-developed financial system
Central bank independence and a clear mandate for price stability
A reasonably well-developed ability to forecast inflation
Absence of other nominal anchors than inflation
Transparent and accountable monetary policy

Source: Jonas and Mishkin (2005).

As regards exchange rate passthrough, which is also sometimes seen as complicating inflation targeting in the emerging markets (see Annex 3.A1), there are indications that the impact of nominal exchange rate changes on inflation in Russia have been moderate since 2000 (see Annex 3.A2).

Finally, in order to avoid early losses of credibility, the CBR may consider gradually strengthening the meaning of its inflation targets. In this regard, the CBR's "Quarterly Inflation Reviews" (QIRs), which have been prepared since the beginning of 2008 along with its "Guidelines for the Single State Monetary Policy", are a useful starting point. It has so far remained somewhat ambiguous whether the inflation projections included in the Guidelines should be interpreted as targets against which the CBR should be benchmarked. To date, the QIRs have not assessed deviations of inflation from the CBR's projections. To the extent that the CBR progressively ceases to target the exchange rate, these projections can be complemented with hard inflation targets. Under fully-fledged inflation targeting, sustained deviation of the inflation forecast from the target would trigger a monetary policy response.

As regards a sound fiscal position, Russia has achieved low public debt levels that make a fiscal dominance of monetary policy unlikely. However, efforts aimed at strengthening medium-term budgetary frameworks and long-term fiscal sustainability (see Chapters 1 and 2) would further strengthen the credibility of an inflation targeting framework in Russia.

Finally, with respect to central bank independence, the CBR is *de jure* independent but *de facto* is in the middle range of central banks of countries with similar income levels (Arone *et al.*, 2007). The degree of central bank independence may rise "endogenously" once inflation targeting has been introduced. As regards central bank transparency, reasonable standards of openness and accountability have been reached (IMF, 2003) in particular as quarterly inflation reports were launched in 2008. In view of a more prominent role of the CBR under envisaged inflation targeting, however, more progress is needed with respect to explaining deviations from the CBR's inflation target and changes of monetary policy. In particular, the CBR might consider accelerating the timeliness and regularity of such explanations. In this context, the announcement of an advanced schedule for monthly meetings of the Board of Directors as well as regular monthly press conferences should be considered as communication tools.

Box 3.2. **Recommendations on monetary and exchange rate policy**

Exchange rate policy should gradually become more flexible in order to allow Russia to conduct its own monetary policy, taking into account domestic macroeconomic conditions. Preparations for inflation targeting should be accelerated as the exchange rate has or to a large extent lost its function as nominal anchor. In particular the authorities should:

- strengthen their commitment to price stability as the primary goal of monetary policy by amending the CBR's mandate in the central bank law;
- gradually increase exchange rate flexibility;
- gradually strengthen the meaning of the CBR's inflation targets;
- accelerate efforts aimed at strengthening the institutional basis for monetary policy making by improving CBR's communication policy;
- accelerate financial sector reforms aimed at financial deepening.

Against the backdrop of these considerations, the authorities' envisaged time frame of a few years for the transition to inflation targeting appears to be reasonable. It should be noted, though, that the increasing of exchange rate flexibility and the strengthening of the CBR's inflation targets should be complemented by a broader process of financial deepening and accelerated efforts to built reliable models for the monetary transmission process in Russia.

As regards the appropriate long-term target for price stability and the speed of disinflation in Russia, several considerations should be taken into account. First, while Balassa-Samuelson effects in Russia are estimated to be relatively small (OECD, 2006), the literature on inflation targeting in emerging markets suggests that there may be case of allowing for inflation rates at around 1-2% higher than in advanced countries (see Annex 3.A1 for a more detailed discussion). Secondly, the optimal speed of disinflation is difficult to determine. In any case, both the target itself and the path to reach it should be subject to a political consensus.

Notes

1. According to the 1995 Central Bank Law, the goal of monetary policy is to "defend the currency, control inflation ...". The Central Bank of Russia stated in 2001 in a monetary strategy document explicitly that resisting nominal appreciation of the rouble is goal of monetary policy. The fact that these two goals of Russia's monetary policy may conflict has been pointed out already in OECD (2002, 2004 and 2006).
2. In February 2005, the Central Bank of Russia (CBR) introduced an operational US dollar/euro basket as a reference for the daily management of the rouble's exchange rate. The weight of the euro in this currency basket, initially set at 10% has been gradually increased to 35% and 45%, broadly mirroring the trade share of the euro area in Russia's total foreign trade. At the same time, the CBR has also diversified its foreign exchange reserves into euro and occasionally intervened in the rouble-euro market.
3. Russia formally introduced full rouble convertibility on 1 July 2006. In practice, however, Russia's capital account has been mostly open already before.
4. It is well-documented in empirical studies that a positive terms-of-trade shock typically leads to and adjustment of the real exchange rate (Cashin, Céspedes and Sahay, 2004).
5. The figure for the half life of the shock to inflation is computed as $\ln(0.5)/\ln(^2)$.
6. See IMF (2007) and references given there.

Bibliography

Amato, J. and S. Gerlach (2000), "Inflation Targeting in Emerging Market and Transition Economies: Lessons after a Decade", *European Economic Review*, 46, pp. 781-790.

Aoki, K. (2001), "Optimal Monetary Policy Responses to Relative-Price Changes,"*Journal of Monetary Economics* 48(2001), pp. 55-80.

Arnone, M. *et al.* (2007), "Central Bank Autonomy: Lessons from Global Trends", *IMF Working Papers*, pp. 1-53.

Ball, L. and N. Mankiw (1995), "Relative-Price Changes as Aggregate Supply Shocks,"*Quarterly Journal of Economics*, Vol. 110 (February), pp. 161–93.

Bernanke, B. *et al.* (1999), *Inflation Targeting: Lessons from the International Experience*, Princeton University Press, Princeton, NJ.

Caballero, R. and A. Krishnamurthy (2005). "Inflation Targeting and Sudden Stops", in Bernanke and Woodford (eds.), *The Inflation Targeting Debate*, National Bureau of Economic Research, Chicago, IL.

Calvo, G. and C. M. Reinhart (2002), "Fear Of Floating", *Quarterly Journal of Economics*, Vol. 107 (2 May), pp. 379-408.

Campa, J. and L. Goldberg (2005), "Exchange Rate Pass-Through into Import Prices", *The Review of Economics and Statistics*, Vol. 87(4), pp. 679-690, MIT Press, Cambridge, MA.

Cashin, P., L.F. Céspedes and R. Sahay (2004), "Commodity Currencies and the Real Exchange Rate,"*Journal of Development Economics* 75, pp. 239-268.

Central Bank of Russia (2008a), *Quarterly Inflation Review Q2 2008*, CBR, Moscow.

Central Bank of Russia (2008b), *Quarterly Inflation Review Q3 2008*, CBR, Moscow.

Economic Expert Group (2007), "Analysis of Relationships between Exchange Rate and Consumer Prices", *mimeo* in Russian.

Edwards, S. (2006), "The Relationship Between Exchange Rates and Inflation Targeting Revisited", *NBER Working Papers*, 12163, April.

European Central Bank (2001), "Framework and Tools of Monetary Analysis", *ECB Monthly Bulletin*, May.

Frankel, J.A. (2005), "Peg the Export Price Index: A Proposed Monetary Regime for Small Countries", *Journal of Policy Modelling* 27, pp. 495-508.

International Monetary Fund (2006), *World Economic Outlook*, chapter IV: "Does Inflation Targeting Work in Emerging Markets?", IMF, Washington, DC, September 2006.

International Monetary Fund (2007), "Russian Federation: Selected Issues", *IMF Country Reports* No. 07/352, October.

International Monetary Fund (2008), *World Economic Outlook*, Chapter III: "Is Inflation Back? Commodity Prices and Inflation", IMF, Washington, DC, October 2008.

International Monetary Fund (2008), *Russian Federation : 2008*, Article IV: "Consultation–Staff Report; Staff Statement; and Public Information Notice on the Executive Board Discussion", *IMF Country Reports No.* 08/309, September.

Jonas, J. and F. Mishkin (2005), "Inflation Targeting in Transition Economies: Experience and Prospects", in Bernanke and Woodford (eds.), *The Inflation Targeting Debate*, National Bureau of Economic Research, Chicago, IL.

Junior, N. and R. Pinto (2007), "Inflation Targeting and Exchange Rate Pass-through", *Econ. Apl.*, Ribeirão Preto, Vol. 11, No. 2, June.

Korhonen, I. and P. Wachtel (2005), "A Note on Exchange Rate Pass-through in CIS Countries", *BOFIT Discussion Papers No.* 2.

Masson, P., M. Savastano and S. Sharma (1997), "The Scope for Inflation Targeting in Developing Countries", *IMF Working Papers* No. 97/130.

Mishkin, F.S. (2000), "Inflation Targeting in Emerging-Market Countries", *American Economic Review*, Vol. 90(2), pp. 105-109, American Economic Association, May.

Mishkin, F.S. (2002), "Structural Issues for Successful Inflation Targering in Transition Countries", paper presented at the 22nd National Bank of Poland Conference on Monetary Policy in the Environment of Structural Change, Warsaw, October.

Mishkin, F.S. and K. Schmidt-Hebbel (2006), "Monetary Policy under Inflation Targeting: An Introduction,"*Central Bank of Chile Working Papers* No. 396, December.

OECD (2002), *OECD Economic Surveys: Russian Federation* , Vol. 2002/05, OECD, Paris, February.

OECD (2004), *OECD Economic Surveys: Russian Federation* , Vol. 2004/11, OECD, Paris, September.

OECD (2006), *OECD Economic Surveys: Russian Federation* , Vol. 2006/17, OECD, Paris, November.

Schmidt-Hebbel, K. and A. Werner (2002), "Inflation Targeting in Brazil, Chile, and Mexico: Performance, Credibility, and the Exchange Rate", *Central Bank of Chile Working Papers No.* 171, July.

Svensson, L. (1997), "Exchange Rate Target or Inflation Target for Norway?", in Christiansen, A.B. and J.F. Qvigstad (eds.), *Choosing a Monetary Policy Target*, pp. 120-138, Scandinavian University Press (Universitetsforlaget AS), Oslo.

Svensson, L. (1998), Inflation Targeting in an Open Economy: Strict or Flexible Inflation Targeting, *Victoria Economic Commentaries*, Vol. 15, No. 1.

Svensson, L. (2006), "Comments on Jeffrey Frankel, Commodity Prices and Monetary Policy", paper presented at the NBER conference on Asset Prices and Monetary Policy, 5-6 May 2006.

ANNEX 3.A1

Inflation targeting in emerging markets and commodity-exporting countries

Inflation targeting can be broadly defined as a strategy in which the central bank publicly announces a numerical medium-term inflation target and adjusts short-term interest rates if its inflation forecast deviates from the inflation target.[1] There is no target level for the exchange rate under inflation targeting, as the exchange rate matters for monetary policy only to the extent that it impacts inflation. As a result, inflation targeting may imply a large degree of exchange rate volatility although empirical studies suggest that exchange rate volatility (nominal or real) is not necessarily higher under inflation targeting (Edwards, 2006; and IMF, 2006).

Inflation targeting has been adopted in about 25 advanced and emerging economies. The shift towards inflation targeting started in the early 1990s in New Zealand, Canada Australia and Norway. Since the late-1990s, the move towards inflation targeting has spread to emerging market economies (*e.g.* Israel, the Czech Republic, Poland, Chile, South Africa and Brazil).[2] In general, inflation targeting is widely seen as successful in achieving price stability over the medium term and in anchoring long-term inflation expectations.[3] Nevertheless, the recent volatility in commodity prices has been a challenge for inflation targeting regimes across the globe as headline inflation rose above inflation targets. However, in countries where central banks have strong credibility, second-round effects and a rise in long-term inflation expectations have hardly materialised (IMF, 2008). In emerging market economies, where central banks in some cases still lack a track-record of credibility, inflation expectations have risen in response to the recent rise in commodity prices until mid-2008 (*e.g.* in South Africa and Turkey).

It has often been argued that inflation targeting can be an appropriate anchor for monetary policy in emerging markets, provided that such countries meet certain preconditions. Such preconditions typically relate to a combination of institutional, technical, economic and financial areas (see Table 3.A1.1). The relevance of these preconditions, both in terms of being necessary or sufficient conditions for achieving price stability after the introduction of inflation targeting, has, however, been controversial. For example, some have argued that most preconditions – such as central bank independence and sound fiscal policies – are not specific to inflation targeting and are relevant also for other monetary policy frameworks (Amato and Gerlach, 2000). In addition, some of the preconditions may be "endogenous", *i.e.* they are more likely to be fulfilled after the establishment of inflation targeting. The adoption of an inflation targeting framework can, for example, strengthen the institutional basis and the credibility of the central bank (IMF, 2006).

Table 3.A1.1. **Preconditions for inflation targeting**

Precondition	May lack for emerging markets	May lack for commodity- exporters	Possibly "endogenous"
Institutional			
Central bank independence	X		X
Strong institutional commitment to price stability	X		X
Technical			
Model-based forecasts of inflation	X		X
Model-based analysis of monetary transmission mechanism	X		X
Reliable data on current inflation and inflation expectations	X		X
Economic			
Moderate inflation rates	X		X
Prudent fiscal policy and low government debt	X	X(?)	X
Low sensitivity to exchange rate and commodity price changes	X	X	
Low degree of dollarization	X		
Low variability of capital account	X	X(?)	X(?)
De-regulated prices	X	X(?)	X(?)
Financial			
"Sound" banking system	X		X
"Well-developed" capital markets	X		X

Source: OECD assessment based on literature cited in this box.

However, certain economic features of emerging market economies are likely to complicate inflation targeting in such countries (Mishkin, 2000). For example, if inflation is still at relatively high levels (*i.e.* in the double-digits), control over headline inflation is difficult and forecast errors are likely to be large. As a result, inflation targets are often likely to be missed, possibly undermining the credibility of the central bank. In addition, emerging market economies often exhibit a high degree of dollarization, in particular as regards the denomination of bank, corporate and household debt. Therefore, many emerging markets cannot afford to ignore the exchange rate when conducting monetary policy as a large depreciation may lead to financial instability.[4] A "benign neglect" of the exchange rate is also often not entirely possible due to a high degree of exchange rate pass-through.[5] However, the degree of pass-through can decline once inflation targeting has been introduced (Edwards, 2006). A high share of administered prices in consumer price indices, on the other hand, makes it difficult for the central bank to control headline inflation. Likewise, an exposure to volatile net capital inflows as well as frequent and large changes of the terms of trade renders inflation targeting in the emerging markets more challenging than in industrial countries.

Whether inflation targeting is an appropriate monetary policy framework for commodity-exporting countries has been subject to debate. Most oil-exporting countries (*e.g.* in the Gulf Cooperation Council countries) have so far preferred to use the exchange rate as an anchor of monetary policy. However, such arrangements are likely to mainly reflect a lack of technical expertise.[6] In fact, large swings in the terms-of-trade of commodity-exporting countries make it difficult to stabilise the nominal exchange rate. Moreover, it is well-documented that such shocks typically lead to a change of the real exchange rate (Cashin, Céspedes and Sahay, 2004) which can occur through changes in the nominal exchange rate or an inflation-differential *vis-à-vis* the trading partners of the country. As inflation tends to be persistent, the real exchange rate may overshoot under a fixed exchange rate regime in response to a positive terms-of-trade shock. As a result, fixed exchange rate regimes may result in alternating inflation-deflation periods (Svensson, 1998).[7]

The optimal monetary response to a terms-of-trade shock – in general and in commodity exporting countries – has remained controversial. Some have argued that a negative (positive) terms-of-trade shock should give rise to a monetary easing (tightening), *i.e.* a depreciation (appreciation) of the currency. In this context, it has been proposed that commodity-exporting countries peg their currency to an export price index, so as to combine the benefits of a nominal anchor with those of a floating exchange rate regime (Frankel, 2005).[8] In response to such proposals, advocates of inflation targeting have stressed that such a framework may lead to excessive changes in the monetary policy stance and entail the risk of deflation in response to a sharp rise in commodity prices (Svensson, 2006).[9] In addition, theoretical work on the optimal monetary policy response to changes in relative prices suggests that it is better to target core rather than broader measures of inflation (Aoki, 2001).

In general, under inflation targeting, the monetary policy response to a rise in the exchange rate (*i.e.* depreciation of the currency) would depend on the nature of the shock (*e.g.* Mishkin, 2002). If it is due to portfolio shifts with no impact on aggregate demand, monetary policy should tighten in order to limit pass-through to inflation. If on the other hand, the depreciation is due to a negative terms-of-trade shock which is also lowering aggregate demand, monetary policy might have to be eased.

As regards the optimal monetary policy response to a sudden stop in capital inflows, Caballero and Krishnamurthy (2005) point out that in advanced emerging market countries – which have achieved a reasonable degree of central bank credibility but are still subject to sudden stops – the raising of interest rates to defend the exchange rate due to "fear of floating" may be optimal from a contemporaneous perspective. In fact, in their model, the raising of interest rates has only a limited impact output as during a sudden stop output in these countries is mainly constrained by a shortage of external borrowing. However, the authors show that ex ante, this response may not be optimal since economic agents anticipating the central bank's tight monetary policy have an incentive to build up currency mismatches (*i.e.* to borrow in foreign currency without holding a sufficient amount of foreign assets).

As regards the appropriate target level for inflation, it is often argued that emerging market central banks should aim for somewhat higher inflation rates than advanced countries due to Balassa-Samuelson effects (Masson *et al.*, 1997). According to Amato and Gerlach (2002) such effects may warrant a 1-2% higher inflation target in the emerging markets. For advanced countries, there is almost unanimous agreement that price stability should not be quantified near zero inflation rates due to downward nominal wage rigidity and the zero-bound on nominal interest rates (Jonas and Mishkin, 2005). As a result, most scholarly papers and central bank practitioners come to the conclusion that an inflation rate of 1-3% corresponds to price stability.

The optimal speed of disinflation in emerging markets should in theory be set to minimize the "sacrifice ratio"*i.e.* the ratio of loss of output to disinflation (Jonas and Mishkin, 2005). While the empirical literature in this area has identified several characteristics which affect the sacrifice ratio (including the structure of the economy, the degree of wage indexation, past history of inflation, the credibility of monetary policy and the openness of the economy), it has been difficult to pin down the optimal speed of disinflation for individual countries. As a result, the literature has often concluded that this decision should be based on a political consensus (Jonas and Mishkin, 2005).

Against the background of the above considerations, many countries – including commodity-exporting countries – have adopted more flexible versions of inflation targeting. By and large, the experience of commodity-exporting countries which have introduced inflation targeting has been positive with the exception of early policy mistakes in response to changes in the exchange rate.[10] On balance, it appears that this overall positive performance of inflation targeting regimes in emerging market and commodity-exporting countries has not been hampered by their export dependency on commodities or their relatively open economies. These successes appear to be largely attributed to four factors. First, most countries have introduced inflation-targeting when a degree of disinflation (often to single-digit inflation rates) had already taken place.[11] Second, many countries have gradually upgraded initially soft inflation targets to hard ones in order to avoid early losses of credibility. Third, the targeted measures of inflation have often excluded food, energy and administered prices. Finally, most countries have continued to smooth exchange rate movements in the early phase of inflation targeting.

In countries where long-term inflation expectations could not yet be fully stabilised, on the other hand, the level of the central bank's credibility has apparently been too low to withstand large exogenous shocks to headline inflation. In addition, policy mistakes due to a lack of rigorous understanding of the monetary transmission process, as well as inappropriate communication strategies in the case of missed targets, may have played a role in these cases.

Notes

1. For an overview of the literature on inflation targeting, see *e.g.* Bernanke *et al.* (1999) and Mishkin and Schmidt-Hebbel (2006).
2. In Chile, an early version of inflation targeting was introduced in 1990 but fully-fledged inflation targeting was implemented only in 1999 (Schmidt-Hebbel and Werner, 2002).
3. For example, Bernanke *et al.* (1999) and Jonáš and Mishkin (2005) show empirically that the adoption of inflation targeting has been associated with an increase in monetary policy accountability and credibility, and a notable decline in inflation expectations.
4. In the literature, this argument is often referred to as "fear of floating" (Calvo and Reinhart, 2002).
5. Under inflation targeting, a depreciation of the currency may be countered by monetary tightening if the pass-through to domestic inflation dominates the possible negative impact on domestic demand (which may depend on the nature of the exchange rate shock).
6. Under an exchange rate peg, such countries cannot pursue domestic goals when setting monetary policy as they import the monetary policy stance of the country to the currency of which they peg. As the business cycle in oil-exporting countries is largely determined by oil price fluctuations, it is unlikely to be synchronised with that of the anchor country, which is typically an oil importer.
7. In practice commodity-exporting countries tend to experience only inflationary periods during upswings in commodity prices, as deflation is often avoided by abandoning the exchange rate peg during downwings of commodity prices.
8. Frankel (2005) suggests that this proposal can also be interpreted as an inflation targeting regime in which the central bank targets the export price instead of the consumer price index.
9. In addition, it has been stressed that the exchange rate under a currency peg to an export price index does not always respond to terms-of-trade changes in the desired direction. A terms-of-trade deterioration which is driven by a rise in export and import prices (where the rise in import prices is larger than that of export prices), for example, would lead under an export-price peg to an appreciation of the currency (Svensson, 2006).
10. For example, Mishkin (2002) argues that the Reserve Bank of New Zealand raised interest rates in response to the East Asian financial crisis in 1997, disregarding its negative impact on aggregate demand. Likewise, the central bank of Chile raised interest rates in 1998. Both countries suffered a recession as a result of these policy mistakes, as they appear to be in hindsight.
11. In the case of Chile, a version of inflation targeting was introduced in 1990 when the inflation rate was still at 20% p.a. However, fully-fledged inflation targeting was introduced only in 1999 when inflation had reached the low single digits.

ANNEX 3.A2

Econometric estimation of the empirical determinants of inflation in the Russian Federation

The estimation of econometric models to economic variables in Russia is in general complicated by the fact that the sample size for such exercises is still relatively small, especially if one takes into account structural breaks, most notably the 1998 crisis. This caveat also applies to the empirical determinants of inflation. In fact, since consumer prices increased by almost 40% month-on-month in September 2008 when the Russian rouble lost more than 100% month-on-month, econometric regressions which include this period suggest that exchange rate pass-through is large (around 0.25) and instantaneous while other important determinants of inflation are insignificant. In view of possible non-linearities in the relationship between the exchange rate and inflation *via* import prices, such estimates may not be very informative for assessing the magnitude of exchange rate pass-through more recently. As suggested by Korhonen and Wachtel (2005) and the Economic Expert Group (2007), a more informative period for this purpose would start in 2000, thus also excluding the phase of post-crisis recovery in 1999.

In the applied literature on exchange rate pass-through,[1] changes in the aggregate price level *p* are usually regressed on their own lags (to account for inflation persistence), lagged changes in the nominal exchange rate *e* to account for exchange rate pass-through, lagged changes of output *y* (*i.e.* postulating a backward-looking Phillips curve) and lagged changes of foreign prices p^*. In addition, other relevant lagged variables *x* are often included in such regressions.

$$\Delta p_t = \alpha + \sum_{k=1}^{n} \beta_k \Delta p_{t-k} + \sum_{k=1}^{n} \gamma_k \Delta e_{t-k} + \sum_{k=1}^{n} \chi_k \Delta y_{t-k} + \sum_{k=1}^{n} \kappa_k \Delta p^*_{t-k} + \sum_{k=1}^{n} \lambda_k \Delta x_{t-k} + \varepsilon$$

A similar auto-regressive-distributed lag (ARDL) model for consumer price inflation in Russia should be augmented by past money supply growth and lagged produced price inflation as the latter have been found in other studies as robust determinants of consumer price inflation (Economic Expert Group, 2007).

Estimation results for monthly data ranging from January 2000 to February 2009 suggest that exchange rate pass-through, measured in terms of the rouble against the dollar/euro currency basket, has been relatively low and affects consumer price inflation with a lag of around 4 months (see Table 3.A2.1). At the same time, money supply (lagged by 7 months) and producer prices (lagged by 4 months) are significant and robust determinants of consumer price inflation. Output growth or international prices are, on the other hand, not statistically significant in such regressions.[2]

 OECD ECONOMIC SURVEYS: RUSSIAN FEDERATION – ISBN 978-92-64-05433-2 – © OECD 200

Table 3.A2.1. **Regression results**

Dependent variable: CPI
Sample: 2000M01 2009M02
Included observations: 110

Variable	Coefficient Std.	Error	t-Statistic	Prob.
CPI (–1)	0.72	0.05	14.38	0.00
M2 (–7)	0.07	0.02	4.11	0.00
PPI (–4)	0.05	0.02	2.81	0.01
BASKET (–4)	0.05	0.02	3.27	0.00
R-squared	0.54643			
Adjusted R-squared	0.533593			

Note: Estimated in monthly, seasonally adjusted percentage chances which are found to be stationary using standard tests for unit roots Accounting for remaining negative serial correlation through an AR (1.5) process in the error process does not materially affect the results.
Source: OECD staff estimates.

Recursive estimates of the exchange rate pass-through coefficient suggest that pass-through has only marginally increased during the period of rouble depreciation against the currency basket (August 2008 – February 2009). Excluding this period from the sample yields a pass-through coefficient of around 0.07 instead of 0.08 (see Figure 3.A2.1).

Figure 3.A2.1. **Recursive estimates of exchange rate pass-through**

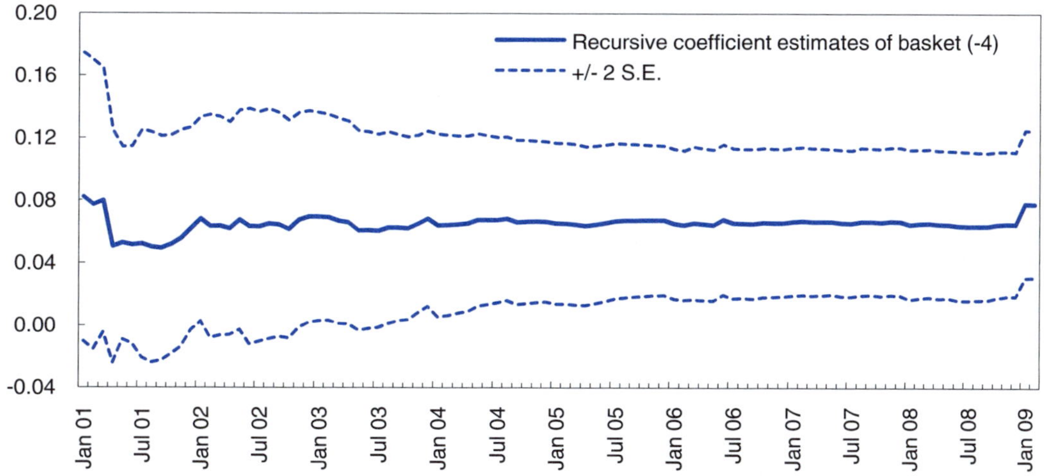

StatLink http://dx.doi.org/10.1787/650213170012

The findings do not change materially once exchange rate pass-through is measured in terms of the rouble's bilateral exchange rate against the dollar or the euro. Likewise, the reported results are broadly the same when core measures of consumer prices are used instead of headline inflation.

Notes

1. See, for example, Junior and Pinto (2007) and Campa and Goldberg (2005).
2. Foreign prices have been approximated by German export prices.

ISBN 978-92-64-05433-2
OECD Economic Surveys: Russian Federation

Chapter 4

Making the banking sector more efficient and resilient

Russia's banking system has grown considerably larger and stronger since the aftermath of the 1998 financial crisis, but even before the onset of the current global crisis it continued to play a limited role in intermediating savings and investment, especially for small and medium-sized enterprises. Moreover, despite important improvements, some weaknesses in prudential supervision remained, and the Russian banking sector continued to have too many very small banks doing little if any banking business. Further consolidation of the sector would both strengthen competition and improve the robustness of the system. This chapter discusses the policy imperatives in the short term, in the face of the crisis, and reforms that could be implemented over the longer term to improve the efficiency and resilience of the financial system and raise Russia's potential growth rate. While the current crisis is painful for the banking sector as well as the broader economy, it may facilitate a restructuring of the system that will be positive in the long run, as well as new approaches to regulation that will make banking less crisis-prone.

The global economic crisis has revealed weaknesses in banking sector, but also brings opportunities

Russia's banking sector is in the midst of its most serious crisis in a decade. Dozens of banks have already merged, come under state ownership, or had their licenses withdrawn, despite the fact that the main upsurge in non-performing loans is still to come, as the economic slowdown hits the financial position of borrowers. The interbank market, which was already segmented, became even more so. Although the authorities moved quickly to offer massive support to bank liquidity and capital, and to provide foreign exchange to meet external debt payments, bank lending nonetheless slowed dramatically, interbank rates stayed high (with many banks shut out entirely), and rouble deposits fell by about 20% between September 1 2008 and April 1 2009.

The ongoing crisis in the banking system, the latest of several since the beginning of transition, would be reason enough to review policy options relating to the Russian banking sector, especially since Russia appeared to be better-placed to resist the global financial crisis than many other countries. As Russia's own past experience and fresh episodes from a variety of OECD and emerging market economies confirm, financial crises are often costly, aggravating and prolonging cyclical slowdowns (Reinhart and Rogoff, 2009; IMF, 2008; Haugh, Ollivaud and Turner, 2009). The deleveraging that occurs as banks try to repair their balance sheets in the face of rising non-performing loans and/or securities losses can aggravate other recessionary forces, and bank bailouts or restructurings can entail massive budgetary costs, undermining fiscal sustainability. Moreover, for countries like Russia with relatively underdeveloped financial systems, financial crises can further damage trust in banks and securities markets, which impedes the catch-up in financial development.[1]

Looking beyond the current financial crisis, however, there is another rationale for examining the banking sector. An extensive literature on finance and growth (*e.g.* King and Levine, 1993; Beck *et al.*, 2000; Aghion *et al.*, 2004; De Serres *et al.*, 2006, Rajan and Zingales, 1998), provides compelling evidence that financial development contributes to faster economic growth. Despite its rapid expansion in recent years, Russia's financial system is still relatively underdeveloped, leaving considerable scope for financial deepening to contribute to long-term growth. There can, of course, be tensions and trade-offs between financial growth and stability, but Russia appears still to be some way from the efficient frontier where such tradeoffs bind, and there is corresponding scope for Russia both to reinforce the stability of the banking sector and boost potential growth *via* further financial deepening.

The general direction of these policy actions – better risk management, more effective regulation, increased transparency, a more level playing field for different categories of bank – is recognised by the Russian authorities, and has been for some time (*e.g.* CBR, 2002; Ministry of Finance, 2007). Progress in these areas underlies much of the banking sector's impressive rebound from the debilitating 1998 crisis. Both in terms of outcomes and processes, the Russian banking sector was getting progressively healthier when the global crisis struck, although some imbalances were starting to build. The current crisis has provided new information about the costs of remaining weaknesses in the system, adding urgency to the reform agenda. In addition, while clearly painful, the crisis may have some salutary effects on the banking system, notably by bringing to an end the period of breakneck lending growth rates.

The global crisis has also revealed, however, that countries with a variety of financial structures and approaches to banking supervision can experience severe financial stress. There have been major bank failures, nationalisations, costly public bail-outs and deleveraging in many economies, including the largest and most advanced OECD countries. This fact cautions against being overly prescriptive as regards ideal models of financial regulation and crisis management.

Development of the Russian banking system – gradual maturation punctuated by crises

Phase I – Early transition: A proliferation of banks, but little effective intermediation

Until the end of the Soviet era there were no private banks, and no competition within the public sector. The banking sector did not intermediate savings and investment on the basis of price signals in a manner conducive to an efficient allocation of capital. The situation changed dramatically however, during the initial transition period, from 1992, as the central bank issued a huge number of banking licenses (Figure 4.1).

There were several specific reasons, beyond the usual considerations governing entry to any industry, to want to establish or acquire a bank during the early years of transition. Banks, unlike other corporations, were allowed to deal in foreign exchange, and could hold correspondent accounts with foreign banks. This meant that owning a bank facilitated capital flight – net private capital outflows were equivalent to more than 5% of GDP a year on average in the 1990s – and/or money laundering.[2] Banks could be used as corporate treasuries for groups of non-financial enterprises. This was attractive given the lack of trust in unrelated parties, which in turn was in large part a function of the low level of confidence in the rule of law and the protection of property rights. Banks also provided a

Figure 4.1. **Number of banks**

End of period

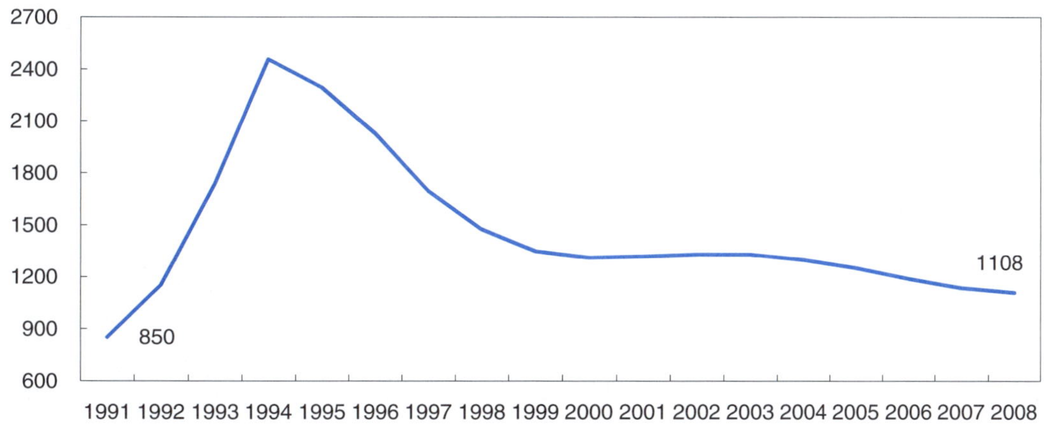

Source: Central Bank of Russia.

StatLink http://dx.doi.org/10.1787/650250822214

vehicle for securities speculation. In addition, given that minimum capital for a bank was set as low as USD 100 000, the proliferation of banks in the early 1990s is understandable.

Some of these reasons for owning a bank were also reasons why the banking sector played only a limited role in intermediating savings and investment in the 1990s. Insofar as they were lenders, banks largely funnelled loans to related companies at rates of interest that had more to do with tax optimisation than true cost of capital. Lending, however, was relatively limited, amounting to little more than a third of bank assets in 1999 (Figure 4.2) – and the ratio of bank assets to GDP remained very low. Bank profits were highly reliant on securities transactions. In particular, during the period of fixed exchange rates from 1995 through the onset of the financial crisis in August 1998, banks were able to borrow dollars and buy government treasury bills (GKOs), earning substantial interest margins.[3]

Figure 4.2. **Lending to total assets**[1]

Percentage

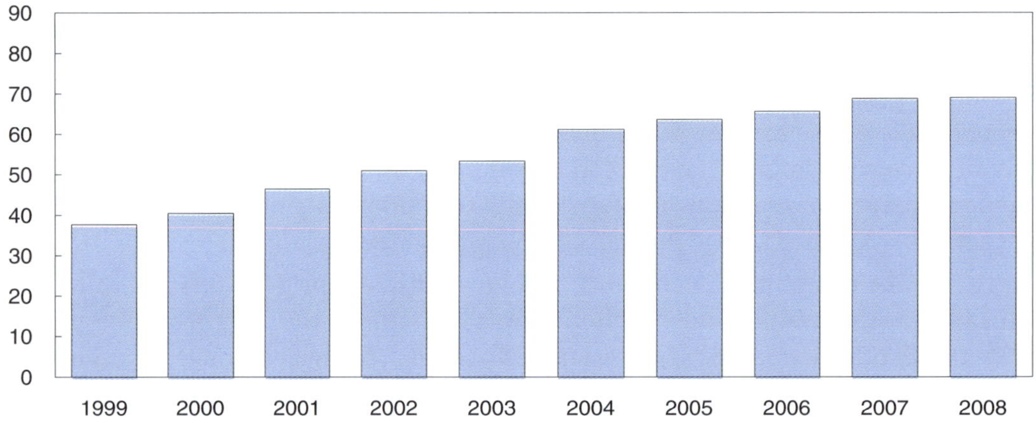

1. Loans, deposits and other funds placed with organisations, individuals and credit institutions.

Source: OECD calculations based on Central Bank of Russia

StatLink http://dx.doi.org/10.1787/650258388011

Pathologies in the banking sector were far from being the only factor in Russia's poor macroeconomic performance in the mid-1990s and descent into crisis in 1998, but they did contribute. Risk management and prudential supervision were weak, accounting standards for banks were below international standards, and ownership of banks was opaque, while screening for fit and proper ownership of banks was largely non-existent. Lending to smaller companies was especially underdeveloped, while consumer and mortgage lending remained embryonic.

Phase II – Recovery from the 1998 crisis and planning for development of the system

The financial crisis that erupted in August 1998 had several crippling effects on banks. The quadrupling of the rouble-dollar exchange rate in a short period was devastating for banks reliant on borrowing abroad to fund purchases of rouble securities, while on the asset side, the government defaulted on its domestic bonds, and went on to impose on holders of the defaulted debt a restructuring involving deep discounts. At the same time, the sharp recession pushed up non-performing loans, and bond and equity prices collapsed. Many banks, including some of the largest private ones, failed. There was a flight of deposits to the public banks (especially Sberbank, the largest bank in the system), which benefitted from a government guarantee – by December 1999, Sberbank alone accounted for some 80% of household deposits.

Following the crisis, however, the banking system began a rapid and sustained rebound. A key factor was the resumption of economic growth, which took off in 1999, as the huge real effective depreciation of the rouble resulted in strong import substitution. With the principal exception of import businesses, the solvency of the corporate sector improved rapidly. In particular, with the oil price rising from the lows of under USD 10 a barrel in 1998 to the high-twenties in 2000, the fortunes of the important energy sector took a sharp turn for the better. Against this favourable macroeconomic background, bank assets, deposits, capital, profits, and market capitalisation all mushroomed (Figure 4.3).

In support of the improved macroeconomic conditions, a number of structural reforms were also underway at this time. In the wake of the crisis numerous changes were made to the banking laws to streamline bank bankruptcy, permit earlier resolution of failing banks, and tighten regulation on fit and proper ownership of banks. Also, in 2001 an anti-money laundering agency was launched and in the following year Russia was removed from the Financial Action Task Force blacklist. In 2002 the CBR released a strategy for the banking sector covering the period through 2008. Among the most important elements of that strategy were the proposals to: require banks to submit financial statements under International Financial Reporting Standards (IFRS) (Box 4.1); introduce deposit insurance for household deposits (Box 4.2); and improve the effectiveness of prudential supervision. The introduction of a deposit insurance scheme was itself intended to be an important step in improving supervision, as banks wanting to join the scheme were effectively subjected to a relicensing.

All groups of banks experienced rapid growth in assets and deposits in the years following the 1998 crisis, so that there was little change in the market share of state-owned banks, domestic private banks, and foreign banks (Figure 4.4). Sberbank's share of household deposits fell from 80% to under 60% between late-1998 and 2002. At the same time, however, Sberbank expanded its share of other deposit and loan segments, as did VTB. The government divested itself of holdings in hundreds of banks, but maintained its much smaller number of majority stakes, and injected equity capital into the major state-owned banks.

The post-crisis recovery period witnessed a gradual but fairly steady consolidation of the sector. After the initial wave of bank failures in the wake of the 1998 crisis, there were very few bank bankruptcies or license withdrawals for reasons of capital insufficiency. Initially, consolidation happened largely *via* the acquisition of regional banks by Moscow-based private banks trying to build national branch networks.[4] Later, the main contributor to consolidation was the removal of licenses from (generally small) banks for money laundering offences. During the period 1999-2004 the number of banks fell from 1 476 to 1 299.

While the growth and strengthening of the banking sector were almost continuous from 1999 onward, there was one significant hiccup in the summer of 2004, when a liquidity crisis claimed a few medium-sized banks and caused a short-lived run on deposits. The episode, though alarming at the time, was not in retrospect of major significance. It did, however, underline the limitations of the CBR's instruments to support liquidity, and highlighted the importance of levelling the playing field between private and state-owned banks as regards deposit guarantees.

Figure 4.3. **Post-crisis recovery of the banking system**

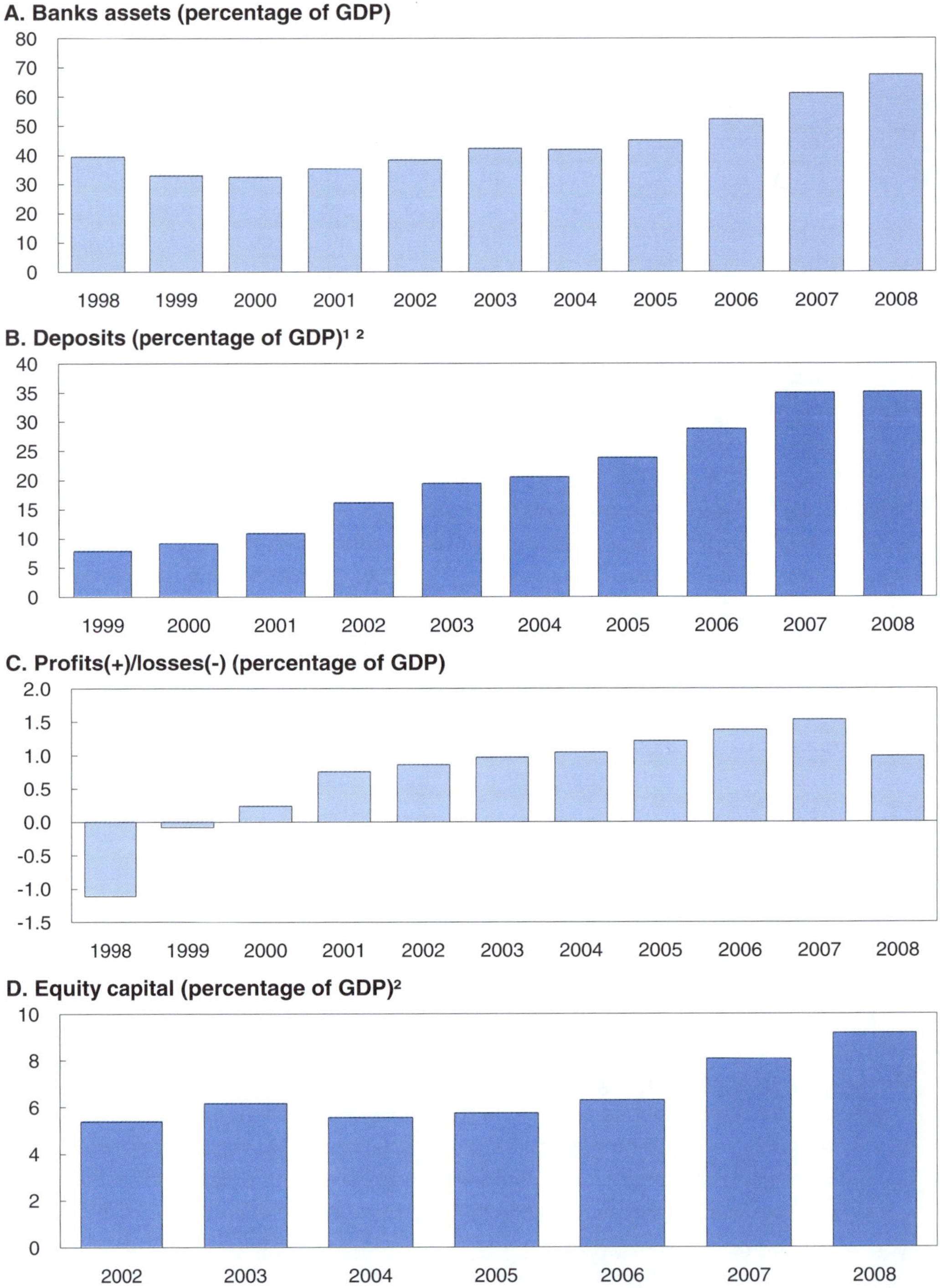

1. Deposits of individuals, individual entrepreneurs and organisations (financial and non-financial). A methodological change in 2002 makes earlier data not directly comparable.
2. Data are available only from 1999 for deposits and from 2002 for equity capital.

Source: OECD calculations based on Central Bank of Russia and Federal Service for State Statistics.

StatLink http://dx.doi.org/10.1787/650271678132

OECD ECONOMIC SURVEYS: RUSSIAN FEDERATION – ISBN 978-92-64-05433-2 – © OECD 20

Box 4.1. The move to International Financial Reporting Standards for Russian banks

IFRS was first used in Russia by large banks issuing Eurobonds or seeking ratings during the 1990s. The CBR required annual IFRS audits and financial statements as from 2004, in addition to the normal Russian Accounting Standards (RAS) accounts for tax purposes.

In September 2002 the CBR created a special committee to introduce IFRS, which included representatives of CBR departments, the Ministry of Finance, and parliament. The CBR began training specialists in its supervisory divisions to regulate banks based on IFRS.

The number of banks preparing financial reports to international accounting standards in 2000 was 125, and this grew to 130 in 2001 and 185 in 2002. Most banks published IFRS financials unwillingly and with several restrictions in 2000, but by 2002 reports were readily available on bank web sites. In order to develop the new accounting methods, train specialists, and select an auditor, many banks in Moscow and the regions began publishing IFRS reports without waiting for it to become mandatory.

From 1 January 2004 Russian banks were required to begin compiling IFRS financial reports once a year and to undergo an audit to international standards.

There are several differences between RAS and IFRS for banks, including the treatment of provisioning, consolidation, disclosure, and valuation of assets. IFRS brings together in a single document a wide range of information necessary to make a credit or investment decision. To achieve similar information using RAS a large number of documents must be prepared that are more cumbersome to use. The typical balance sheet for second-tier accounts to RAS includes 400-500 entries, the income statement includes 150-200 entries, and most other forms are less bulky but are riddled with unclear symbols, codes, and so on. Analyzing such a mountain of information, especially for a period of several years, requires proper software and highly trained specialists. It is no wonder that for most creditors RAS are extremely difficult to use. Moreover, this information is often inaccessible to the outside creditor and collecting other information requires consulting various sources.

On the other hand, financial reports prepared to RAS are often useful in analysing a Russian bank, especially because they are available at higher frequency. The most important purpose for examining Russian financial reports is to determine how a bank looks at various periods during the year, not just at the end of the year. For example, banks' liquidity usually increases noticeably at the end of the year, and auditors rarely mention discrepancies between end-year indicators and the typical level of liquidity during the year.

Phase III – Improved regulation and growing strength, though with emerging imbalances

The major implementation phase of the joint CBR-government medium-term strategy for the banking sector, released in 2002, was 2004-06. Among the main elements of the strategy were: the introduction of deposit insurance, including the use of screening criteria for admittance to the scheme that amounted to a new licensing procedure; the disclosure to the CBR of banks' shareholder structure; the requirement that banks report financial data to the CBR on an IFRS basis; making the methods of calculating loan loss reserves more similar to IFRS; the streamlining of prudential ratios; the sale by the state of most stakes owned in banks; tightened procedures for increasing authorised capital; and the creation of a system of credit bureaus. Also, in 2007 the CBR returned to a previous system (abandoned out of concerns about the scope offered for corruption) system of bank "curators",

Box 4.2. **Deposit insurance in Russia**

The Central Bank of Russia began accepting applications to join the deposit insurance system from 27 March –27 June 2004, when 1 137 banks indicated they would like to join. A list of the first group of banks to join the deposit insurance system was published on 21 October 2004 and by end-March 2005 the Central Bank banking regulation committee had completed consideration of applications by all 1 137 banks under all criteria.

The committee approved 819 banks to join the deposit insurance system (including repeat applications). It also granted deposit licenses to seven banks that had not previously operated on the retail market. As a result the deposit insurance system included 824 banks at the close of the first quarter of 2005. These banks held 98% of deposits by individuals in Russian banks and accounted for 90% of the assets in the banking system.

Eighteen banks that filed applications to join were rejected and lost their banking licenses, while another 51 banks that had previously accepted deposits from individuals opted against participating in the deposit insurance system. Household deposits are of no interest for the business of some banks (*e.g.* investment banks, and certain subsidiaries of foreign banks). Other banks that for one reason or another have yet to join the deposit insurance system may still do so.

The deposit insurance agency regularly conducts public opinion surveys about depositor behaviour and deposit insurance awareness. The *2008 Survey* revealed that only 38% of the population is aware of existence of deposit insurance in Russia.

Figure 4.4. **Ownership structure of the banking system**

Share in total assets

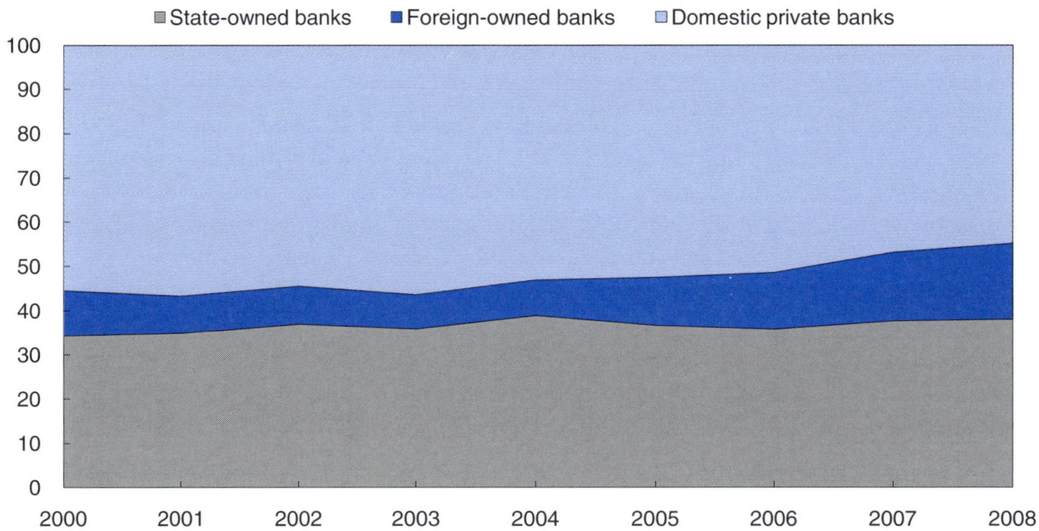

Source: Interfax.

StatLink http://dx.doi.org/10.1787/650276548588

i.e. CBR officers responsible for monitoring individual bank and being a channel through which the bank can voice its concern or questions to the CBR.

All of the principal measures in the 2002 strategy document were implemented, and all contributed to the improved soundness of the banking system until the onset of the global financial crisis. On the other hand, the measures in some cases could have gone further. In particular, screening for deposit insurance turned out to be largely a missed chance to weed out weak banks and achieve rapid consolidation of the sector, which would have eased the burden of prudential supervision for the CBR. Very few banks, and none of any significance, were turned down for entry to the system. Sberbank joined the scheme in 2005. As to the sale of state-owned stakes in banks, shares in hundreds of banks were sold, but the three largest banks remained state-owned, and significant new state banks or quasi-banks – the Russian Development Bank and the agriculture bank – were created. Reform in that area therefore amounted to a focussing of state ownership rather than a withdrawal.

While banking reforms were important, the biggest reason for the rapid expansion and rising profitability of the banking sector during this period, as had been the case in the first few years following the 1998 crisis, was the benign macroeconomic climate. Indeed, the later period saw even more favourable economic conditions for the growth of the banking sector. The strong rise of the oil price from 2004 through mid-2008 resulted in huge current account surpluses which were the main driver of domestic liquidity. With the CBR using massive foreign exchange intervention to resist nominal appreciation of the rouble against the dollar-euro basket, especially during a period in which the dollar was falling against the euro, banks and corporates increasingly saw the rouble-dollar exchange rate as a one-way bet. Given also the low interest rates and compressed spreads for emerging market borrowers generally and Russian borrowers in particular, given Russia's strong macroeconomic fundamentals, Russian entities had both the incentive and the ability to borrow in dollars and invest or lend in roubles. Thus, in addition to the current account surpluses there were latterly net capital inflows as well (Figure 4.5), which also fed through to bank liquidity and domestic demand. Meanwhile, the strong rise in the equity and housing markets spurred lending and boosted profits of banks, and this lending growth attained dizzying and indeed worrisome proportions (Figure 4.6).

Figure 4.5. **Net private capital flows**

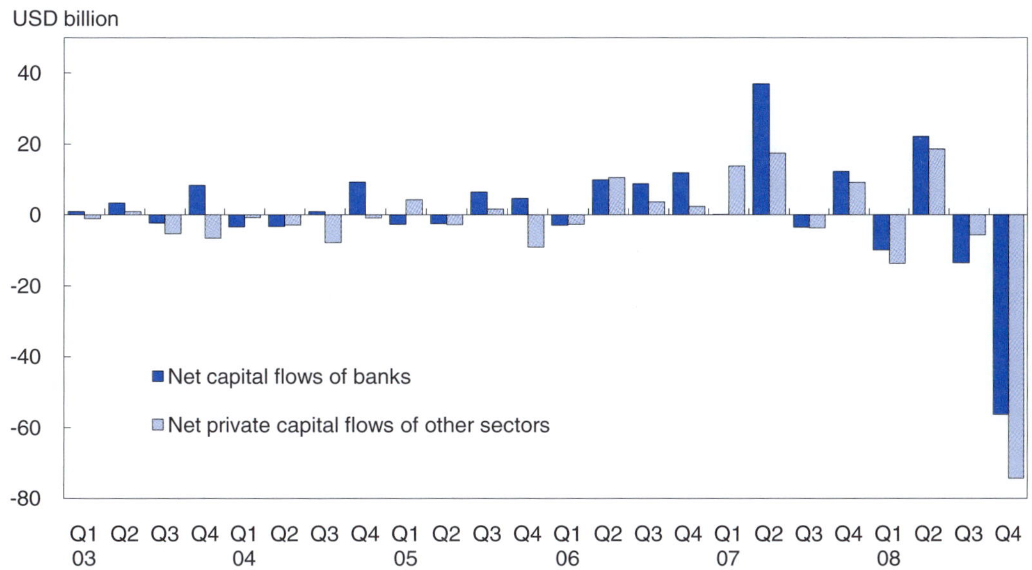

Source: Central Bank of Russia.

StatLink http://dx.doi.org/10.1787/650300458038

Figure 4.6. **Growth of bank lending in real terms**

Change in bank loans deflated by CPI[1]

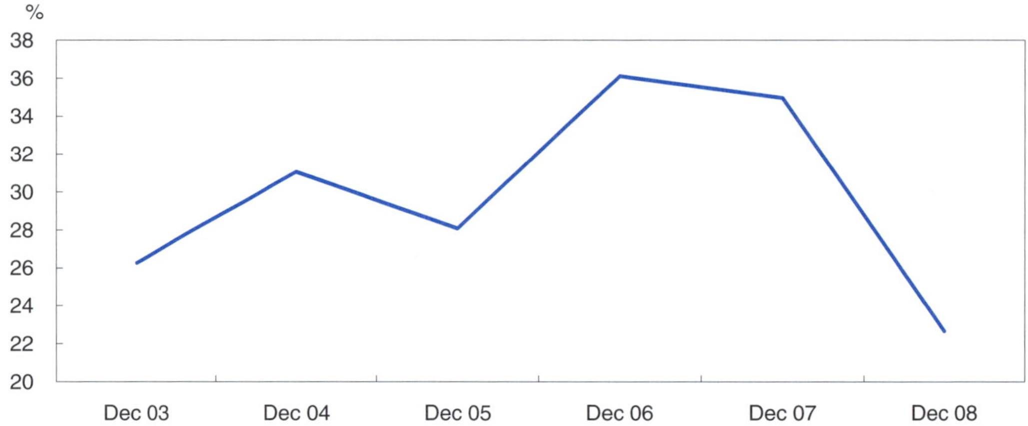

1. Loans, deposits and other funds placed with organisations, individuals and credit institutions.

Source: OECD calculations based on Central Bank of Russia.

StatLink http://dx.doi.org/10.1787/650330661615

As a result of the sustained economic boom and the advances on the regulatory front, the banking sector achieved a dramatic expansion in the years leading up to the 2008 crisis. Deposits rose nearly seven-fold between 2002 and 2007, increasing from 16% to 35% of GDP. Bank assets likewise grew strongly as a percentage of GDP, moving Russia out of the category of emerging economies with the most underdeveloped banking sectors, although it still lagged behind a number of other Eastern European economies. Bank capital increased massively, despite the measures taken to limit the artificial inflation of capital, while efficiency as measured by cost-income ratios or return on assets improved markedly, to levels that were towards the upper end of international comparators (Figure 4.7).

While most dynamics of the sector were clearly positive, there were for several years some indications of growing imbalances. The speed of expansion of lending in general and certain segments in particular gave rise to fears about credit risk management and the possibility of a bust to follow the boom. The explosive growth of consumer lending was one salient area of concern. This market grew from a negligible share of overall loans to 20% in the period 2000-07 (Figure 4.8). Lending to construction and real estate also grew extremely rapidly, fuelling a bubble in housing prices, especially in Moscow and to a lesser extent St. Petersburg and other major cities. Residential real estate prices in Moscow rose from about USD 1 000 per square meter in 2002 to USD 3 000 at the start of 2006 and USD 6 000 in the summer of 2008. This growth far outstripped increases in rental rates.

Another alarming feature of the last few years leading up to the crisis was the rate of growth of banks' external debt. Gross foreign liabilities of banks grew from 12.5% of total liabilities in 2004 to 20.4% in mid-2007, before access to international markets began to be disrupted (Figure 4.9, Panel A). That exposure was also relatively concentrated among the large and medium-sized private banks. Subsidiaries of foreign banks also maintained relatively high levels of foreign liabilities, but these were considered less worrisome as for the most part they were liabilities to the parent bank. State-owned banks as a group and Sberbank in particular had less exposure to external debt (Figure 4.9, Panel B), although the second largest bank, VTB, was an exception to that rule. At the level of the banking system

Figure 4.7. **Banking sector development and efficiency**

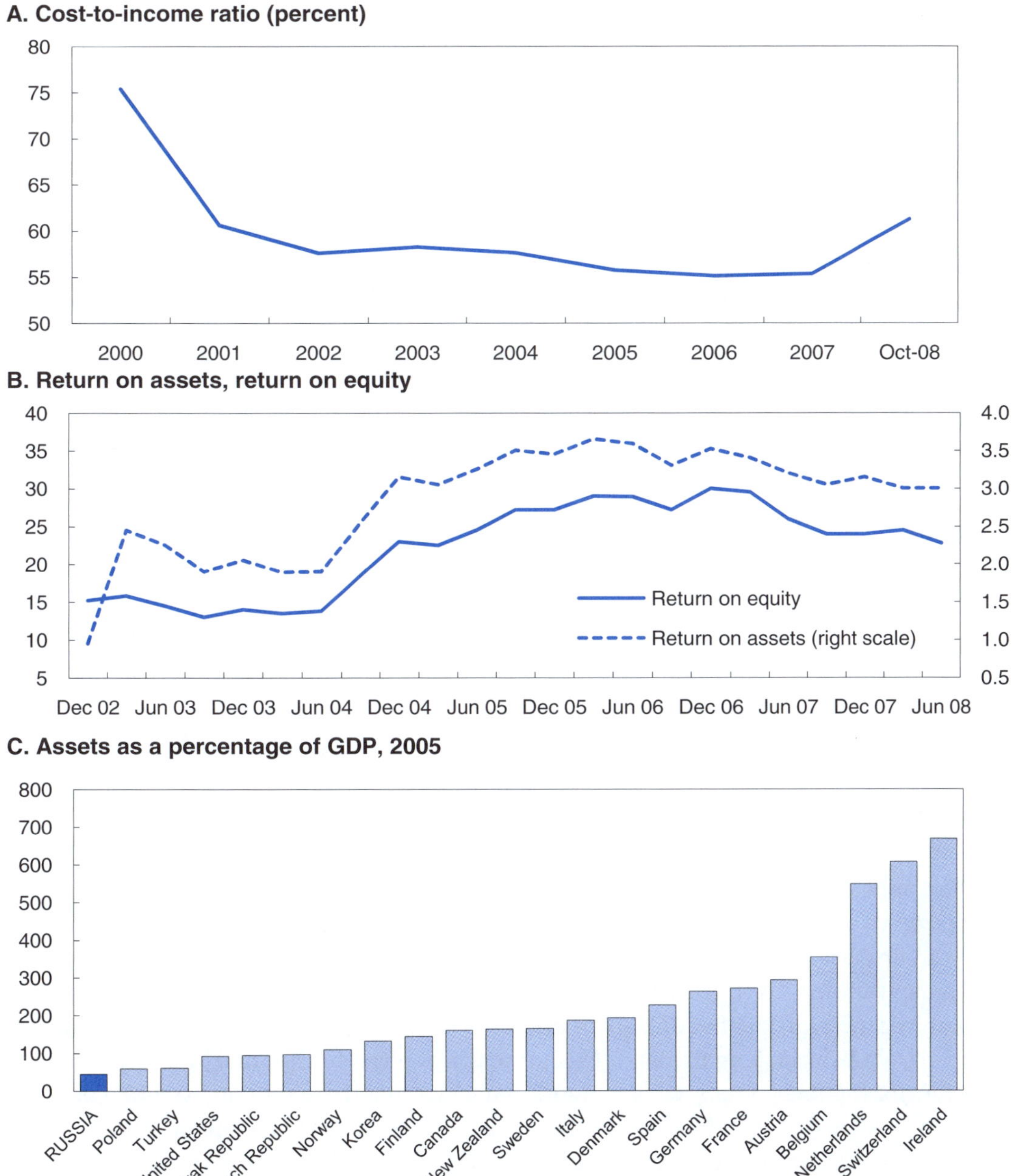

Source: OECD calculations based on OECD Bank Profitability database, Interfax 100 database, OECD Economic Outlook 84 database, Federal Service for State Statistics and Central Bank of Russia.

StatLink http://dx.doi.org/10.1787/650334830766

as a whole, foreign liabilities were not particularly large by international standards (Figure 4.9, Panel C), although until mid-2007 they were rising at an accelerating rate.

Phase IV– The current crisis

Until the collapse of Lehman Brothers in September 2008, Russia's financial system appeared to be weathering the worsening international conditions quite well. The unfolding of the subprime crisis in the United States in the summer of 2007 had already

Figure 4.8. **Consumer lending**

End of period, as a percentage of total[1]

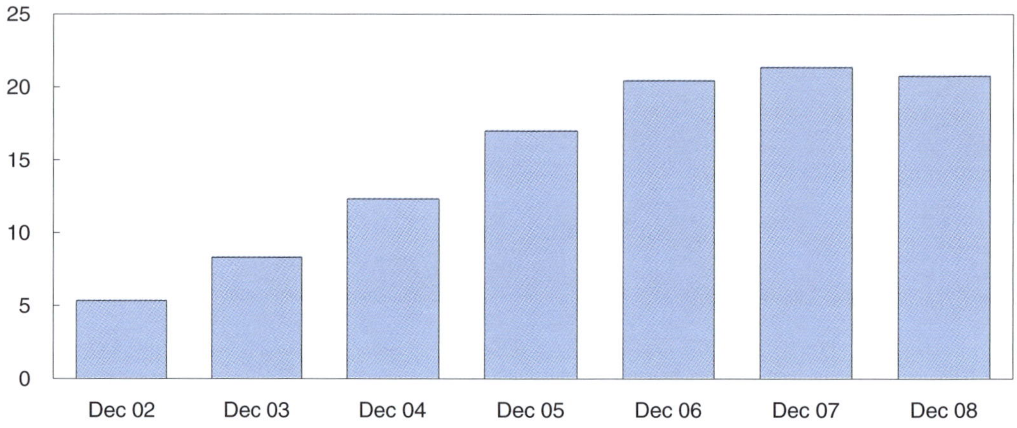

1. Total lending is loans, deposits and other funds extended to organisations, individuals and credit institutions.

Source: OECD calculations based on Central bank of Russia and Federal Service for State Statistics.

StatLink http://dx.doi.org/10.1787/650367633103

dented appetite for risk in international capital markets, reducing Russian banks' ability to fund themselves abroad. In the autumn of 2007 the CBR and the government reacted quickly to sustain liquidity in the system, *via* the expansion of the list of eligible securities for CBR refinancing (the Lombard list), the auctioning of government deposits to commercial banks, and a reduction in reserve requirements in October 2007. Most indicators of system-level liquidity, capital, and profitability remained healthy through August 2008, and Russian banks sporadically regained access to foreign borrowing, such as in the second quarter of 2008 (Figure 4.10, Panel A). Interbank interest rates remained sharply negative in real terms until late 2008 (Figure 4.10, Panel B).

The appearance of stability and continued growth in the Russian banking system after the first wave of turbulence in international markets in August 2007 may have been at least partly an artefact of overly vigorous official support for the sector early on, which delayed but arguably ultimately aggravated the impact of the crisis on the banking sector. Liquidity support beginning in the fall of 2007 permitted a further leg of unfunded loan expansion, with the state banks taking the lead. This process was given further fuel by the intermittent reopening of the foreign borrowing window. It may be that there was no systemic liquidity shortage in August 2007, and an excessive official reaction allowed incipient imbalances to grow. The counterargument is that even if most banks did not suffer from liquidity shortages in 2007, allowing even a few banks to fail could have provoked panic among depositors and precipitated a systemic crisis. The counterfactual is of course unknowable.

In any event, when the global crisis suddenly intensified in September 2008, it had a surprisingly large impact on the Russian financial system, given Russian banks' limited direct exposure to the roots of the international crisis and their still relatively modest reliance (on average) on access to international capital markets. The population's shaky confidence in Russian banks was weakened. The shares of quoted banks fell by nearly 90% from their peaks (Figure 4.11, Panel A). Given also pressure on the rouble arising in large part from the steep fall in the oil price, rouble deposits reversed their strong growth trend of the past ten years (Figure 4.11, Panel B).[5]

 OECD ECONOMIC SURVEYS: RUSSIAN FEDERATION – ISBN 978-92-64-05433-2 – © OECD 2009

Figure 4.9. **Exposure to foreign liabilities**

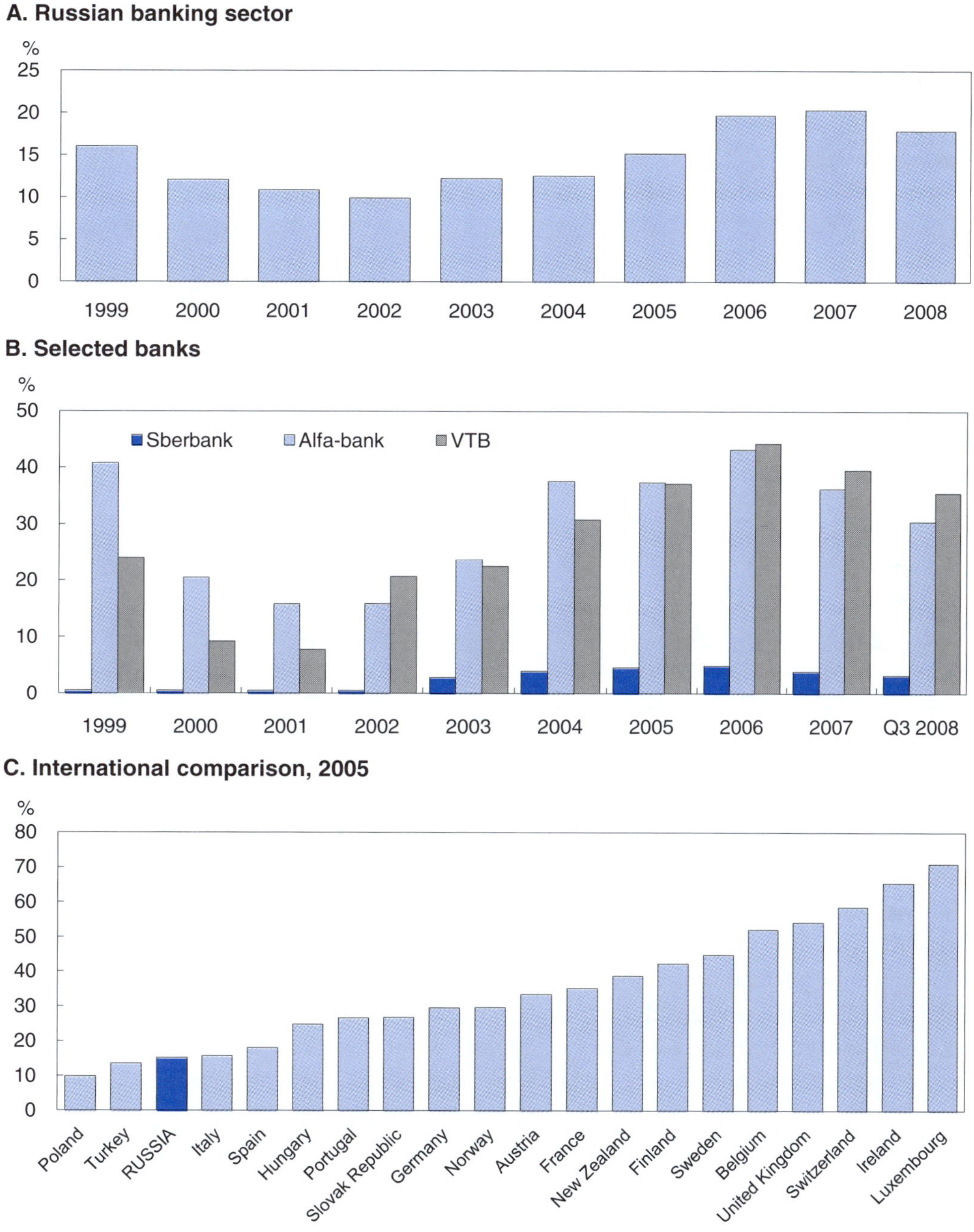

Source: OECD calculations based on OECD Bank profitability database, Central Bank of Russia and Interfax.

StatLink http://dx.doi.org/10.1787/650416278164

The initial effect on the banking sector came *via* the securities markets. Sharp falls in share prices had already got underway, given net sales by foreign institutions from emerging markets in general, the sharp fall in commodity prices after their peak in July 2008, and some negative Russia specific factors such as the conflict with Georgia in August 2008 and the TNK-BP saga. A number of banks, exposed to securities markets (especially *via* the use of multiple repos – see Box 4.3), quickly found themselves in difficulty, and began to default on obligations in the interbank market. These banks were

Figure 4.10. **Banking system liquidity**

Source: OECD calculations based on Central bank of Russia.

StatLink http://dx.doi.org/10.1787/650421565362

swiftly either acquired *via* state action/support or closed, and their obligations to other banks were honoured. Even though these stricken banks did not include any of systemic importance, the impact on sentiment among depositors and other banks was marked. This in turn was in part on account of the legacy of crises, which makes sentiment of the Russian population fragile, leading to bigger deposit withdrawals than elsewhere (especially compared to OECD countries). The net deposit withdrawals in late-2008 were especially marked for private second-tier banks, but affected even state- and foreign-owned banks.

Although the banks were very much in the forefront of sectors affected by the global financial crisis, part of the reason for the heavy impact of the crisis on the banking system is that it quickly became much more than just a financial crisis. In Russia's case, the 75% fall in the oil price over a matter of 5 months radically undermined the macroeconomic health of the country. It meant, among other things, a dramatic worsening of the position of Russian corporates, which exposes banks to higher loan losses (and which may also mean that apparently balanced foreign exchange positions of banks wind up being unbalanced as and when foreign currency loan defaults come through). Lower economic growth reduces the creditworthiness of borrowers, cutting lending growth and impacting on non-performing loan rates. Fears of rapid depreciation of the rouble became a significant factor in deposit withdrawals and shifts to foreign currency deposits by both households and firms.

Figure 4.11. **Crisis impact on banks**

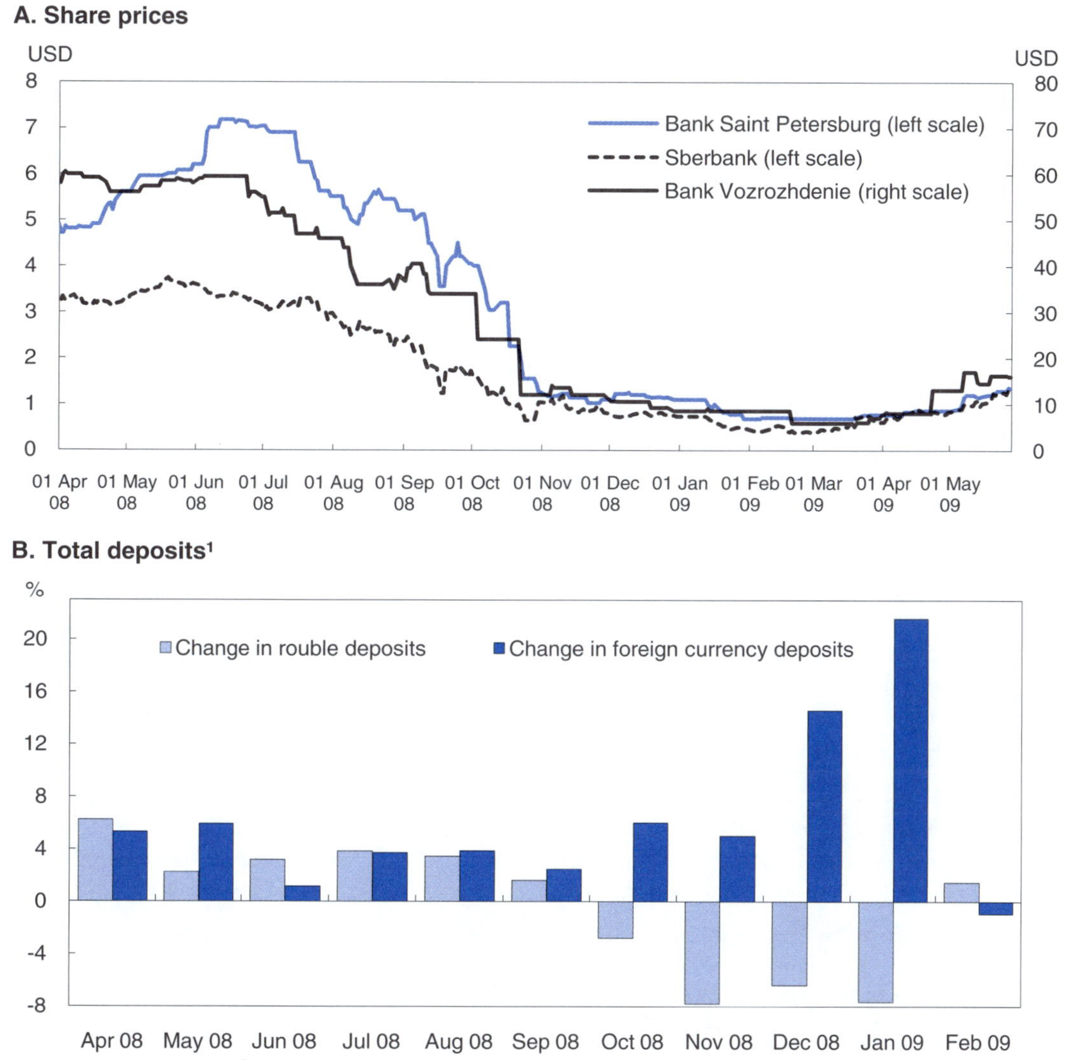

1. Total deposits of individuals + organisations + credit institutions + individual entrepreneurs.

Source: Datastream and OECD calculations based on Central Bank of Russia.

StatLink http://dx.doi.org/10.1787/650481157812

Significant as it has been, the impact of the global crisis on the Russian banking system may also appear to have been greater than it really was. The authorities' keenness to be seen to be taking decisive action (see Box 4.4 for a listing of actions taken in response to the crisis to shore up the banking system) may have meant that some actions were taken before they were needed. For example, subordinated loans were made available to banks in large amounts to support capital positions, but as of March 2009 no major Russian bank had fallen below the 10% capital adequacy requirement. Likewise, the facility to provide foreign currency for external debt repayments has not been fully taken up and seems mostly to have been accessed by enterprises and banks which had not exhausted their own capacity to make such repayments. Larger banks were generally relatively liquid, well capitalised, and with limited exposure to a drying up of foreign capital flows. But doubts about some banks, mostly second-tier, caused the interbank market to seize up and led

Box 4.3. **Gaming the system – selected schemes for circumventing prudential and tax regulations**

Inflating authorised capital. Banks often used loan schemes to increase equity capital and align it with risk-weighted assets according to CBR requirements. A CBR regulation N215-P of March 2003 on the method for determining the capital of banks introduced the concept of "improper assets", which aimed at ruling out the use of loan schemes to form capital. Improper assets include cash assets and other assets originating directly or indirectly from assets provided by the bank or other individuals, if the bank directly or indirectly assumed risks arising through the provision of these assets. In identifying instances or symptoms that capital was formed using improper assets the CBR can demand banks to provide documented proof that improper assets were not used in forming capital or make the appropriate changes to capital within a specified period. This measure in principle addresses the problem, but in practice is hard to implement effectively

Multiple repos. Under this scheme, a bank holding bonds (yielding, say, 8%) pledges them at a discount for a loan at a lower interest rate (*e.g.* 6%), using the proceeds to buy the same bonds. The newly acquired bonds are likewise pledged and so on. It emerged at the onset of the 2008 crisis that some banks and financial companies had used such a scheme 5-6 times to leverage returns. Such iteration could roughly double the initial 8% bond return, but at the cost of greatly increased market risk. When the markets fell in August-September 2008, some market players lost virtually all of their assets and were not able to meet their payment obligations to other participants in the market, which resulted in a chain reaction through the system. The sharp rise in counterparty risk provoked the seizing-up of the interbank market, other than for the largest banks.

Tax optimisation. Banks often have associated companies located in regions with favourable tax regimes. An associated company located in such a region that owns a bank building or other property can save on property tax. Lease payments for the use of the building, although they have no impact on profit under IFRS, reduce it under RAS, which is what counts for tax purposes. The associated company in a holding company often serves as the profit centre, and manages the bank's securities portfolio. The bank receives minimum income on a loan to this company and most profit on operations with securities remains on the balance sheet of the associated company. Another option is for the associated company to receive a loan from the bank and place the money on deposit in the bank. Interest on the loan is lower than the deposit rate, which reduces pretax profit according to Russian accounting standards. Claims on associated companies can be shown in correspondent accounts in banks, loans to banks and companies, or notes, and liabilities can be shown in deposits, notes, correspondent accounts, and loans of other banks. Several companies, including offshore companies and Russian banks, may be involved in such schemes.

authorities to flood the system with liquidity to prevent bank failures and spreading of panic.

Despite the efforts of the authorities to sustain bank lending, rouble M2 fell quite sharply between end-August 2008 and end-March 2009. Although there have been signs of stabilisation, with the rouble strengthening and international reserves rebounding, Russia is still in the crisis phase and the outcome is uncertain. There have still been no major bank failures, and deposit runs have been limited, and apparently mainly associated with fears about the value of the rouble rather than bank stability. Vigorous action has been taken to

Box 4.4. **Anti-crisis measures to support the banking system**

- Reduction of reserve requirements 18 September and 18 October, boosting bank liquidity by approximately RUB 400 billion.
- Auction of government deposits to banks. Originally RUB 1.1 trillion, later expanded to RUB 1.5 trillion.
- Increased CBR repo transactions, beginning in September 2008. Average daily amounts increased roughly five-fold after early September, peaking in late January 2009.
- Permission for CBR to extend uncollateralised credit to banks with designated credit ratings. Amount extended rose to more than RUB 1.9 trillion in February 2009, before falling back to about RUB 700 billion by early June.
- Amendment to 2008-10 Budget to allow government to deposit money from National Welfare Fund with VEB, which was to buy back shares of enterprises controlled but not wholly-owned by the state, up to RUB 75 billion in 2008 and RUB 175 billion in 2009.
- Set-aside of USD 50 billion to help companies (*via* VEB) refinance foreign loans falling due. USD 9 billion disbursed by end-2008.
- Permission for CBR to compensate banks for losses on interbank loans through end-2009.
- VEB authorised to provide subordinated loans of RUB 450 billion to banks other than Sberbank, with CBR authorised to provide up to RUB 500 billion to Sberbank.
- Acquisition (*via* VEB, VTB and state-owned enterprises) of failing private banks (*e.g.* Globex, Kit Finance, Sobinbank, Svyaz).
- Raising of deposit insurance limits to RUB 200 000 from RUB 100 000, and at 90% up to RUB 700 000 from RUB 400 000.
- Raising of interest rates paid to banks by CBR on deposits.
- Restarting of CBR 90-day repos, after earlier being discontinued for lack of demand.
- Amendment of 2008 Budget to provide for capital injections of RUB 200 billion to the Deposit Insurance Agency (in order to allow it to restructure or liquidate failed banks) and RUB 60 billion to the State Mortgage Agency.
- Guarantee by State Mortgage Agency of mortgage bonds and lending, up to RUB 500 billion.
- Recapitalisation of RosSelkhozbank (agriculture bank) and RosAgroLeasing.
- Government guarantee of bank loans to corporates, up to 70% of loans; amount available RUB 300 billion.
- Announcement of further possible injections of capital into banks, up to RUB 1.4 trillion.

sustain bank liquidity and solvency and avoid a sharp reduction of lending. But more bad news, such as rising non-performing loans, the possible failure of one or more of the larger banks, and bigger bank runs could be in the pipeline. Although, unlike some other crisis-hit countries, pre-crisis leverage levels were not obviously excessive, further deleveraging therefore remains possible.

Strengths and weaknesses of the current system

While the full impact of the crisis has yet to be seen, the starting situation was favourable: on most indicators of systemic health the situation as of end-2008 was much improved on earlier years. While the usual caveat about the integrity of the data apply, and while 2008 clearly represented a cyclical peak, in some respects Russia appears to compare favourably with relevant peers on measures of financial depth, efficiency, and stability.

Strengths

Overall, the Russian banking system is, or at least was at the onset of the current crisis, relatively well capitalised. In addition, almost all of the largest banks are either state-owned or are subsidiaries of foreign banks (Table 4.1). In both cases, stability is in principle bolstered by the existence of owners capable of supporting the banks in the event of difficulties, although the scale of upheaval in advanced country banking systems has underlined the risk that foreign banks may not be able or willing to support their Russian subsidiaries. Indeed, it has become clear that they may even seek to use them as a source of liquidity. The presumed existence of back-up resources for state- and foreign-owned banks is reflected in the fact that their capital adequacy ratios are lower than for domestic private banks on average, since the latter may require more of a capital buffer.

Table 4.1. **Top ten banks by ownership type**

Bank	% of total banking assets	Ownership
Sberbank	23.7	State
VTB	8.0	State
Gazprombank	4.7	State
Rosselhozbank	2.9	State
Bank of Moscow	2.8	State
Alfa-bank	2.5	Private domestic
UniCredit Bank	2.1	Foreign
Raiffeisenbank	2.1	Foreign
VTB-24	2.0	State
Rosbank	1.7	Foreign

Source: Central Bank of Russia and OECD calculations.

Likewise, until the onset of the crisis Russian banks on average had levels of profitability that were relatively high and rising (Figure 4.7, Panel B). It is to be expected that these ratios will fall sharply in the context of the financial and economic crisis gripping Russia and many other countries at present, but on a pre-crisis basis, Russian banks were quite profitable and increasingly efficient: cost-to-income ratios were on a declining trend through early 2008 (Figure 4.7, Panel A).

Russian banks have low direct exposure to troubled US assets such as mortgage bonds and derivatives, and they have not engaged in complex lending practices with structured products, a practice which has proved so dangerous in a number of advanced countries. Also, the US-style "sub-prime" mortgage market is virtually non-existent in Russia. During the real estate boom in Russia some zero-down-payment mortgage loans emerged for transactions in Moscow and St. Petersburg, but such loans were extended only to customers demonstrating the ability to make the payments. The lack of exposure to these sorts of risk is no doubt primarily a function of the relative lack of sophistication of Russian banks rather than superior risk management or tight regulation, but it is nonetheless a boon to stability in the current environment.

Although the picture for some individual banks is quite different, the banking sector as a whole has a fairly balanced exposure to different sectors, with none accounting for more than 20% of total lending. The energy and metals sectors have been underrepresented in the loan portfolios of Russian banks, as the largest companies have been able to attract cheaper and longer-term resources from international banks and capital markets. This underweighting has been unintentional, but is not necessarily a disadvantage in circumstances of very weak commodity prices, as seen in late 2008 and early 2009. Total lending to real estate and the construction sector has grown very rapidly in recent years and, at around 11% of bank assets, is the 3rd largest sectoral exposure, after trade and finance. This level remains fairly modest in international comparison, however.

While consumer and mortgage lending have mushroomed in the past few years, they did so from a near-zero base. Total mortgages at the end of 2008 amounted to less than 4% of GDP, far lower than in OECD countries. Consumer loans have virtually doubled annually in recent years, but still only amounted to 20% of total loans outstanding at end-2008.

On the liability side, Russia's ratio of retail to total deposits, at around 40%, is relatively high in international terms, suggesting a relatively stable funding base. For Sberbank, probably still the only systemic bank, the ratio is still higher, at approximately 65%. Moreover, the average maturity of retail deposits has risen substantially over the past 10 years, indicating a rising degree of stability. Also, while the average tenor of deposits remains short (and household deposits of any term can by law be withdrawn on demand), so too is that of loans, so that Russian banks on average have a relatively low maturity gap: the average original maturity of liabilities is 1.4 years, not much less than the 1.6 year average maturity of assets. Thus, when faced with liquidity shortages, Russian banks can typically shrink their balance sheet quite rapidly.

Despite the big increase in 2006-07, the share of foreign liabilities is still only about 20%, relatively low by comparison with other emerging markets, and the share for Sberbank is in the low single digits. Moreover, with external loans not being rolled over and access to new borrowing – largely withdrawn, foreign liabilities have recently begun to fall: the CBR estimates that banks' foreign liabilities fell by about USD 28 billion in the fourth quarter of 2008 (while their foreign assets were built up by a similar amount). The system as a whole therefore does not exhibit excessive vulnerability to continued disruption of access to international capital markets, although there are a number of banks with much greater than average resort to foreign liabilities which are being forced to find other funding or shrink their balance sheets quickly to survive.

At least on the face of it, loan loss provisions are relatively high. At end-September 2008 provisions were equivalent to 3.9% of assets.[6] Although the ferocity of the economic crisis could well overwhelm this cushion loan losses in the 1998 crisis peaked at around 15% of total loans – it is quite large in the context of past experience and international norms.

Weaknesses

Notwithstanding the many improvements made over the past decade or so, there are significant remaining weaknesses in prudential supervision. Banks continue to report that inspectors have insufficient understanding of banking and banking risks, and that supervision is still largely form-over-substance. This may reflect insufficient resources and/or training for bank supervisors. Meanwhile, although the authorities have consistently affirmed their aim to implement Basel II, there has never been a formal objective for the date by which this would be achieved, and the informal timetable has already slipped by several years. It is currently hoped that implementation will be achieved in 2011, but progress in preparing for that shift appears to be slow. In addition, as in other countries, the arrival of the current economic and financial crisis suggests that there are weaknesses in the existing approaches to banking supervision (both as regards Basel I and Basel II), with in particular too much pro-cyclicality and insufficient weight put on liquidity as against capital adequacy.

Russia appears to have too many banks (Figure 4.12), and in particular too many small banks. The theoretical relationship between bank concentration and banking system fragility is ambiguous. On the one hand, concentration may reduce competition, resulting in higher profits, which makes banks more resistant to adverse shocks. Also, having fewer banks to monitor may facilitate prudential supervision in a concentrated banking system reducing the risk of systemic crisis. In addition, to the extent that banks in a consolidated system are on average larger than those in a diffuse system, they may benefit from greater diversification and/or economies of scale, making them less prone to failure. Moreover, Russia's experience suggests that the vulnerability of smaller banks can spark broader crises of confidence, and so can at times be a drag on the sound part of the system. Banks which are relatively small and weak may be, in part for those reasons, overly aggressive and prone to failure, which can poison trust in the whole system and lead to a seizing up of interbank lending. As against this, it is argued that concentrated banking systems will be more prone to "too big to fail" effects, which aggravates moral hazard and increases banking system fragility (Mishkin, 1999). Beck *et al.* (2006) provide cross-country empirical evidence which supports the consolidation-stability link, and Rati *et al.* (2008), in another cross-country study, find that consolidation is favourable for access to finance.[7]

Interestingly, although Beck *et al.* (2006) find that consolidation is favourable to systemic stability, they find the same for measures of competition, and other research suggest that the two are not necessarily in conflict.[8] Russia appears to have too little of both. Despite the very large number of banks, effective competition in Russian banking is still limited, although it has picked up in recent years. The banking sector is quite

Figure 4.12. **Number of banks – international comparison**

2005

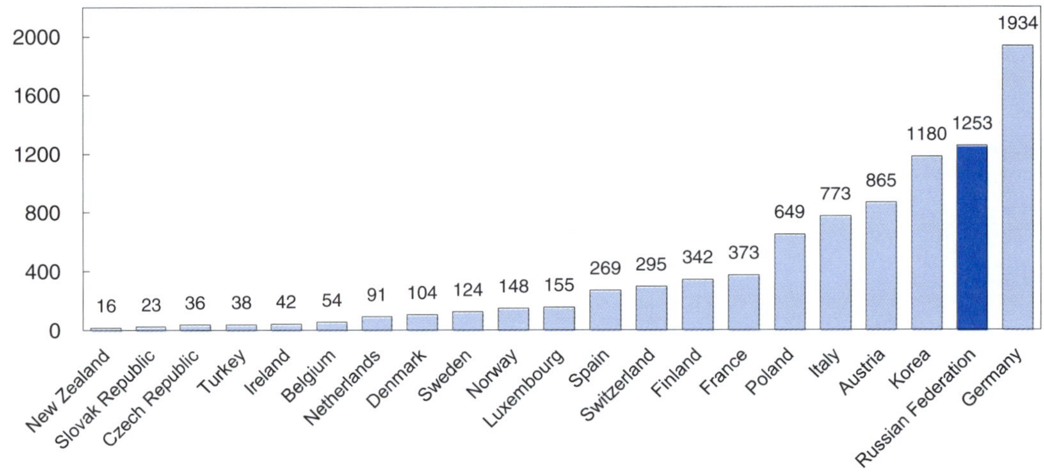

Source: OECD Bank profitability database and Central Bank of Russia.

StatLink http://dx.doi.org/10.1787/650487378736

concentrated by various measures (*e.g.* shares of top 5 banks in total assets, deposits, and capital) and Sberbank remains the clear market leader in most areas. The relatively high margins enjoyed by Russian banks, albeit positive for building capital and resilience, may be one sign of less-than-vigorous competition.[9] Sberbank, which benefits from cheap funding and favourable access to foreign borrowing on account of its state backing, has not faced a strong challenge in the most profitable market segments.

Capital adequacy represents a mixed picture. Average ratios of capital to risk-weighted assets as of 2008 showed little sign of danger, but may have represented a cyclical high, while questions persist about the measurement of capital. Bank capital has grown rapidly in the past 10 years, but has largely just kept pace with growth of assets, so that capital adequacy ratios have not changed much, leaving Russia around the middle of its peer group. The capital cushion is especially small for some medium-sized private banks, which is the group that has tended to produce the most bank failures.

The situation with capital adequacy pre-crisis is a reminder of the fact that the relatively reassuring level of most system-level indicators is no protection from a systemic crisis, even leaving aside doubts about the quality of the statistics. The recent liquidity crisis shows that even isolated difficulties can spread *via* uncertainty about the soundness of counterparties. In such an environment, the already segmented interbank market can seize up, spreading liquidity shortages. The reliance of a few banks on foreign borrowing for funding points to one source of vulnerability in this respect, as does the heavy exposure of some banks to securities markets, consumer lending, and lending to individual cyclical sectors like construction.

The fact that households are legally able to withdraw their term deposits on demand has long been a much-debated feature of the Russian banking system. This provision of the Civil Code means that regardless of the nominal maturity of a deposit, banks are forced to see it as a demand deposit. This remains a potentially serious source of vulnerability for banks, making it harder to limit maturity mismatches, although to date there is little evidence of it having played a big role in either the underdevelopment of the sector or of financial instability.[10] Whatever the significance of this Civil Code provision, however, there is clearly a relative lack of long-term funding.

Although lending concentration has declined markedly, it remains relatively high, and it is questionable whether the full extent of such concentration is accurately measured. Such concentration can be to single borrowers, single sectors, related parties, or on types of loans, such as uncollateralised loans. Certainly the concentration of banks' loan portfolios has fallen. An Interfax Rating Agency study in 2001 showed that the largest 10 loans typically comprised 40% of the loan portfolio of even large Russian banks, whereas as of 2008 this figure was down to 15%.

Risk management in Russian banks remains underdeveloped. Only the largest few dozen banks use risk management to manage their businesses. For many other banks, the high reliance on a few customers and the connected nature of many transactions means that risk management considerations are trumped by the perceived need to retain good relations with key borrowers and/or depositors.

Notwithstanding the improvements that have been made, the Russian banking system continues to suffer from a relative lack of transparency. It remains the case that not all links between banks and related parties are revealed, which obscures the extent to which such parties may be afforded favourable treatment in the event of difficulties, leaving other creditors and/or shareholders bearing the burden of losses. Although this problem is well known, the reality is hard to pin down. The authorities remain reliant on the willingness of shareholders to disclose. This problem is not unique to Russia, but it does seem to be particularly pronounced there. A culture of transparency remains to be entrenched.

Despite the strong growth of lending in the long economic upswing from 1999 through 2008, the Russian banking sector still does relatively little intermediation of savings and investment, especially for small and medium-sized enterprises (SMEs). According to Rosstat, only about 10% of corporate investment is financed by bank loans, up strongly from only 3% in 2000, but still very small in relation to retained earnings and other financing sources. One issue in this respect is financial reporting in the non-financial sector; unlike banks, other enterprises do not have to prepare financial statements according to IFRS, and only a small number (largely those issuing bonds or equity abroad) do so. Russian accounting standards, while useful for some purposes, are less transparent in several respects.

The problem of corruption, recognised at the highest levels of government, may be another factor that impedes the development of the banking sector. Using regional data, Weill (2009) finds that corruption has a depressing effect on lending, and Russia continues to rate poorly on international surveys of perceived corruption. This is course an issue that has much wider implications than just banking (see Chapter 5 for a discussion of corruption and product market regulation).

Although not a weakness of the Russian banking system as such, another clear danger at present is the sheer size of the shock now facing the system. Regardless of the reserves accumulated, the diversification of borrowers and depositors, the rebalancing of assets, or the limiting of currency mismatches, the financial market turmoil already experienced and the economic slowdown underway will stress many banks. A rise in non-performing loans similar to that experienced in the 1998 crisis would require a substantial injection of capital into the banks to prevent widespread insolvencies. Some banks could also experience serious losses from securities holdings and/or exchange rate movements.

Dealing with the current crisis and reducing the probability of future ones

In the short term, the authorities are faced with the challenge of preserving stability of the financial system in the face of a sharp worsening of economic conditions while minimising deleterious effects on long-run efficiency. Avoiding a collapse of the banking system is rightly a high priority of the authorities.

Many of the actions taken since the onset of the crisis are sensible from the point of view of bolstering the banking system and maintaining confidence, and so far, most signs are reasonably encouraging, notwithstanding the scale of the shock. Rouble deposits (and cash, and therefore M2) did decline in the last quarter of 2008 and early-2009, when pressures on the exchange rate eventually led first to a gradual and then a virtually unchecked depreciation against the dollar-euro basket. Moreover, non-performing loans began to turn upward, and bank profit growth fell sharply. So far, however, the liquidity and solvency of systemic banks has remained adequate. In the meantime, since late-January the rouble has stabilised and indeed strengthened against the dollar-euro basket, which if maintained could induce a large flow back into rouble deposits, permitting continued growth of rouble lending.

The relative pre-crisis solidity of the banking system, the fact that only a few banks are of systemic importance, and the reasonably favourable outcomes to date (given the scale of the global crisis) suggest that one near-term danger is overloading the crisis response with potentially harmful measures. In Russia's case, these would include excessive aggravation of moral hazard and further expansion of the state's already extensive involvement in banking. Clearly, as in other countries there may be a case in current circumstances for the judicious use of government guarantees of some assets, capital injections, and even perhaps nationalisations if necessary to preserve the functioning of the system. With state banks already holding nearly half of banking system assets and no private bank accounting for more than 2½ per cent, however, there are few if any private banks which would have to be saved to keep the system functioning. Costly support for or acquisition of non-systemic banks should be avoided. As and when further banks fail in coming months, the *presumption should be in favour of speedy liquidation and a pay-out of depositors.* More consolidation of the banking sector is likely to improve competition and banking efficiency and reduce the burden of supervision borne by the CBR.

One aspect of a creeping expansion of the role of the state in banking is the increased capitalisation and additional tasks for VEB. As discussed in chapter 5, VEB is one of the half dozen recently-created special-status state corporations whose governance falls short of OECD standards, and as such its growing importance as a lender, investor, and vehicle for rescuing banks and corporations is a potentially worrying development. The government should either provide for VEB to be licensed and regulated like other financial institutions or reduce its role.

While the state's control of the largest banks is in some ways an advantage in a crisis situation, since it is easier to maintain lending levels, it also carries dangers. In particular, there is a temptation to direct lending to favoured large (and often state-owned) enterprises, thus weakening competition. Care should be taken to maximise the extent to which loans are allocated on a commercial basis, even if pressure is exerted to maintain overall lending levels. If anything, in Russia, it is small and medium-sized enterprises which are credit-deprived and should benefit from any favourable treatment.

Beyond minimising the costs and duration of the current economic and financial crisis, Russia faces two broad challenges as regards making the banking system more resistant to crises in the future. The first is to converge on existing best practice as regards the implementation of prudential supervision. The second, which faces not only Russia but many other countries, including the most advanced, is to address defects in bank regulation which amplify economic cycles and give insufficient weight to liquidity considerations.

Better implementation of the existing supervision framework could involve a number of features. *To begin with, more and better-trained supervisors would be helpful. Consolidation of the sector would help in this respect, as scarce resources could be spread over a smaller number of banks. Also, it may be useful to explicitly divide the Russian banking sector into tiers subject to different levels of supervision, to allow resources to be more focussed on the larger banks. In addition, there is scope for further streamlining of formal requirements on banks, while increasing substantive assessment of risks. In the longer term, Russia might benefit from moving away from supervision by legal form of the regulated entity to supervision by objectives*, as is done in some OECD countries. Currently, the CBR is responsible for banking supervision and the Federal Financial Markets Service oversees financial markets, while the Ministry of Finance supervises insurance. The global crisis has pointed up gaps in such systems of regulation. Some advanced countries have adopted regulation by objectives (Netherlands, Australia), while others (*e.g.* Sweden and the United Kingdom) have adopted a unified framework with a single financial services regulator.

As regards moving toward a more countercyclical framework for bank supervision, it is widely acknowledged that there is a global need for a more macro-prudential approach, one which takes more account of systemic risks while continuing to consider bank-specific ones (*e.g.* Borio and White, 2004; Borio and Shim, 2007; Turner, 2009; G30, 2009). This is certainly true for Russia. Difficult issues arise with efforts to make banking regulation more countercyclical, for example the problem of ascertaining where the economy is in the cycle at any given moment, but the dangers of inaction are more obvious than ever. *Capital requirements and/or provisioning rules should be made counter-cyclical and capital requirements should be allowed to vary across banks to reflect each bank's contribution to systemic risk. In addition, stress tests should include assessments of shocks which hit the financial system as a whole, so that counterparty and market risk deteriorate along with credit risk.* There will be ongoing efforts to reform international rules to strengthen existing supervision approaches, and *Russia should play an active role in these discussions, but without waiting to implement its own reforms to make bank regulation less procyclical.*

Another important aspect of international efforts to improve prudential supervision of banks is the need for more regulation of liquidity to put it on a more equal footing with capital adequacy. One possible reform would be to *require banks to prepare periodic liquidity assessments for review by the CBR, with the CBR to give liquidity guidance to banks on an individual basis.*

Certain actions beyond bank supervision would be useful in furthering greater resilience of the system. While the repeated crises in the Russian banking sector do not have a single cause, one common thread is the low confidence of the population in banks (and the rouble) and the low levels of trust between banks. This suggests the need for more transparency and more confidence in the strength of regulation and the rule of law. Also, while it may still be too early to tell, it is not clear that deposit insurance has had the hoped-for confidence-building effect on depositors. One problem appears to be that the public remain largely unaware of the existence of the system, or of the amount of protection offered. A survey by the Deposit Insurance Agency in 2008 found that only 38% of individuals were aware of the system of deposit insurance. *Greater efforts to publicise the deposit insurance scheme and its protections are called for in current circumstances. It is also important to ensure timely payouts of insured deposits in the event of bank failures as the downturn progresses.*

Achieving a deeper and more efficient banking system

Over the longer term, the banking system could do more to contribute to sustained rapid economic growth, especially in conjunction with a liberalisation of product markets, with greater competition throughout the economy. To begin with, the fragility of the system revealed by successive crises hurts confidence in the system, hindering the growth of deposits, the intermediation of savings, and the efficient allocation of capital – imprudent practices in booms will worsen the busts and provoke more bank crises. In addition, the current structure of the sector leaves unexploited economies of scale and holds back vigorous competition between larger, more equal groups.

One reform which would be likely to boost efficiency in the long run is the gradual withdrawal of the state from the banking sector. There is no clear long-term rationale for state

Box 4.5. Recommendations for making the banking system more efficient and resilient

Crisis response measures

- Facilitate and encourage consolidation of the sector, *via* speedy resolution of failing banks, facilitation of mergers, and higher minimum capital requirements.
- Avoid expanding the use of directed lending, especially to large and/or well connected borrowers – to the extent that pressure is put on banks to lend, the opportunity should be taken to expand the share of SMEs in total loans.
- Publicise deposit insurance to raise awareness of its provisions, and ensure speedy and full (*i.e.* in accordance with law) payout of depositors in case of failures during crisis, especially if any larger banks fail, in order to strengthen public confidence in the Russian banking sector.

Strengthening prudential supervision

- Improve the quality of on-site supervision, including *via* increased resources for staffing and training.
- Explicitly divide the Russian banking sector into tiers subject to different levels of supervision, to allow scarce resources to be more focussed on the larger banks.
- Further streamline formal requirements on banks, while strengthening risk assessments.
- Play an active role in international efforts to improve financial regulation.
- In parallel with such efforts, explore ways of making capital adequacy requirements countercyclical, such as *via* dynamic provisioning rules, higher capital adequacy requirements in cyclical upswings, and capital requirements that vary across banks according to their contribution to systemic risk.
- Expand the use of stress testing, including more testing of system–wide shocks affecting counter–party and market risks.
- Seek improved ways of regulating liquidity and responding to shortages for individual banks. Require banks to prepare periodic liquidity assessments for review by the CBR, with the CBR to give liquidity guidance to banks on an individual basis.

Improve the regulatory environment for banks

- Amend the Civil Code provision allowing term deposits of households to be withdrawn on demand.
- Expand the use of IFRS financial reporting, including for non-banks.
- Develop a system of personal bankruptcy.

Improve the structure of the banking sector

- Outline a long-term privatisation strategy for the state-owned banks.

ownership, while there is substantial evidence from elsewhere for greater efficiency of private banks (*e.g.* La Porta *et al.*, 2000). On the other hand, there is no urgent need in Russia for large-scale privatisation, especially in light of the fragmentary evidence that public banks in Russia are not less efficient than private ones (Karas *et al.*, 2008). Moreover, there is clear evidence that state banks have been beneficial for systemic stability in periods of crisis, while a period of depressed asset prices is hardly opportune for divesting stakes in state-owned banks. In the near term, the priority is to work on levelling the playing field and bolstering effective competition. A plan for streamlining state involvement in banking when conditions are more propitious should be developed, however. *Particularly given the likelihood of a further increase of the share of state-owned banks in total assets as a result of the economic crisis, the authorities should outline a long-term strategy for reducing their dominance.* As noted above, the growing role of VEB is particularly problematic, given the shortcomings of its corporate governance.

Another reform that would assist with financial deepening is to allow for true term deposits for individuals, by amending the Civil Code provision which allows term deposits of households to be withdrawn on demand. An effective lengthening of the maturity of liabilities would permit banks to address the shortage of longer-term loans.

The use of IFRS financial reporting is beneficial for transparency and should be expanded, including for non-banks. This would help banks make meaningful assessments of credit risk at lower cost than now, and would also improve the transparency of ownership in the corporate sector, which in turn would facilitate the task of identifying related party lending, deposits, and ownership links.

As credit to households continue to grow in future as a proportion of total bank lending, *it will be increasingly important to develop a system of personal bankruptcy*, to facilitate certainty regarding creditor rights.

Notes

1. Russia has seen the rapid evolution of securities markets and other non-bank financial activity, especially in the past 8 years or so, but banking still accounts for almost all financial intermediation.
2. In the Russian context most "money laundering" by banks constitutes the transfer abroad of funds associated with violations of tax laws, rather than the legitimisation of the proceeds of illegal activities.
3. The spread between domestic rouble yields and dollar rates reflected the low (but rising) probability of a devaluation – the so called peso problem – permitting supra-normal profits for holders of rouble securities as long as the devaluation didn't happen.
4. Among the major groups formed at that time *via* the acquisition of regional affiliates was the MDM-Bank group, which included Conversbank and Petrovsky, among others, and the Uralsib group, which included Nikoil and Avtobank.
5. Part of the growth of foreign currency deposits in November and December 2008 reflects valuation effects as a result of the depreciation of the rouble.
6. The Financial Sector Assessment programme update conducted by the IMF and World Bank asserted that the amended rules for loan loss provisioning gave excessive discretion to the banks in determining the level of provisions (IMF, 2008), allowing bank capital to be overstated. The CBR's response pointed out that the changes nonetheless resulted in higher provisions on average than under the previous system.
7. The alternative view on small banks in Russia is that, if they abide by all prudential norms and are not found to be breaking the law, then they are doing no harm, and if they continue to exist then they must be sufficiently efficient. It is also often noted that many small banks are regional, and may be delivering local banking services that would be absent altogether or monopolised in the absence of these banks. As has been seen in many countries in the context of the current economic crisis, however, prudential norms may be procyclical and pay insufficient attention to liquidity sufficiency, while small banks may continue to exist for reasons other than their efficiency: most of the license withdrawals over the past 5 years have been of very small banks found to have been engaged in illegal activities.
8. Claessens and Laeven (2004) find no evidence that increased concentration is associated with anticompetitive activity in the banking sector, and Demirgüc-Kunt *et al.* (2004) find no positive relationship between concentration and net interest rate margins.
9. The high lending margins could also reflect a risk premium, but they seem implausibly large, especially compared to other emerging market economies.
10. There is anecdotal evidence that after the outbreak of the current crisis, some distressed banks defied the Civil Code provision, betting that the time taken to mount a legal challenge would give them enough breathing space to bolster liquidity, and that they would in the end only face manageable fines for breaking the law.

Bibliography

Aghion, P., P. Howitt and D. Mayer-Foulkes (2005), "The Effect of Financial Development on Convergence: Theory and Evidence", *The Quarterly Journal of Economics* 120(1), pp. 173-222.

Beck, T., R. Levine and N. Loayza (2000), "Finance and the Sources of Growth", *Journal of Financial Economics* 58 (1-2), pp. 261-300.

Beck, T., A. Demirgüc-Kunt and R. Levine (2006), "Bank Concentration, Competition and Crises: first Results", *Journal of Banking and Finance* 30(5), pp. 1581–1603.

Bordo, M.S. and P.L. Rousseau (2006), "Legal-political Factors and the Historical Evolution of the Finance-growth Link", *NBER Working Papers* No. 12035.

Borio, M.S and W. White (2004), "Whither Monetary and Financial Stability? The Implications of Evolving Policy Regimes", *BIS Working Papers* 147.

Borio, C. and I. Shim (2007), "What can (Macro-)prudential Policy do to Support Monetary Policy?", *BIS Working Papers* 242.

Central Bank of Russia (2002), "Strategy for the Development of the Banking Sector of the Russian Federation", *Vestnik of the Bank of Russia*, January.

Claessens, S. and L. Laeven (2004), "What Drives Bank Competition? Some International Evidence", *Journal of Money, Credit and Banking* 36, pp. 563–583.

Demirgüc-Kunt, A., L. Laeven and R. Levine (2004), "Regulation, Market Structure, Institutions, and the Cost of Financial Intermediation", *Journal of Money, Credit and Banking* 36, pp. 593-626.

Group of 30 (2009), *Financial Reform: A Framework for Financial Stability*, Group of 30, Washington, DC, *www.group30.org/pubs/recommendations.pdf*.

Haugh, D., P. Ollivaud, and D. Turner (2009), "The Macroeconomic Consequences of Banking Crises in OECD Countries", *OECD Economics Department Working Papers* No. 683, OECD, Paris.

IMF (2008), *Russian Federation – Financial System Stability Assessment – Update*, IMF, Washington, DC.

Karas, A., K. Schools and L. Weill (2008), "Are Private Banks more Efficient than Public Banks? Evidence from Russia", *BOFIT Discussion Papers* 3/2008, Bank of Finland, Helsinki, *http://ssrn.com/abstract_id=1121709*.

King, R.G. and R. Levine (1993), "Finance, Entrepreneurship, and Growth: Theory and Evidence", *Journal of Monetary Economics* 32(3), pp. 513–542.

La Porta, R., F. Lopez-de-Silanes and A. Shleifer (2002), "Government Ownership of Banks", *The Journal of Finance*, Vol. 57, No 1, pp. 265-301.

Ministry of Finance of the Russian Federation (2005), *Стратегия развития банковского сектора Российской Федерации на период до 2008 года* (Strategy of the development of the banking sector of the Russian Federation for the period up to 2008).

Mishkin, F. (1999), "Bank Consolidation: a Central Banker's Perspective", *NBER Working Paper* 5849, *www.inter.org/papers/w5849.pdf*.

Rajan, R.G. and L. Zingales (1998), "Financial Dependence and Growth", *American Economic Review*, Vol. 88, No. 3 (June 1998), pp. 559-586, *www.jstor.org/action/showPublication?journalCode=amereconrevi*.

Rati, R.A., S. Lee and Y. Seol (2008), "Bank Concentration and Financial Constraints on Firm-level Investment in Europe", *Journal of Banking & Finance* 32, pp. 2684-2694.

Reinhart, C. and K. Rogoff (2009), "The Aftermath of Financial Crises", *NBER Working Paper No. w14656*, *http://papers.ssrn.com/sol3/papers.cfm?abstract_id=1329274*.

De Serres *et al.* (2006), Growth and Financial Intermediation, *OECD Economics Department Working Papers* No. 506, OECD, Paris.

Turner, A. (2009), "The Financial Crisis and the Future of Financial Regulation", The Economist's Inaugural City Lecture, *www.fsa.gov.uk/pubs/speeches/at_21jan09.pdf*, 21 January 2009, *www.fsa.gov.uk/pages/Library/Communication/Speeches/2009/0121_at.shtml*.

Weill, L. (2008), "How Corruption Affects Bank Lending in Russia", *BOFIT Discussion Papers* 18, Bank of Finland, Institute for Economies in Transition, Helsinki.

ISBN 978-92-64-05433-2
OECD Economic Surveys: Russian Federation

Chapter 5

Improving regulation in Russia's goods and services markets

This chapter uses the OECD's product market regulation (PMR) indicators to assess the extent to which the regulatory environment in Russian Federation is supportive to competition and to draw attention to the areas where further reform efforts would pay dividends. The results of estimating these indicators suggest that, despite improvements in some areas, many aspects of Russia's regulatory framework are still restrictive and there is considerable scope for enhancing economic performance by bringing regulation into line with best practices. In particular, the scores indicate that reducing the role of the state-enterprise sector in markets that are inherently competitive and reinvigorating efforts to liberalise foreign trade and direct investment regimes would benefit Russia's economic performance. In some network sectors, recent regulatory changes have significantly improved the scope for competition. However, ongoing work needs to focus on separating competitive and monopoly market segments and eliminating barriers to entry. In addition, the authorities need to develop the capacity and strengthen the hands of the sectoral regulators. Introducing an overarching competition policy would also help bring the issue of competition to centre stage and spread a competition ethos through different levels of government.

The promotion and protection of competitive markets is enshrined in the Constitution of the Russian Federation and, according to surveys of Russian entrepreneurs, is seen as one of the key tasks of government. And with good reason – the extent to which regulation promotes or hinders competition in markets for goods and services has been found to be an important determinant of economic growth in both developed and developing countries. Reflecting the importance of competition, the Russian government has made considerable progress over recent years in improving the regulatory environment to enhance the role of competitive market forces. For example, in October 2006 a new competition law came into force, for which the Federal Antimonopoly Service acts as the principal enforcement institution. Beginning in 2003, the regulation of electricity markets was also comprehensively reformed. However, in spite of these and other significant improvements in the regulatory framework, a range of business surveys continue to highlight regulatory uncertainty and a business climate that is less supportive of private sector competition than in OECD countries and some other emerging markets.[1]

This chapter uses the OECD's indicators of product market regulation (PMR) to assess the degree to which Russia's regulatory environment is conducive to competition in goods and services markets and to highlight areas where further reform efforts would pay dividends. These indicators are based on a standardised procedure that has been used extensively on OECD members and a number of other countries to evaluate the stance of product market regulation in key areas. The chapter begins by briefly outlining the PMR indicator methodology and presenting the overall indicator results for Russia. It then assesses the extent of competition in Russian product markets before briefly reviewing some of the recent literature on the linkages between the regulatory environment, competition and economic performance. The chapter then presents the detailed PMR indicator results for Russia along with a number of policy recommendations that would increase product market competition and improve economic performance.

The OECD's PMR indicators[2]

The OECD's PMR indicators assess the extent to which the regulatory environment promotes or inhibits competition in markets where technology and market conditions make competition viable. These indicators have been used extensively over the last decade to benchmark regulatory frameworks in OECD and a number of other countries and have proven useful in encouraging countries to implement structural reforms that enhance economic performance.

The PMR indicator system summarises a large number of formal rules and regulations that have a bearing on competition. These regulatory data cover most of the important aspects of general regulatory practice as well as a range of features of industry-specific regulatory policy, particularly in the network sectors. This regulatory information feeds into 18 low-level indicators that form the base of the PMR indicator system (Figure 5.1). These low-level indicators are progressively aggregated into three broad regulatory areas:

Figure 5.1. **The structure of the PMR indicator system**

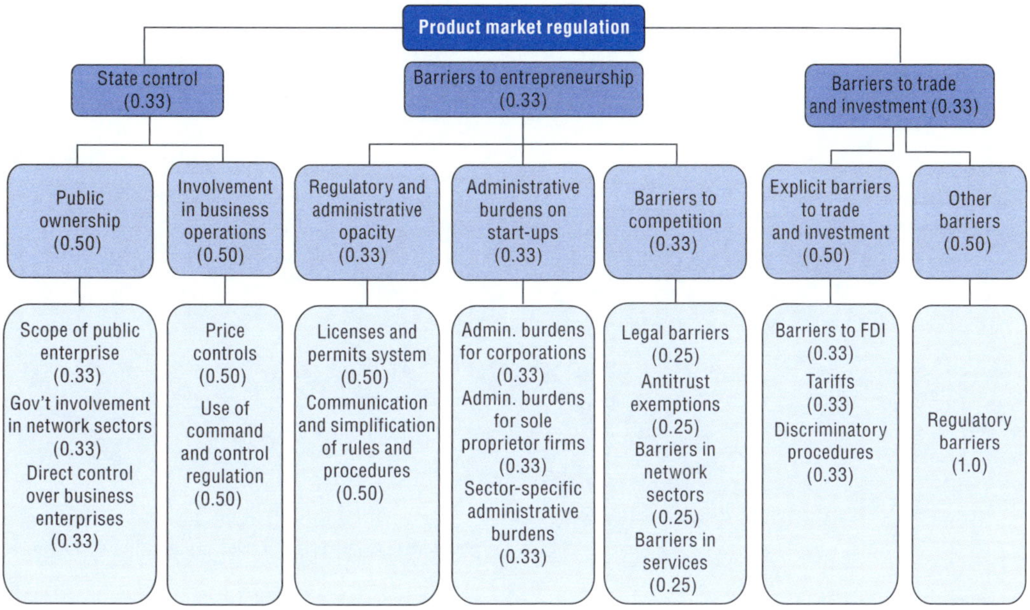

i) state control; *ii) barriers to entrepreneurship*; and *iii) barriers to international trade and investment*. In turn, at the top of the structure, the overall PMR indicator serves as a summary statistic of the general stance of product market regulation.

The PMR indicators have a number of characteristics that differentiate them from other indicators of the business environment. First, in principle, the low-level indicators only record "objective" information about rules and regulations, as opposed to "subjective" assessments of market participants as in indicators based on opinion surveys. This isolates the indicators from context-specific assessments and makes them comparable across time and countries. Second, the PMR indicators follow a bottom-up approach, in which indicator values can be related to specific underlying policies. One of the advantages of this system is that the values of higher-level indicators can be traced with an increasing degree of detail to the values of the more disaggregated indicators and, eventually, to specific data points in the regulation database. This is not possible with indicator systems based on opinion surveys, which can identify perceived areas of policy weakness, but are less able to relate these to specific policy settings.

The overall intensity of product market regulation in Russia: an international comparison

Estimating the PMR indicators for Russia reveals that, despite liberalisation in some areas, product market regulations are, on average, highly restrictive. The *overall level of regulation* is significantly higher and restricts competition to a greater extent than in any of the OECD country, including the emerging market economies within the OECD area (Figure 5.2).[3] All three of the high-level sub-components of the overall PMR index are high in Russia relative to comparator countries, particularly *state control* and *barriers to international trade and investment* (Figure 5.3). As will be expanded on below, this implies much scope for improving the regulatory environment and reaping considerable benefits in terms of improved economic performance.

Figure 5.2. **The overall indicator of product market regulation**

2008

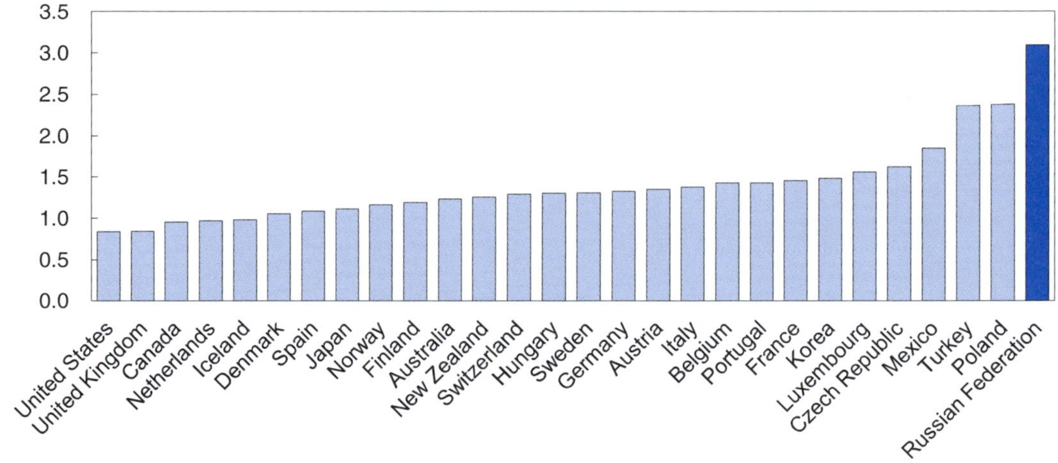

Note: Index scale of 0-6 from least to most restrictive.

StatLink http://dx.doi.org/10.1787/650504614728

Figure 5.3. **The overall PMR indicator and main sub-indicators**

2008

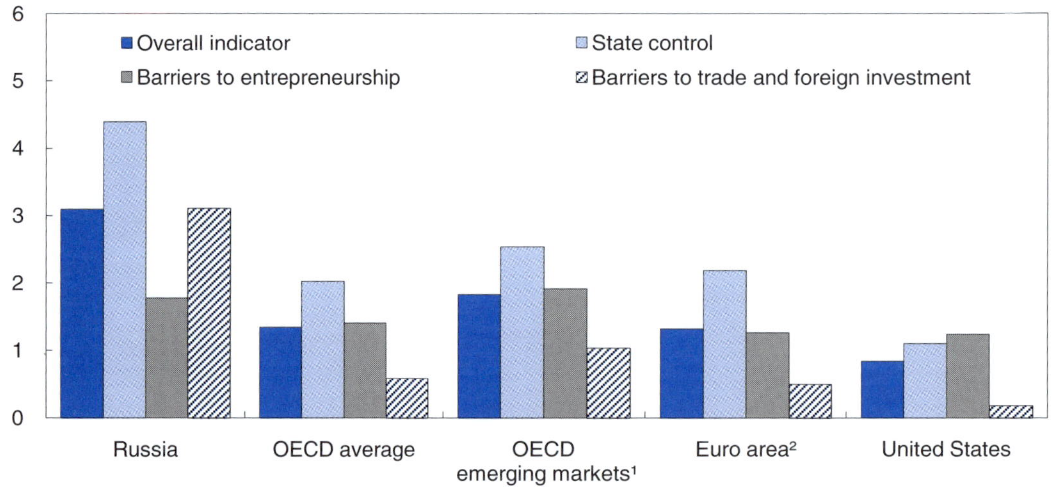

1. Czech Republic, Hungary, Korea, Mexico, Poland, Turkey.
2. Austria, Belgium, Finland, France, Germany, Italy, Luxembourg, Netherlands, Portugal, Spain.

Note: Index scale of 0-6 from least to most restrictive.

StatLink http://dx.doi.org/10.1787/650507751718

The extent of product market competition in Russia is generally weak

Between 2001 and 2007 the share of highly concentrated markets in Russia increased from 43 to 47%.[4] Although differences in methodology and sectoral coverage make comparison difficult, this is a high incidence of concentrated sectors compared to OECD countries and these results are indicative of an economy dominated by a relatively small number of large companies.

Substantial falls to 2005 in the number of firms producing a given percentage of Russian GDP also signals an alarming decrease in competition among Russia's largest firms (Table 5.1). As well as reflecting the strong growth of these firms, this also indicates ongoing industry

Table 5.1. **Number of largest firms producing a given share of GDP**

Share of GDP	2003	2004	2005	2006
10%	52	19	10	11
20%	710	207	69	90
30%	7 128	2 248	474	620
40%	97 937	36 601	4 320	5 364
50%	–	94 621	87 906	102 443

Source: Federal Antimonopoly Service (2008).

consolidation and vertical integration of supply chains. With political support, the dominance of large conglomerates has also been spreading across market segments as they acquire non-core assets and diversify product lines. More positively, the trend of increasing dominance may have reversed slightly since 2005, perhaps reflecting the beneficial impact of recent policy changes to stimulate competition. However, whether measured by the share in GDP or employment, the significance of large firms in the Russian economy is much greater than in many OECD and other countries. Small and medium-sized enterprises (SMEs) in Russia account for about 20% of total employment and generate an even smaller share of output, while for most OECD economies both figures exceed 50% (OECD 2008a).

In addition to highly concentrated industries, the formation of cartels adversely impacts on competition in Russian product markets. With markets typically characterised by a small number of large firms, the temptation is to increase profits by reducing effective competition between market participants. Indeed, the Federal Antimonopoly Service considers cartel formation to be one of the major threats to competition in the Russian economy and estimates that as many as one in five industries may be prone to cartel activity. In part, cartel formation reflects former policy settings that encouraged market division – for example, in the 1990s different regions were assigned to individual oil companies (Federal Antimonopoly Service, 2008).[5]

More encouragingly, some indicators suggest that product market competition may be improving along several dimensions. Surveys of entrepreneurs indicate that the level of competition in markets is, in many cases, perceived to be fierce and growing in intensity (Federal Antimonopoly Service, 2008). Competition from imports has also increased over recent years. However, openness to imports remains at a much lower level than in OECD countries, including the emerging market economies within the OECD, as well as emerging markets outside the OECD (Figure 5.4).

Another feature of Russian product markets that dilutes the benefits of competition is a business preference for dealing with well-known counterparts and a reluctance to change suppliers. According to the Institute of Economies in Transition surveys, enterprises regularly cite established relations between producers and consumers as the main obstacle to competition[6]. A lack of trust also encourages firms to seek control over suppliers, leading to a significant degree of vertical integration, even in markets where vertical integration is not typical in other economies (Bessonova, 2009). This reduces competition further and erodes its benefits.

In summary, empirical work on Russian product markets typically depicts a limited degree of competition that may have even decreased until recently for large firms at the national level. At the regional level, given internal barriers to trade, the degree of product market competition is even weaker across all industries (OECD, 2006; Bessonova, 2009). In

Figure 5.4. **Openness to imports: An international comparison**

Imports of goods and services as a share of GDP, 2005-07

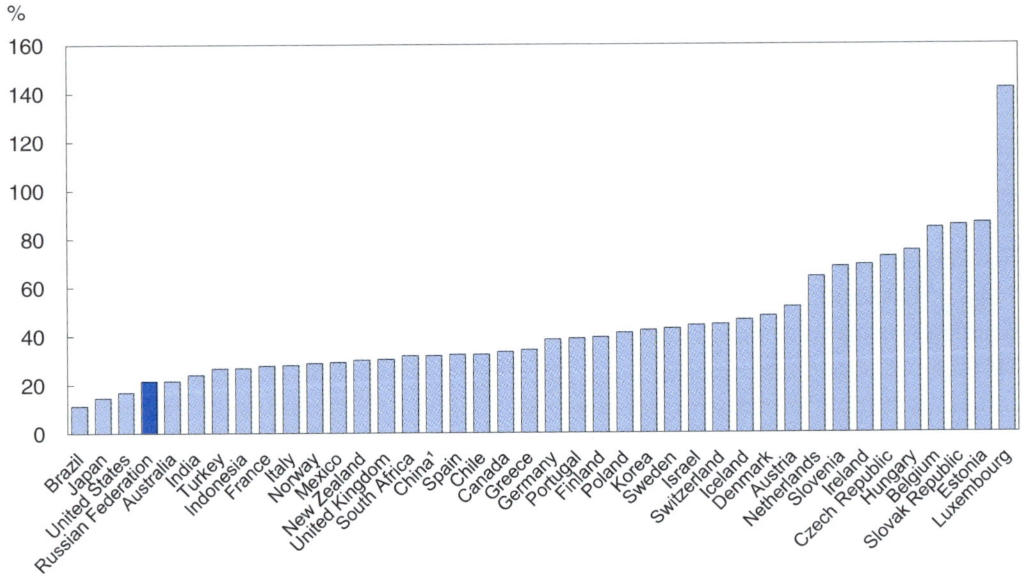

1. 2005-06.

Source: OECD Economic Outlook 84 database and World Bank, WDI database.

StatLink http://dx.doi.org/10.1787/650546370310

many regional markets it is still typical to have a few incumbent firms operating in cooperation with regional or local officials. As well as reflecting corruption and rent-seeking behaviour, these arrangements often also arise as a result of limited fiscal autonomy at lower levels of government. Many of the regional governments and municipalities pursue their social objectives through shadow budgets that employ the quasi-fiscal services of large incumbent enterprises operating in their territory. These arrangements typically translate into effective barriers to entry from outside competition. In part, this is a legacy of Soviet-era history during which product markets were characterised by massive distortions resulting from policies that granted monopoly concessions, protected incumbents from foreign competition and provided extensive state support to key sectors. *More fiscal autonomy would help breaking the dependence of regional governments on a limited number of local firms for revenue raising.*

Product market competition improves economic performance

An increasingly diverse range of theoretical and empirical studies suggest that the generally low level of competition among Russia's largest firms has a negative impact on economic performance. In general, pro-competitive reforms have been found to have important beneficial effects on GDP *per capita* through a number of different channels, including increased productivity.[7] In particular, lower entry costs tend to improve resource allocation by facilitating the movement of capital from low to high productivity firms and sectors (Arnold *et al.* 2008).[8] Increased competition can also substitute for effective corporate governance by acting as an "incentive scheme" for managers, motivating efforts to improve efficiency (Aghion *et al.*, 1999, 2002). By the same token, monitoring firm performance also becomes easier in a competitive environment where other firms provide points of reference.

As well as static effects, increased competition can have dynamic affects on productivity growth by influencing firms' incentives to innovate and adopt new technologies.[9] This raises the possibility of product market regulation and competition influencing the extent to which new technologies and production techniques flow from more to less productive economies. At the firm level, the impact of competition may differ depending on the level of productivity relative to global technological leaders. Recent evidence suggests that an increased threat of new entry from foreign competitors will spur domestic firms that are relatively close to the world technological frontier to increase innovation so as to escape competition. On the other hand, domestic firms with very low productivity may be unable to "catch up" to the leading global firms and appropriate the benefits of innovation. As a result, these firms may face a "discouragement effect" and *reduce* innovation given an increased entry threat from more productive firms. At the sectoral and economy levels, however, the impact of increased competition on innovation and aggregate productivity is positive as weaker incumbents shrink or close and more productive incumbents and new firms innovate (Aghion and Bessonova, 2006).[10] This highlights the key role of product market liberalisation in improving the efficiency with which resources are channelled from low to high productivity firms.

Product market liberalisation can have large effects in transition economies

Although much of the work on the impact of regulation on productivity catch-up has developed outside the context of transition economies, a number of studies find that regulation is also an important determinant of economic performance in these countries. For example, Aghion *et al.* (2002) argue that transition economies are likely to have a relatively large number of state-owned or newly privatised firms run by "satisficing" managers that are more interested in minimising effort than maximising profits. As regulation becomes more conducive to competition, these firms are confronted with the need to restructure and innovate in order to survive. At the same time, competitive pressures encourage new profit-maximising firms to innovate to gain a lead over their competitors. Accordingly, the impact of reform on economic performance is likely to be relatively large in transition economies.

A number of empirical studies of transition economies find that competition is generally beneficial for economic performance. In particular, in countries where the industrial structure was characterised by a high degree of concentration – typically transition economies – the positive impact of competition on productivity growth is found to be relatively strong (OECD, 2006; OECD, 2007). Greater foreign competition, through increased FDI and import penetration, has also been found to increase the likelihood of a firm in a transition economy innovating whereas state ownership has the inverse affect (Carlin *et al.*, 2001; Gorodnichenko *et al.*, 2008). More generally, soft budget constraints and state ownership have been found to mitigate the positive effects of improvements in the business environment on firm restructuring and performance (Carlin *et al.*, 2001; Aghion *et al.*, 2002). This implies that unconditional state support for firm survival needs to be removed if transition economies are to reap the full benefits of product market liberalisation.

In the Russian context, empirical studies imply that increased domestic and foreign competition would help improve firm performance and lead to significant economic benefits. In a sample of almost 15 000 firms covering 75% of employment in the industrial sector, Brown and Earle (2000) found that the "big bang" liberalisation in 1992, which improved product and labour market regulation as well as transport infrastructure, generated large positive effects on total factor productivity (TFP). In addition, private sector firms were found to perform better than state-owned enterprises (SOEs) even after correcting for selection bias.

Bessonova *et al.* (2003) use firm-level data from 1995-2001 to assess the impact of trade and FDI liberalisation on the efficiency of Russian firms in the industrial sector. They find that competition with foreign imports and goods produced by foreign-owned firms in Russia increased the speed with which domestic firms are restructured and improved productivity. These authors also find that the effects of liberalising trade and investment depend on other policies, including financial sector reform, measures to increase labour mobility and reductions in regional bureaucracy. These results mirror those of a number of OECD studies that find FDI is an important link between product market regulation and productivity catch up.[11] Bessonova (2009) updates the dataset to 2005 and finds that increased penetration of foreign companies has a positive effect on the productivity performance of the most efficient firms but a negative effect on Russia's relatively inefficient firms. This highlights the importance of effective policies to lower barriers to exit so that inefficient firms can close down, allowing resources to flow to more productive areas of economic activity.

These results highlight the potential contribution that regulatory reforms aimed at enhancing competition would make to Russia's long-term economic prospects. Given that competition among Russia's largest firms is relatively weak, greater product market competition would lead to substantial improvements in productivity and other aspects of economic performance. As discussed above, the overall PMR indicators suggest that the regulatory environment currently hinders competition and can be improved in a number of ways. The following section uses the detailed PMR indicator results to outline a number of policy recommendations that would increase competition in Russian product markets and thereby improve economic performance.

The detailed PMR indicator results and policy recommendations[12]

State control over economic activity is pervasive

Reflecting the communist history of the Soviet era, the extent of *state control* in the Russian economy remains extensive as a result of a high degree of state ownership and control over economic activity. According to the PMR indicators, the extent of state control in Russia is higher than in any OECD country (Table 5.2, Figures 5.A2.1-5.A2.5). Over recent years, the policy of the Russian government with respect to state-owned enterprises has been aimed at increasing its stake in strategic enterprises to a controlling level and privatising minority stakes of firms in non-strategic sectors. Reflecting this, the number of majority stakes of the federal government increased from 25% of total holdings in 2005 to 61% in 2008 (Sprenger, 2008). A related development is the emergence of large state-controlled conglomerates which have in some cases been established through the consolidation of existing SOEs[13].

The government has also established a number of state corporations that have the special legal status of a non-commercial organisation and are not subject to the Bankruptcy Law nor controlled by the Audit Chamber of the Russian Federation.[14] Disclosure rules for these entities are also less stringent than for joint-stock companies. Despite their non-commercial status, several state corporations pursue commercial

Table 5.2. **The extent of state control**

2008

	Russia	OECD average	OECD emerging markets[1]	Euro area[2]	United States
State control	4.39	2.03	2.54	2.19	1.10
Public ownership	4.28	2.91	3.46	3.08	1.30
Scope of public enterprise sector	4.64	3.10	3.54	3.23	2.25
Direct Control over business enterprises	4.19	2.86	3.67	2.93	0.68
Government control in infrastructure sectors	4.02	2.76	3.18	3.08	0.99
Involvement in business operations	4.50	1.15	1.61	1.30	0.90
Use of command and control regulation	4.00	1.52	1.94	1.88	1.30
Price controls	5.00	0.78	1.29	0.71	0.50

1. Czech Republic, Hungary, Korea, Mexico, Poland, Turkey.
2. Austria, Belgium, Finland, France, Germany, Italy, Luxemburg, Netherlands, Portugal, Spain.

Note: Index scale of 0-6 from least to most restrictive.

activities. The Federal Antimonopoly Service considers the state corporations to be one of the major threats to competition, together with cartels, network industries and anticompetitive behaviour of the authorities.

The state enterprise sector is large

According to data from the Federal Service for State Statistics, 9% of all registered firms were fully state owned in 2007 while 2% had mixed ownership.[15] However, SOEs tend to be bigger than private-sector companies so these figures understate the extent of government control over economic activity. In a survey of 822 Russian enterprises conducted by the Higher School of Economics Moscow and the Institute of Economic Research of Hitotsubashi University Tokyo in 2005, the median number of employees of SOEs was 880 compared to 414 for private firms. The corresponding figures for sales volume was 350 million roubles and 195 million roubles respectively. So according to both statistics, SOEs are, on average, roughly twice as large as private sector firms.[16] A more recent statistics also shows that SOEs tend to be relatively large; in regular enterprise surveys conducted by the Institute of Economy in Transition, Moscow, 58% of SOEs surveyed in 2006-08 employed more 1 000 people, compared with 30% in enterprises with a different form of ownership.

In terms of the employment share, around 10% of all employees worked for fully state-owned companies in 2007 with another 7% employed by companies with mixed state and private-sector ownership (Figure 5.5A). Although methodological differences make exact comparison difficult, this is high relative to OECD countries (OECD, 2005a). In terms of fixed asset investment, 32% is carried out by the public sector (both general government and SOEs) (Figure 5.5B). Despite widely held perceptions that the size of the state enterprise sector is increasing in Russia, both measures have been in decline over recent years, although the bulk of privatisations were carried out in the 1990s. At the same time, the government has been increasing its level of ownership among the largest Russian companies listed on the stock exchange. According to Troika Dialog (2008), the share of market capitalisation of the Russian equity market controlled by the state has increased from 24% in 2004 to 40% in 2007.[17] A related development is the emergence of large state-controlled conglomerates which have in some cases been established through the consolidation of existing SOEs. These companies usually occupy dominant market positions in their areas of activity with the scope for private sector participation, including by foreign investors, tightly controlled. This, in conjunction with guaranteed government

Figure 5.5. **The size of the public enterprise sector**

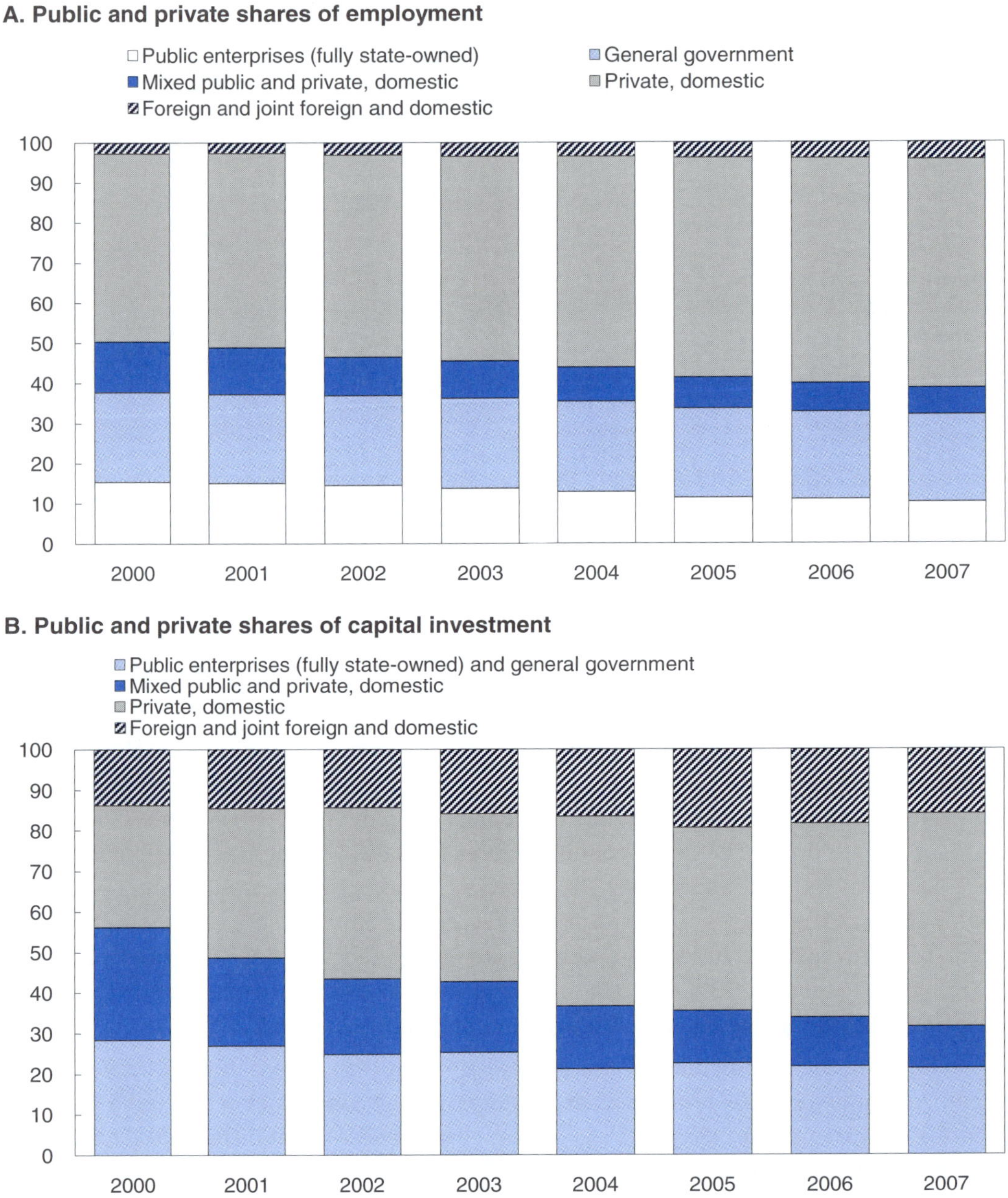

Source: ILO, Federal Service for State Statistics and OECD estimates.

StatLink http://dx.doi.org/10.1787/650575174608

support, leads to a lack of incentives to increase efficiency, reduce costs and innovate. In combination with the results outlined above of increasing market concentration among Russia's largest companies, this highlights the negative impact of increasing government ownership on competition in key sectors of the Russian economy.

As well as being relatively large in size, SOEs operate across a diverse range of sectors, many of which are inherently competitive (Figure 5.6). Indeed, according to the PMR indicators, Russian SOEs are more ubiquitous across different sectors of the economy than in all OECD countries with the exception of Poland (Table 5.2, Figure 5.A2.1).

Figure 5.6. **The state-owned share of listed companies by sector**

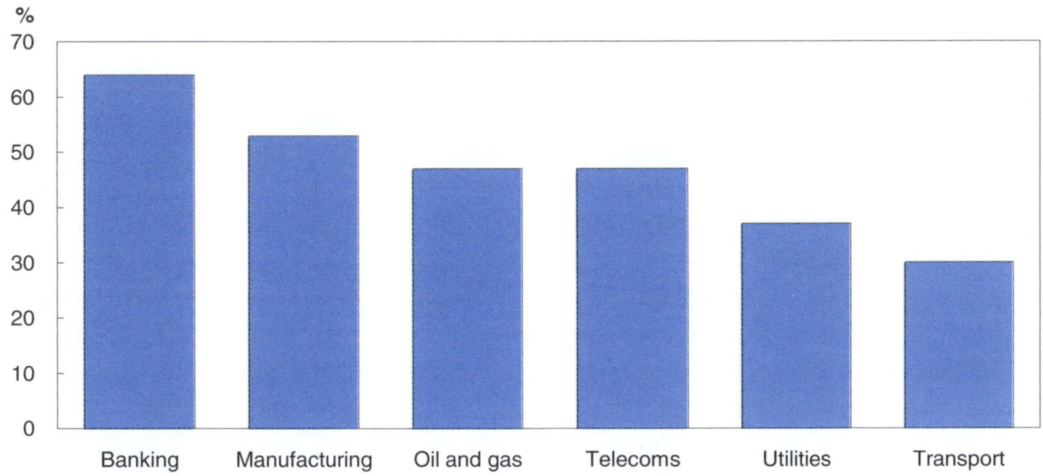

Note: As of 21 November 2007.

Source: Troika Dialog (2008).

StatLink http://dx.doi.org/10.1787/650603186727

Improving the corporate governance of the SOEs

The results of the PMR indicator exercise also imply that the Russian government exercises considerable control over SOEs that goes beyond normal ownership oversight. This can have a negative impact on competition in the sectors in which SOEs operate. First and foremost, because government is a major market player, policymaker and regulator in network industries, there is often no clear separation between the ownership function and other functions that influence market conditions. For example, the government uses its ownership role to pursue its industrial policy objectives and has recently announced that it will use the SOEs to create vertically integrated industrial structures that are robust to international competition.

As well as having to fulfil non-commercial obligations, the governance of many SOEs is also adversely affected by political interference and the use of civil servants as board members. In many cases, government representatives on SOE boards are instructed by the associated ministry on how to vote on strategic issues and there are widespread reports of Russian government officials using their influence on SOEs to promote political or individual goals that often diverge from commercial motives and investor interests. In general, these instructions are not made public. In some sectors the government holds a golden share' granting it veto power over the strategic choices of the incumbent state-owned firm. Because they dominate some markets, political interference in the operation of the SOEs not only threatens their profitability but also adversely influences overall market conditions. Last year, the government announced that it would promote the appointment of independent directors, not bound to vote according to government instructions, to SOE boards. In July 2008, independent directors were appointed to 11 SOE boards. *This positive development needs to be expanded across a larger number of SOEs.*

There are a number of other ways in which corporate governance in the state enterprise sector could be improved to ensure a level playing field and government neutrality in its dealings with the private sector (Box 5.1). *First, the commercial and non-commercial roles of the SOEs need to be transparently unbundled with the latter transferred back to the relevant line ministry. Any remaining legitimate non-commercial obligations and responsibilities that SOEs are required to undertake in terms of public services should be clearly mandated by laws or regulations.* These obligations should be disclosed to the general public and the related costs should be covered by government in a transparent way. This would make the SOEs more attractive to potential buyers and thus is an important prerequisite for economically effective privatisation. In the interests of a level playing field with the private sector, soft budget constraints for the SOEs, which arise as a result of access to subsidies from budget and off-budget state funds, need to first be hardened before being reduced and eliminated. As discussed above, soft budget constraints have been found to mitigate the benefits of improved product market regulation. SOEs should also be exposed to competitive conditions in access to finance and government procurement policies, which currently tend to favour the SOEs. Insulating SOEs from competitive conditions will only serve to prolong the existing inefficiencies.

Once the rule of law has improved in Russia, consideration should be given to moving towards a more centralised model of SOE management where SOEs are put under the responsibility of an investment agency. This would facilitate a more unified and consistent ownership policy, distance SOEs from excessive political control, simplify the often elaborate and non-transparent structures currently in place to supervise and control SOEs and ensure equitable treatment of non-state shareholders by preventing politicians and government bureaucrats from pursuing objectives outside the SOE's commercial interests. A centralised management model would also improve standards of transparency and disclosure as well as corporate responsibility more generally, which have been relatively low in Russia, not only compared to OECD countries but also other emerging markets (OECD, 2008b).[18] However, centralising the ownership function of the SOEs requires full accountability to parliament and a high level of transparency so as to avoid the political capture of the investment agency.

Privatisation needs to be restarted

Since the late 1980s, the privatisation experiences of many developed and developing countries have shown that private ownership typically leads to improvements in firm profitability, output and efficiency (*e.g.* Megginson and Netter, 2001; Kikeri and Nellis, 2004). In the Russian context, despite serious deficiencies in the privatisation process, the evidence suggests that privatisation has still resulted in improvements in firm performance. Although studies of former SOEs vary widely in their assessment of the size of the benefits of privatisation, virtually all report improvements in firms' sales and productivity performance. In addition, compared to SOEs, privatised firms in Russia are more flexible in response to shifts in demand, more innovative and more likely to adopt modern management techniques quickly (OECD, 2005c; Tompson, 2002). Stock market listing for SOEs has also been found to improve their transparency, although having publicly traded debt can also enhance transparency (Kochetygova *et al.*, 2005). Despite the benefits, however, privatisation in Russia has slowed over recent years. Although the privatisation of small and medium-sized SOEs has continued, there have been only a few major privatisation transactions over the last three years, mostly auctions of generation companies as part of the reform of the electricity sector.

A significant obstacle to further major reductions in the government's portfolio of SOEs is restrictions on privatisation and foreign ownership in a range of sectors and firms that are deemed to be strategic. In 2004, a presidential decree was issued with a list of more

Box 5.1. **Corporate governance of state-owned enterprises in OECD countries**

The characteristics of state-owned enterprises (SOEs) raise specific challenges for their governance. Firstly, SOEs are often protected from two major threats that are essential in policing management behaviour: the threat of takeover and bankruptcy. Secondly, accounting and disclosure may be oriented towards public expenditure control and not up to private sector standards. Without appropriate governance arrangements to counter these characteristics the management of SOEs may have more discretion than in the case of private firms and demands on the government's budget for investment and expansion programmes may become excessive.

Governments of OECD countries have faced complex issues and trade-offs in reforming the corporate governance of state-owned enterprises. Achieving a sound organisation and effective exercise of the ownership function within the state administration requires an ownership policy that is active while at the same time avoiding undue interference in day-to-day management. In addition, the chain of accountability needs to ensure that the boards and management of SOEs make responsible decisions with appropriate information disclosure to the public. It is also necessary to clearly separate state ownership from the regulatory and policy-making roles and ensure that efficient decision making processes are in place.

The report *Corporate Governance of State-Owned Enterprises: A Survey of OECD Countries* (OECD, 2005a) provides a comprehensive inventory of current practices and recent experiences in reforming governance arrangements for SOEs in OECD countries. Reform has focused on a number of areas including the way in which the boards of SOEs are nominated, their composition, functions, and the way they perform their main tasks. Disclosure rules, for the SOEs themselves and the ownership entity within government, have also been reformed in a number of countries as have provisions to protect minority shareholders, where they exist, and the way in which SOEs relate to stakeholders.

Incentive structures and the ways in which senior executives in SOEs are nominated and remunerated has also been the target of reform. Provided they are soundly structured and effectively implemented, governance reform can improve SOE efficiency and access to capital, while contributing to fair competition by ensuring a level-playing field between companies in the private and public sectors. Better corporate governance of SOEs can also strengthen overall public governance through better transparency and improve fiscal discipline. OECD experience has also shown that good corporate governance of SOEs is an important prerequisite for effective privatisation, since it makes the enterprises more attractive to prospective buyers and enhances their commercial value.

To help governments meet the challenges of public sector governance the OECD has published guidelines on the corporate governance of SOEs (*OECD Guidelines on Corporate Governance of State-Owned Enterprises*, OECD, 2005b). In broad terms, these guidelines cover the following areas: *i*) Ensuring an Effective Legal and Regulatory Framework for SOEs; *ii*) The State Acting as an Owner; *iii*) Equitable Treatment of Shareholders; *iv*) Relations with Stakeholders; *v*) Transparency and Disclosure; *vi*) The Responsibilities of Boards of State-Owned Enterprises. These guidelines complement the OECD's Corporate Governance Principles (Revised 2004) and have been widely endorsed and welcomed by OECD and non-OECD governments.

than 1 000 strategic enterprises that require the approval of the president for privatisation and new share issues. The list includes enterprises operating across a wide range of sectors, such as the energy sector, the aircraft industry, shipbuilding, car manufacturing, banking and forestry. *This list is extensive and leaves only a relatively limited number of sectors completely outside of state control. As such, it constrains the prospects for future significant privatisation and needs to be cut back.* In addition, the law on strategic industries that came into force in May 2008 requires government approval for acquisitions that would result in foreign control over a company operating in one of 42 sectors deemed to be strategic (Box 5.3). On the other hand, the transformation of unitary enterprises, which do not have ownership shares but are fully controlled by federal, state, or municipal governments, into joint-stock companies is making them more transparent, and may be a first step towards a later privatisation.[19]

Once the corporate governance of the SOEs has been improved, the privatisation programme needs to be stepped up, especially in the competitive sectors of the economy. Offering more opportunities for a positive contribution from the private sector and for beneficial competition would be more in line with the government's declared strategy of modernising and enhancing the competitiveness of the Russian economy. Although the method of privatisation will need to be assessed on a case-by-case basis, mixed sales, which combine strategic sales with public share offerings, have the potential advantages of developing strong corporate governance structures and introducing new management and technology into the company. For SOEs operating in network sectors in which there are monopoly elements, the regulatory environment needs to be consistent with private ownership and competition prior to privatisation (see below).

The line between the public and private sectors is blurred

The PMR indicators also signal a high level of government involvement in the private business sector. In part, this reflects a prevalence of command and control type regulation that can give rise to seemingly arbitrary policy decisions. For example, the Russian government owns an exceptionally large number of golden shares' in private-sector companies that allow it to have seats on boards even when it does not own any conventional shares. These golden shares, which allow the government to veto the firm's commercial decisions, were often created as part of the privatisation of firms operating in sectors deemed to be of strategic importance. Data presented in Sprenger (2008) indicate that on 1 January 2007, the Russian government owned golden shares in 181 companies in which it had no conventional equity stake. There are also cases where regional and municipal governments appoint board members for privately owned firms despite not holding any conventional or golden shares.

Allowing the state to exercise a level of control beyond the level of risk implied by its ownership stake carries with it the potential for abuse. *Government should, therefore, eliminate the use of golden shares and disclose shareholder agreements and capital structures that allow it to exercise control over a firm that is disproportionate to it equity stake.*

Other aspects of Russia's regulatory regime also indicate a high prevalence of "command and control" type regulation. For example, universal service obligations are used more extensively in Russia compared to OECD countries. In addition, alternative approaches to command and control regulation that are designed to influence incentives are not routinely assessed as part of the policymaking process. If the Russian government wishes to encourage a vibrant private sector it will have to rely less on direct intervention in the economy and instead work towards creating a quality regulatory environment.

Barriers to entrepreneurship restrict private sector development

Low *barriers to entrepreneurship* are an important condition for creating competitive markets. Russia performs well in some of the regulatory areas covered by this indicator (Table 5.3), reflecting the implementation of major reform of business regulation early this decade[20] and ongoing efforts to improve the efficiency of the public bureaucracy. In particular, the indicator of regulatory and administrative opacity is comparable with the average for OECD countries. This reflects improvements in the communication and simplification of rules and procedures including the introduction of plain language drafting and systematic procedures for publicising new regulations. The indicator of the licence and permits system is also around the average for OECD emerging markets, following the introduction of one stop shops (OSSs) that deal with applications for notifications and licenses. However, despite these efforts, the administrative burden that the government places on entrepreneurs starting a new business, whether they are corporations or sole traders, is still very high and acts as an obstacle to new entry. These high indicator values could also be indicative of more widespread inefficiencies in government administration and reflect ongoing difficulties in reforming the public administration, creating new regulatory institutions and implementing market orientated forms of regulation.

Table 5.3. **Barriers to entrepreneurship**

2008

	Russia	OECD average	OECD emerging markets[1]	Euro area[2]	United States
Barriers to entrepreneurship	1.78	1.41	1.91	1.26	1.24
Regulatory and administrative opacity	1.00	1.00	1.18	0.64	0.19
Licenses and permit system	2.00	1.78	2.00	1.20	0.00
Communication and simplification of rules and procedures	0.00	0.22	0.35	0.09	0.38
Administrative burdens on start ups	2.32	1.53	2.70	1.61	0.99
Administrative burdens for corporations	2.33	1.62	2.79	1.60	0.75
Administrative burdens for sole proprietor firms	3.00	1.61	2.75	1.78	1.25
Sector-specific administrative burdens	1.64	1.35	2.55	1.46	0.97
Barriers to competition	2.01	1.69	1.87	1.53	2.53
Legal barriers	2.00	1.07	1.14	0.81	1.14
Antitrust exemptions	1.16	0.50	0.61	0.00	2.25
Barriers to entry in network sectors	2.22	1.94	2.29	1.69	3.07
Barrier to entry in services	2.67	3.25	3.43	3.61	3.64

1. Czech Republic, Hungary, Korea, Mexico, Poland, Turkey.
2. Austria, Belgium, Finland, France, Germany, Italy, Luxemburg, Netherlands, Portugal, Spain.

Regulatory and administrative opacity has improved…

The indicators of *regulatory and administrative opacity* in Russia compare favourably internationally, reflecting continuing efforts to improve the effectiveness of public administration. A programme to reduce administrative burdens imposed by the state on enterprises and citizens has been launched by the Ministry of Economic Development. This programme includes explicit quantitative targets for burden reduction and uses a range of different strategies, including extensive use of ICT. Another initiative designed to reduce red tape is the introduction of OSSs for providing information on notifications and licenses. In some cases, OSSs are also used to issue or accept notifications and licenses. The essential idea of the OSSs is that potential investors only need to be in contact with a single entity to complete all the necessary paperwork and applications in a streamlined and coordinated process, rather than having to go through a labyrinth of different government bodies. In practice, given the impracticalities of assuming full control of the approval process, OSSs tend to act as a coordination mechanism between relevant government authorities.

To be effective in reducing administrative burdens, OSSs need to be implemented along with other reforms geared towards cutting red tape. In the absence of such measures, OSSs run the risk of simply adding another layer of bureaucracy to the approval process. Indeed, because OSSs provide a focal point for investment clearance, they can act as important catalysts for improving administrative processes and cooperation across government departments.

Closely related to the OSS concept is the idea of "deemed clearance", under which licenses are issued automatically if the licensing office does not act by the end of the statutory response period. Deemed clearance regimes are not currently used in Russia but can be an effective method of enhancing the single window concept if they are set and implemented judiciously. However, the administrative system must be reformed to the point where it is capable of meeting these statutory response periods. The objective is not to circumvent regulation but to implement and enforce it as efficiently as possible.

... but administrative burdens on start ups remain excessive and act as a barrier to entry

The PMR indicators demonstrate that despite continuing efforts to improve the functioning of the public bureaucracy, *administrative burdens on start ups* remain high compared with other countries (Figures 5.A2.7 and 5.A2.8 in the Annex). The number of mandatory procedures involved in the creation of new companies, as well as the number of agencies involved and the total cost of start-up procedures are higher in Russia than in most OECD economies. By way of confirmation, the World Bank's *Doing Business* indicators, which also assess administrative burdens on start ups, rank Russia 65th out of 181 countries in 2008 in terms of the ease of setting up a new business. This is a deterioration of 13 places compared to the results for 2007.

Administrative reform needs to support the regulatory environment

As noted before, various enterprise surveys point out that despite a considerable progress with deregulation, administrative burden remains high. This suggests that barriers to entrepreneurship in Russia stem not from formal regulations but in large part from informal and often corrupt practices on the part of government officials. This increases compliance costs, especially for small firms, and discourages firm expansion into the formal sector, thus restraining competition and productivity.

With an interventionist tradition and administrative structures that have in many cases not kept pace with economic liberalisation, a significant reengineering of administrative processes is needed to improve the functioning of the Russian government bureaucracy. Reforming formal laws and regulations will have only a minimal impact on economic performance in the absence of major improvements in the functioning of state institutions. The public bureaucracy needs to become much more transparent, accountable, and efficient so as to simplify the interaction between government and firms and citizens.

Establishing a coordinated programme of administrative reform to improve the functioning of the public bureaucracy requires institutional change and is complex and time consuming. In addition, a long-term strategy for regulatory reform needs to be explicit, coherent and supported by the highest levels of government. Recognising the scope of this challenge, most OECD governments have established regulatory oversight bodies with "whole-of-government" responsibility for regulatory policy. One advantage of this approach is that it promotes a consistent and systematic method of reform across the entire administration. In addition, OECD experience has been that regulatory reform will often fail if left entirely to ministries, implying that a degree of centralisation can improve the chances of successful reform.

The Russian government is well aware of the importance of improving the quality of public administration and, as discussed above, has moved some way towards becoming a more service-oriented facilitator of private-sector entrepreneurship. At present, however, although ministries are obliged to consult with other government departments before drafting new laws, there is no centralised oversight body charged with reviewing regulatory proposals to ensure they do not impose unnecessary or unreasonable administrative burdens on firms and citizens. This important task would involve the use of regulatory impact analysis (RIA) to assess the benefits and costs of significant proposed new regulation. A regulatory oversight body could also develop guidelines on the standards of good regulation and the use of alternatives to traditional command-and-control regulation. Once developed, individual ministries would need to adhere to these principles of regulatory quality in their area of competence. New ways of measuring the impact of administrative regulation would also need to be developed to identify areas of high administrative burden (OECD, 2006). An oversight body could also help to better integrate the administrative functions of the federal and regional governments, thereby ensuring that progress in regulatory reform is more uniform across the Federation.

A centralised and fully-functional regulatory oversight body would go against a tradition of ministerial independence in regulatory matters and could therefore meet with strong resistance. This implies the need for a careful balancing act between cooperation and confrontational relationships with ministries. The need for political support means that the relevance of regulatory reform to larger social and economic goals must be clarified and clearly communicated to all concerned. Ideally, the objectives of the regulatory oversight body should be outlined as part of an explicit regulatory policy that sets out reform priorities and the tools and institutions used by government to shape their regulatory power. The OECD experience has been that countries consistently make greater progress when they have an explicit regulatory policy. As noted in OECD (2002b), "the more complete the principles, and the more concrete and accountable the action programme, the wider and more effective the reform".

Underdevelopment of small and medium-sized enterprises is one sign of the presence of formal and informal barriers to entrepreneurship

Smaller businesses are particularly vulnerable to bureaucratic interference as they are less able to bear the costs of administrative burdens than larger enterprises. The underdevelopment of small and medium-sized enterprises (SMEs) in Russia compared to OECD economies indicates that despite substantial efforts to improve the operating environment for small businesses, barriers to entrepreneurship remain high. The Russian government recognises the importance of SMEs in fostering competition and addressing social problems and over recent years devoted significant efforts to promote SME development. Important legislative initiatives have been implemented and more are in the pipeline (Box 5.2).

The government efforts to develop SMEs are welcome. As usual, implementation of the adopted measures will remain a key issue. The limit on foreign ownership for SME support, a novelty of the 2007 law, is, however, a surprising development. While such a restriction also exists in a few OECD member countries it may nevertheless be worthwhile to reconsider this move, not the least because of an unintended side effect: possibly burdening the large number of resident former Soviet Union citizens running small businesses in Russia.

Corruption is endemic and stifles entrepreneurship

Overly complex administrative procedures also increase discretion within the government bureaucracy, thereby facilitating corruption opportunities. Consistent with high administrative burdens, Russia is ranked 147th out of 180 countries in the Transparency International 2008 Corruption Perceptions Index. This is Russia's worst performance for eight years and puts it on a par with Bangladesh, Kenya and Syria, and indicates that corruption and bribery are so widespread that they are perceived to be a normal part of business activity.[21]

Combating corruption remains a major reform challenge. Reflecting this challenge, an Anti-corruption Council headed by President Medvedev was established, and the National Plan on Counteracting Corruption approved in July 2008. A series of anti-corruption bills have been adopted since, including the Federal Law "On Counteracting Corruption" and various amendments to the existing laws. The implemented legislative initiatives aimed at strengthening public control over politicians and senior bureaucrats, such as a requirement to publicise incomes and financial assets of their family members, as well as measures to prevent and manage conflict of interest, are welcome. Increasing the transparency and accountability of state institutions is an important part of the solution to the problem of rampant corruption. *Administrative reform needs to mitigate the potential for corruption by minimising uncertainty and subjective decision making within the government administration.* Further reductions in licensing and other formal regulatory burdens would reduce bureaucrats' opportunities to extract bribes from private-sector firms. Judicial and civil service reforms would improve the fairness, transparency and efficiency with which remaining regulations are administered.

An important consideration with efforts to reduce corruption is that they filter down department hierarchies and are effectively implemented at the lower levels. Training seminars, performance based pay scales, and promotions based on merit would all help in this regard.

Government disregard threatens the effectiveness of competition policy

The disregard for competition law by the authorities is apparent from the fact that 53% of the total number of violations of antitrust law in 2007 were committed by various levels of the Russian government. These violations cover a range of actions including combining functions of executive authorities and economic entities, making anticompetitive agreements , restricting the free movement of goods and transferring assets to the private sector without a competitive tender. 80% of the violations were committed by the regional and municipal authorities. Those actions distort the markets and can have a catastrophic effect on competition. Breaches of the law by regional authorities seeking to protect local

Box 5.2. **Government policy on small and medium-sized enterprises**

The share of GDP produced by SMEs in Russia is estimated at around 13-17%, significantly below the level in most OECD countries. Small and medium-sized businesses, including individual entrepreneurs, account for only about a fifth of total employment, again substantially below most OECD economies. The government views SME development as a major priority for economic policy. The programme on long-term socio-economic development of the Russian Federation targets an increase in the share of SMEs in GDP and employment to 30% by 2020. Over this period, the government envisages a steep rise in the number of SMEs accompanied by structural changes, with more SMEs present in healthcare, science, information services and utilities, and relatively fewer in retail trade, a sector where a significant proportion of SMEs currently operates.

The framework for government SME policy was outlined in the new law on SME development adopted in 2007. The law defines an SME as a business entity meeting the following criteria: *1)* state and foreign ownership together does not exceed 25%; *2)* ownership by non-SME entities together does not exceed 25%; *3)* headcount does not exceed 250 employees for medium-sized enterprises, 100 for small enterprises and 15 for microenterprises; *4)* annual turnover does not surpass the threshold set by the government once every five years. The following turnover thresholds were set in 2008: 60 million roubles a year (*i.e.* USD 2.6 million at that time, but less than USD 2 million a year later) for micro enterprises, 400 million roubles for small and 1 billion roubles for medium enterprises. The breakdown by three types of SMEs, which was previously absent from legislation, is identical to the norms adopted in the European Union (EU). The thresholds for employment are similar to those applied in the EU, and the turnover thresholds are also in line with the EU practices, although fixing such a threshold for 5 years may prove restrictive in Russia's high-inflation environment. The implementation of this norm is, however, postponed until 1 January 2010, so until this date the government may revise the current threshold.

Beyond definitions, the law stipulates a number of measures that should be implemented to advance SME development, including simplified accounting and taxation, special treatment as suppliers for government procurement, protection against excessive inspections, aid with property, and financial and advisory support. The law itself does not provide any specifics beyond the definition of SMEs and therefore additional legislative acts outlining specific measures were needed. Little happened in the months following adoption of the law on SME development, but shortly after his inauguration in May 2008 President Medvedev signed a decree on urgent measures to eliminate administrative barriers to entrepreneurship that required a speedy development of such legislation. Several legislative initiatives have been implemented since. In July 2008, a law was adopted giving SMEs pre-emptive rights to purchase state property they have leased for at least three years. A new law came into force on 1 May 2009, which limits scheduled inspections of SMEs to one every three years, while any unscheduled inspection now requires an authorisation of the Prosecutor General. The same law introduces a notification mechanism for 13 types of business activities including retail trade, hotel and restaurants and publishing. Other implemented measures include reduced tariffs for access to electrical grids and the extension of the obligatory state contract quota of 10-2% reserved for small businesses to purchases by municipalities.

Box 5.2. **Government policy on small and medium-sized enterprises** *(cont.)*

Since the onset of the crisis, the government has intensified its efforts to support small business, with an aim of casting immediate measures to alleviate the consequences of the crisis into the medium-term framework of SME development. The government pledges an increase in budget expenditures to 10.5 billion roubles in 2009 directed at SME support, such as grants to new entrepreneurs, development of microfinancing and interest rate subsidies. 30 billion roubles will be injected into the capital of *Vneshekonombank* which should be used to finance commercial banks and a variety of non-bank financial entities working with SMEs. More measures are in the pipeline, including reducing the list of products requiring certification, support for SMEs involved in innovation, non-discriminatory access to gas infrastructure, etc. The government will also work on improving already adopted legislation, for example, on the pre-emptive rights of SMEs to buy out state property they occupy.

markets from outside competition constitute an administrative barrier to entry that can result in monopolised markets at the regional level.

Several legislative initiatives implemented over the last few years have sought to reduce the opportunities for anticompetitive behaviour of the authorities. The 2005 law on government procurement has fostered transparency of government purchases of goods and services in particular by introducing the requirement for placing information about prospective tenders on the internet. In order to strengthen the effectiveness of the use of government funds and to prevent discriminatory practices, the 2006 competition law introduced antimonopoly control of the state and municipal aid. The law outlines an exhaustive list of the types of the state aid considered to be legal and requires the competition authority's approval of granting such aid. The amendments to the competition law adopted in 2008 make obligatory a competitive tender for most transactions involving state property. These are positive developments, however, the fact that many violations of competition law by the authorities were committed by repeat offenders in 2007 suggests that the sanctions for infringements are currently inadequate. The proposed amendments to the Administrative Code that would impose sanctions against the government officials for breaking competition law, including penalties and a ban to occupy a government position for up to three years, are welcome.

The regulatory regime is highly variable across network sectors

In some of the network sectors Russia scores comparatively well in the PMR framework with indicator scores below the OECD average in 2007. In other sectors, however, the regulatory regime is assessed to be highly restrictive (Figure 5.7).

In the electricity sector, since 2003, the government has pursued a strategy of unbundling and partially privatising the incumbent, RAO UES. Prior to reform, the electricity sector was highly vertically integrated with RAO UES controlling all large-capacity non-nuclear generation assets, 72 regional utilities with local monopolies on distribution and supply, and the transmission system (OECD, 2004; OECD, 2008b). Under the reform agenda, the transmission grid and system operation have been hived off into two separate companies, both of which are 100% state-owned. Electricity generation assets have been dispersed into a number of separate companies, all of which were initially owned by RAO UES. By end-2007, nearly all newly created generation companies had been

Figure 5.7. **Level and heterogeneity of regulation in network sectors**

Contributions of each sector to aggregate indicator

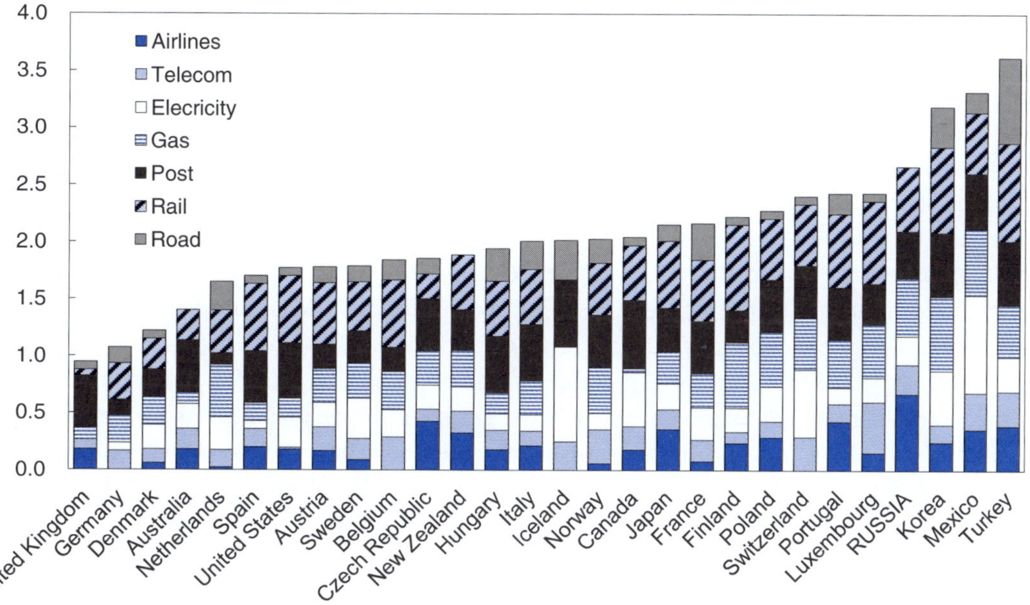

Source: OECD indicators of regulation in energy, transport and communications (ETCR).

StatLink http://dx.doi.org/10.1787/650612146284

listed on the stock exchange and the state and RAO UES had divested some of their holdings in these companies. By end-June 2008 RAO UES's divestment was complete and the company ceased to exist. However, the state is estimated to retain between one quarter and one third of national generation capacity in 2008, including 100% ownership of all nuclear plants (OECD, 2008b); reflecting recent acquisitions, state ownership of generation assets has increased to more than 50% (Renaissance Capital, 2009).

In addition to unbundling and partial privatisation, price formation policies in the electricity sector are also being reformed. In the wholesale electricity market, 95% of contracts between distributors and generation companies are regulated by the Federal Tariff Service while the remaining 5% are traded on a limited spot electricity market. Regulated prices are being increased to bring them more into line with market levels and cross-subsidisation eliminated. The government also plans on liberalising retail markets in parallel with the wholesale market and the goal is to have all electricity prices set be the market by 2014. Given current investment requirements and expected robust demand growth, private sector participation in the electricity sector is imperative, implying that this reform schedule must be adhered to or, ideally, accelerated.[22]

The mobile telecom market is also reasonably well regulated with minimal barriers to entry. As a consequence, this market is predominantly comprised of private sector firms, including some with foreign involvement. In a number of cases, these companies have successfully expanded into the Commonwealth of Independent States region.[23] In contrast to mobile telecoms, the fixed-line market remains under state control. The state-owned and vertically-integrated incumbent, Svyazinvest, has controlling stakes in the seven regional fixed-line telecoms companies and in Rostelcom, which has a monopoly in long-distance and international calls. Privatisation of Svyazinvest has been under discussion for a long while, but so far the government has maintained monopoly ownership. The introduction of competition into the telecoms market has brought large benefits in most OECD countries and should be pursued in Russia.

In a number of other network sectors, very little effort has been made to introduce competition. For example, the regulatory environment in the gas sector has become less conducive to competition over recent years. In 2005, the government increased its holdings in Gazprom to a controlling interest. At the same time, Gazprom has pursued an active acquisition policy, which extends well beyond its core activities, and increased its dominance in the domestic gas market. Gazprom has a monopoly over the gas transport network as well as Russian gas exports. In a number of transport sectors, competition problems remain rife. In the air transport sector, some international routes are served by only one operator with pre-agreed fares, number of flights and landing slots. The air cargo market is highly concentrated. Urban passenger transport markets are usually dominated by local carriers which enjoy a monopoly courtesy of the municipal authorities, who depend on licence fees for revenues. Despite earlier reforms in rail transport, a number of problems, such as cross-subsidisation from freight to passenger services, continue to impede private entrants. Developing the transport infrastructure would aid in the elimination of barriers to intraregional trade and expand markets.

The Federal Antimonopoly Service reports a large number of violations of law across infrastructure sectors. In conjunction with a high level of government ownership in a number of sectors and regional monopolies, this implies a need for strong and independent regulation. Although regulators exist for a number of sectors, they are subordinated to the ministry of the sector they regulate in virtually all cases. Furthermore, in many cases the ministry can give instructions to the regulator and overturn its decisions. As well as separating the ownership function from line ministries, the separation of the regulatory function from the policy making and ownership functions in infrastructure sectors with a monopoly element is an equally important prerequisite for establishing efficient markets, attracting increased private sector participation, and reducing the risk premium required by private investors.

Independent regulators need to strike a balance between promoting efficiency gains and attracting investment while protecting consumers from potential monopolist abuses and firms from political interference. This is no easy task, and delegating regulatory powers to independent bodies is not without risks. For example, an independent regulator might slow structural change or become captured by firms in the sector, losing the sense of a broader market vision. To mitigate these risks and generate the expected benefits of a high quality regulatory environment, independent regulators need to be based on proper institutional design within strong governance frameworks. Independence should go hand-in-hand with accountability, stability and expertise. Accountability requires that the decision-making process be transparent and subject to clear and simple procedural requirements and checks and balances, including opportunities for public hearings and appeal provisions. In OECD countries, regulators have been most effective and credible when their independence and roles are made explicit in a distinct statute with well-defined functions and objectives.

Improving the competition policy framework

The competition policy framework has been steadily improved over recent years. In 2007, the Federal Antimonopoly Service was given the power to negotiate fines and grant leniency in combating cartels, powers which have become common practice in a number of OECD countries. In addition, with 43% of competition law abuses committed by repeat offenders in 2007, the penalties for infringing competition law were increased substantially and calculated as a percentage (from 1 to 15%) of the offending company's turnover in the market where the law was breached. Given the generally weak state of competition in Russian product markets, these are all positive developments. However, *if the Federal Antimonopoly Service is to effectively fulfil its important role, its operational power needs to be bolstered to allow greater use of inspections and the collection of physical evidence in antitrust cases.*

Competition policy involves more than dealing with monopolies, mergers and anticompetitive practices in the business sector. In particular, the framework needs to be able to ensure that policy proposals issued by the government are compatible with competitive markets. An additional challenge in the case of Russia is to ensure that different branches of government respect and are bound by competition law. *A useful development in this regard would be to introduce a policy to ensure that all levels of government and economic regulatory agencies take the competition dimension into account when formulating policy.*

The introduction of such a policy would be a key event that would help bring the issue of competition to centre stage and spread a competition ethos through different levels of government and the private sector. A properly designed policy to support free and fair market competition should emphasise the removal of entry barriers, ensure competitive neutrality between public and private sector enterprises, establish access regimes for network facilities, provide for justification and notification when there is a need to deviate from established principles of competition, and require all government bodies to undertake a competition audit of all existing and proposed policies. As discussed above, a competition policy should also set out the overarching framework for the regulation of infrastructure sectors with monopoly elements. A programme targeted at reducing violations of antitrust laws by federal and local government should also be initiated and compliance activities of the Federal Antimonopoly Service stepped up along with increased advocacy of competition in government. Enacting such a policy would demonstrate the government's commitment to competition and act as a creditable signal that the objectives of regulatory policy are not going to change.

Despite some improvements, barriers to international trade and investment remain high

To a significant extent, Russia's long-term economic development depends on innovating through adapting production techniques and know-how developed abroad. Both international trade and foreign direct investment encourage domestic firms to incorporate foreign technologies into the production process, thereby facilitating technological diffusion. Equally, foreign affiliates tend to be more capital and skill intensive and invest more in research and development than domestic firms in the same industry (Keller, 2004; Keller and Yeaple, 2003). As a result, foreign affiliates tend to grow more quickly and make a larger direct contribution to productivity growth in comparison to domestic firms (Criscuolo, 2005) and more outward-oriented countries consistently grow more quickly than relatively closed countries (Srinivasan and Bhagwati, 1999). However, in spite of the potential benefits of international openness, the indicator of *barriers to international trade and investment* signals a high degree of restrictiveness across the board in Russia compared to OECD countries (Table 5.4). As well as directly improving the performance of the Russian economy, a deeper integration into the global economy *via* increased trade and FDI would also provide an important catalyst for ongoing domestic reform. For these reasons, Russian membership in the WTO and other international and bilateral agreements needs to be actively pursued.[24]

Table 5.4. **Barriers to international trade and investment**

2008

	Russia	OECD average	OECD emerging markets	Euro area	United States
Barriers to trade and investment	3.11	0.59	1.04	0.50	0.18
Explicit barriers to trade and investment	2.62	0.99	1.70	0.87	0.37
Foreign ownership barriers	3.50	1.29	1.68	1.38	1.11
Discriminatory procedures	1.38	0.54	1.09	0.24	0.00
Tariffs	3.00	1.13	2.33	1.00	0.00
Other barriers	3.60	0.18	0.38	0.13	0.00
Regulatory barriers	3.60	0.18	0.38	0.13	0.00

1. Czech Republic, Hungary, Korea, Mexico, Poland, Turkey.
2. Austria, Belgium, Finland, France, Germany, Italy, Luxemburg, Netherlands, Portugal, Spain.

Note: Index scale of 0-6 from least to most restrictive.

Tariff barriers need to be reduced and simplified

Since the state monopoly on foreign trade was removed in 1992, tariffs have progressively replaced non-tariff barriers as the principal instrument for regulating foreign trade. This has increased the transparency of trade barriers and eliminated some corruption opportunities. As part of its bid for WTO membership, Russia has also accelerated the harmonisation of its trade regulation with international norms. However, the trend towards trade liberalisation engenders staunch resistance from administrators and sectoral interest groups. As in other countries, such resistance is particularly hard to counter in economic downturns, as the recent sharp increase in Russian tariffs on imported cars attests.

Assessing the structure of Russia's tariff system is complicated by the widespread use of a combined tariff system under which customs officials apply the maximum of the *ad valorem* or specific tariff on imported goods.Shepotylo and Tarr (2007) estimate that Russia has over 11 000 tariff lines, of which about 1 700 use the "combined" tariff system. Taking this tariff structure into account, the authors find that average tariff rates in Russia increased from 2001 to 2003 but were then broadly stable between 13 and 14.5% to 2005. This average tariff rate is somewhat higher than in most other middle-income countries and significantly higher than in virtually all OECD countries. Further, despite the implementation of a programme to simplify the tariff structure in 2000-01, the dispersion in tariff rates is also found to have increased significantly since the beginning of the 2000s, indicating a less uniform tariff structure.

Widespread exemptions and variability in the tariff structure result in an inefficient allocation of resources.[25] In addition, increased diversity in the tariff structure encourages lobbying and rent-seeking behaviour and, in the Russian context, presents an opportunity for corruption. *In addition to the gains from lower average tariffs, substantial efficiency gains would result from having just one tariff rate.*

Reductions in FDI barriers would increase productivity

Given its abundant natural resources and large domestic market, Russia has significant potential for attracting FDI inflows. Since 2003, FDI inflows have been growing strongly, more than doubling in 2006, and Russia is now one of the world's leading FDI recipients. Almost half of FDI inflows are in the mining and quarrying sector. In a UNCTAD survey for 2007-08,

Box 5.3. **The 2008 Law on Strategic Industries**

The long-awaited federal law on "Procedures of Making Foreign Investments in Business Entities of Strategic Importance to National Defence and Security of the State" entered into force in May 2008. The law imposes prior governmental approval for foreign acquisitions which would result in 50% and more foreign ownership in a company operating in one of 42 designated strategic sectors. The threshold for foreign acquisitions is reduced to 25% if the foreign investor is a state-owned company, to 10% in the case of foreign investment in mineral exploration and extraction companies and to 5% in such companies if the foreign investor is a foreign state-owned company. The 42 strategic sectors include: defence-related activities, high-technology and dual-purpose sectors (space-related technologies, aviation and activities involving nuclear and radioactive materials) and public communication services (radio and TV broadcasting and printing). In addition, the law concerns natural monopolies as defined by the Russian legislation, except electrical power, municipal heating and postal services.

The 16-member Commission which carries out approval procedures is chaired by the Prime Minister and includes several ministers and heads of public agencies, in particular the Federal Security Service and the Federal Antimonopoly Service, also responsible for implementation of the Commission's rulings. After the registration of the request and its consideration by the Federal Security Service, the Commission has three months to the applicants of its decision with a possible extension of an additional three months.

In introducing the law on strategic sectors, the Russian government has sought to address concerns shared by many other countries to protect essential security interests. It also responded to foreign investors' expectations who wished to see former case-by-case authorisations replaced by clear rules. By defining the sectors and the size of foreign transactions concerned and codifying the conditions of approval procedures, Russia's legislation is in line with the transparency and predictability requirement, one of the three sound policy principles identified in the ongoing discussions within the OECD on policy measures addressing the essential security objectives.

However, Russia's legislation differs from OECD recommended best practices in several important aspects. The sectoral coverage of the Russian law is considerably broader than in OECD countries, which limit essential security interests to the safeguard of the national defence, public order and health. Rather than referring to the monetary thresholds of foreign investment transactions used by OECD countries implementing prior screening procedures, Russia's approach takes into account the share of foreign ownership, differentiated according to the category of investors and sectors. In addition to imposing high restrictions on foreign investment in selected sectors, notably in mineral exploration and extraction, such a complex scheme risks to be perceived as particularly constraining and discouraging to potential foreign investors. Furthermore, taking into consideration the possible extension, the delays for notification of the decisions to the applicants are longer in Russia than in OECD countries applying prior evaluations.

In its current form the new law does include any provisions on the public announcement of approval decisions. Some OECD countries, notably Australia and the United States, have an *ex post* reporting mechanism indicating the number of applications received and the proportion of approvals.

1. For a more detailed description of the law see the 2008 OECD Investment Policy Review of the Russian Federation: Strengthening the Policy Framework for Investment, Chapter 2, OECD, Paris, July 2008.
2. Freedom of Investment, National Security and "Strategic" Industries: Progress Report by the OECD Committee, available at *www.oecd.org/daf/investment/foi*.

Box 5.4. **Policy recommendations for reforming Russia's product and services markets**

Reduce political interference in the operation of state-owned enterprises (SOEs) and private sector firms:

- "Unbundle" the non-commercial objectives of the SOEs and consolidate them to the relevant government department. Any remaining non-commercial objectives that SOEs are required to undertake should be clearly mandated by law or regulation.
- Improve standards of transparency and disclosure in SOEs. Eliminate all exemptions, explicit or implicit, for the state corporations from various laws, and make them subject to the standard accounting and reporting principles.
- Once corporate governance has been improved, intensify the privatisation programme. In network sectors with a monopoly element, ensure that regulation is consistent with private ownership prior to privatisation.
- Revise and reduce the list of firms for which privatisation requires the approval of the President.
- Dispose of golden shares in both SOEs and private firms, increase the independence of government representatives and accelerate appointments of independent directors on SOE boards.

Reduce barriers to entrepreneurship and increase competition:

- Continue reforming the public administration and cutting red tape. Work towards increasing the transparency and accountability of the public administration.
- Minimise uncertainty and the need for subjective decision making within the government administration so as to reduce corruption opportunities.
- Create an overarching department to facilitate this work and coordinate between different arms of government. This department will also carry out Regulatory Impact Analysis to assess significant new regulatory proposals.
- Introduce "deemed clearance" regime under which licenses are issued automatically if the licensing office does not act by the end of the statutory response period.
- Address weaknesses in the tax and regional funding regimes to break the dependence of regional governments on a limited number of local firms for revenue raising.
- Increase the operational powers of the Federal Antimonopoly Service.
- In network sectors, continue separating the competitive and monopoly market segments and eliminate barriers to entry. Develop the capacity of the regulators and make them stronger.
- Introduce an overarching competition policy to support free and fair market competition.

Liberalise the trade and foreign investment regimes:

- Lower FDI and tariff barriers.
- Move towards a uniform tariff rate.
- Increase the openness and predictability of the foreign investment regime. Review the list of strategic sectors.
- Ensure a level playing field between domestic and foreign firms with respect to government procurement and access to subsidies.
- Consider introducing provisions to encourage regulators to use internationally harmonised standards and certification procedures wherever possible and appropriate and avoid unnecessary trade restrictiveness.

the Russian Federation is ranked as the fourth most attractive destination for FDI after China, India and the United States (UNCTAD, 2007).

Although inflows of FDI have, until recently, been robust, barriers to foreign ownership are estimated to be high in Russia compared to OECD countries. In part, this reflects the enactment of the law on strategic sectors which came into force in May 2008. This law defines 42 sectors in which control by foreign investors requires prior authorisation from a government commission (Box 5.3). Although this law increases transparency and is less *ad hoc* than the previous regime, its sectoral coverage is broader and notification delays longer than OECD recommended practice (OECD, 2008b).

The emergence of large state-controlled conglomerates with dominant market positions also acts as a barrier to FDI inflows. The scope for foreign investors to acquire equity in these conglomerates or participate in government procurement contracts in the sectors they occupy is strictly limited. There is also evidence of differential treatment of foreign businesses with respect to government procurement and eligibility for government subsidies. Finally, the PMR indicators also signal a lack of provisions encouraging regulators to use internationally harmonised standards and certification procedures or avoid unnecessary trade restrictiveness.

Notwithstanding explicit barriers to FDI, the overall regulatory environment in Russia is perhaps the most significant impediment to greater inflows of FDI. A growing body of recent research has found that the regulatory environment is a key determinant of FDI. As shown in Nicoletti *et al.* (2003), regulatory policies that restrict market access in one way or another negatively influence the share of foreign direct investment in OECD countries. Conway *et al.* (2006) also find that the employment share of foreign affiliates in manufacturing sectors is higher in countries with relatively more liberal product market environments. Accordingly, reducing state interference in economic activity and carrying out necessary administrative and regulatory reforms would not only increase domestic investment and productivity, but also increase foreign investor interest in the Russian Federation.

Notes

1. A summary of recent surveys of Russia's business climate is given in OECD (2008).
2. For a detailed description of the PMR indicators and the results for OECD countries see Nicoletti *et al.* (2000), Conway et al. (2005) and Wölfl et al. (2009). A full description of the PMR indicators methodology applied to Russia can be found in Conway *et al.* (2009).
3. By design, all the indicators in the PMR system range from 0 to 6 from least to most restrictive of competition.
4. Calculated on the basis of 119 markets, for which data from Rosstat are available for both 2001 and 2007. Concentration ratios are calculated using the HHI and CR3 methodologies. A highly concentrated industry is defined as one in which the Herfindahl-Hirschmann Index (HHI) is greater than 2000.
5. The Federal Antimonopoly Service reports that cartel formation is most problematic in the following sectors: wholesale and retail trade in oil products, agriculture and retail trade, banking (consumer credit), the pharmaceutical industry, building materials, metallurgy and the chemical industry.
6. Another major impediment from the enterprises perspective are high transport cost.
7. See Nicoletti and Scarpetta (2003) and Conway *et al.* (2006). Enhanced product market competition can also contribute to GDP *per capita* growth by increasing employment (Blanchard and Giavazzi, 2003; Nicoletti and Scarpetta, 2005). As restrictions are eased and competition increases, firms earn lower product market rents, activity is expanded and employment rates tend to rise. However, employment

in some of the large firms, particularly in the network sectors, where previous regulations were conducive to over-manning, may be adversely affected by deregulation.

8. Arnold *et al.* (2008) find that the negative effect of anti-competitive regulation on the efficiency of resource reallocation is particularly pronounced in ICT-intensive sectors that have a high potential for exploiting new general-purpose technologies.

9. For a recent survey of theoretical and empirical studies on the effects of competition on innovation, see Aghion and Griffith (2005).

10. Accordingly, increased threat of entry increases cross-firm differences in performance and turnover. A number of empirical studies find evidence that more competition increases the heterogeneity of firm performance. Aghion *et al.* (2005) find that entry liberalisation (de-licensing) in Indian states led to an increase in within-industry inequality in output, labour and total factor productivity. Sabirianova *et al.* (2005) also find support for heterogeneous effects of firm entry on firm performance in Russian and Czech industrial firms. In OECD countries, Arnold *et al.* (2008) find that that the result of liberalisation increasing heterogeneity in firm performance also holds in OECD countries.

11. See Nicoletti *et al.* (2003), Conway *et al.* (2006).

12. Results for all of the low-level indicators for Russia vis-à-vis OECD and other countries are given in the Annex.

13. Examples include the United Aircraft Construction Corporation and the United Shipbuilding Corporation.

14. The six new state corporations founded in 2007 are: Development Bank (Vneshekonombank), Rosnanotekh, Rostekhnologii, Rosatom, Olimpstroi, and the Fund for Assistance in the Reform of Housing and Public Utilities. The deposit insurance agency was also established as a state corporation, in 2004, and a previous entity set up to manage the assets of failed banks following the 1998 crisis was subsequently wound up. No new corporations have been founded since 2007. See Sprenger (2008) for a more detailed description.

15. The Federal Service for State Statistics uses the following classification of ownership forms: fully state-owned; mixed state and private, domestic; private domestic; foreign and joint foreign and domestic. Fully state-owned include general government and SOEs: where possible, distinction between the two was made in the data presented in the survey. Mixed state and private does not differentiate between majority and minority state holdings. Joint foreign and domestic may include enterprises that have both state and foreign ownership. Enterprises owned by SOEs are classified as private. Based on this classification, some large state-controlled companies are not included either into fully state-owned or mixed state and private categories. Examples include Gazprom, the largest Russian company; Gazprom Neft, a subsidiary of the Gazprom group; Rosneft, one of the largest companies in the Russian oil industry.

16. Cited in Sprenger (2008).

17. This increase reflected: increases in government minority holdings to controlling interests (*e.g.* Gazprom, Russia's largest company by market capitalisation), previously private enterprises being bought by SOEs, and large SOEs undertaking initial public offerings.

18. Kochetygova *et al.* (2005) find that the transparency of Russian SOEs is worse than the 10 largest listed Russian companies and much worse than state-owned firms in western Europe and the North America. They also report that disclosure by Russian SOEs is prone to one-off lapses at critical junctures, which have a major bearing on companies' strategies and performance. These lapses usually occur when significant stakeholder interests are at risk and undermine Russia's ability to attract capital at competitive rates, to build efficient and trusted institutions, and maximize its economic growth.

19. Unitary enterprises are regulated under the Law on State and Municipal Enterprises. They generally do not disclose financial information but are audited by the Audit Chamber of the Russian Federation. They have only limited rights over their property and many types of transitions that they undertake have to be approved by the corresponding government agency.

20. A series of Federal Laws adopted over this period simplified rules and procedures related to the entry of new businesses and reduced the administrative burden on existing companies. See OECD (2002a), OECD (2006), Yakovlev and Zhuravskaya (2008).

21. See OECD (2006) for a review of other available indicators on corruption.

22. A full description of reform in the electricity sector is given in Annex 5.A1.

23. For example, MTS, the largest Russian mobile operator, controls the leading mobile companies in the Ukraine, Belarus and Uzbekistan.

24. Russia is currently the largest economy outside of the WTO.

25. See Tarr (2002) for a discussion on the benefits of a uniform tariff structure.

Bibliography

Aghion, P., M. Dewatripont and P. Rey (1999), "Competition, Financial Discipline, and Growth", *Review of Economic Studies*, 66, 825-852.

Aghion, P., W. Carlin and M. Schaffer (2002), "Competition, Innovation and Growth in Transition: Exploring the Interaction between Policies", *William Davidson Working Papers*, No 501, *www.wdi.umich.edu/files/Publications/WorkingPapers/wp501.pdf*.

Aghion, P. and R. Griffith (2005), *Competition and Growth*, The MIT Press, Cambridge, Massachusetts.

Aghion, P. *et al.* (2005) "Entry Liberalization and Inequality in Industrial Performance" *Journal of the European Economic Association*, Papers and proceedings, 3(2-3): 291-302.

Aghion, P. and E. Bessonova (2006), "On Entry and Growth: Theory and Evidence", *Revue de l'OFCE, 2006/3*, No. 97 bis.

Arnold, J., G. Nicoletti and S. Scarpetta (2008), "Regulation, Allocative Efficiency and Productivity in OECD Countries: Industry and Firm level Evidence", *OECD Economics Department Working Papers*, No. 616, OECD, Paris.

Bessonova, E., K. Kozlov and K. Yudaeva (2003), "Trade Liberalization, Foreign Direct Investment, and Productivity of Russian Firms", paper prepared for a CEFIR conference on Negotiating Russia's WTO accession: strategic lessons from multilateral trade liberalization and club enlargement, *www.cefir.ru/papers/WP39.pdf*.

Bessonova, E. (2009), "Competition, Foreign Investment, and the Efficiency of Russian Industrial Firms", mimeo.

Blanchard, O. and F. Giavazzi (2003), "Macroeconomic Effects of Regulation and Deregulation in Goods and Labor Markets", *Quarterly Journal of Economics*, vol. 118, No. 3, pp. 879-907.

Brown, D., and J. Earle (2000), "Competition and Firm Performance: Lessons from Russia", CEPR *Discussion Papers* No. 2444, May 2000.

Carlin, W. *et al.* (2001), "Competition and Enterprise Performance in Transition Economies: Evidence from a Cross Country Survey", *CEPR Discussion Papers*, No. 2840.

Conway, P., V. Janod and G. Nicoletti (2005), "Product Market Regulation in OECD Countries: 1998 to 2003", *OECD Economics Department Working Papers*, No. 419, OECD, Paris.

Conway, P. *et al.* (2006), "Product Market Regulation and Productivity Convergence", Economic Studies, No. 43, pp. 39 76, OECD, Paris, *www.oecd.org/dataoecd/62/31/40505949.pdf*.

Conway, P., T. Lysenko and G. Barnard (2009), "Product Market Regulation in Russia", OECD Economics Department Working Papers, OECD, Paris, forthcoming.

Criscuolo, C. (2005), "The Contribution of Foreign Affiliates to Productivity Growth: Evidence from OECD Countries", STI Working Papers 2005/8, OECD, Paris.

Federal Antimonopoly Service (2008), *Доклад "О состоянии конкуренции в Российской Федерации" за 2007 год (Report on the State of Competition in the Russian Federation in 2007)*, Moscow, *www.fas.gov.ru/competition/goods/20916.shtml*.

Gorodnichenko, Y., J. Svejnar and K. Terrell (2008), "Globalization and Innovation in Emerging Markets", *NBER Working Papers*, No. 14481.

International Energy Agency (2005), *Russian Electricity Reform: Emerging Challenges and Opportunities*, OECD/IEA, Paris.

Keller, W. (2004), "International Technology Diffusion", *Journal of Economic Literature*, Vol. XLII (September 2004), pp. 752 82.

Keller, W. and S. Yeaple (2003), "Multinational Enterprises, International Trade, and Productivity Growth: Firm Level Evidence from the United States", *IMF Working Papers 248*.

Kikeri, S. and J. Nellis (2004), "An Assessment of Privatization", *The World Bank Research Observer*, Vol. 19, No. 1.

Kochetygova, J. *et al.* (2005), "Transparency And Disclosure By Russian State Owned Enterprises", Standard & Poor's Governance Services, Prepared for the Roundtable on Corporate Governance organized by the OECD in Moscow on 3 June 2005, *www.oecd.org/dataoecd/9/59/35175841.pdf*.

Megginson, W. and J. Netter (2001), "From State to Market: A Survey of Empirical Studies on Privatization", *Journal of Economic Literature*, Vol. 39, No. 2, pp. 321 89.

Nicoletti, G., S. Scarpetta and O. Boylaud (2000), "Summary Indicators of Product Market Regulation with an Extension to Employment Protection Legislation", *OECD Economics Department Working Papers*, No. 226, *www.oecd.org/dataoecd/21/13/1880867.pdf*.

Nicoletti, G. and S. Scarpetta (2003), "Regulation, Productivity and Growth: OECD Evidence", *Economic Policy*, Vol. 36, pp. 11 72.

Nicoletti, G. et al. (2003), "The Influence of Policies on Trade and Foreign Direct Investment", *Economic Studies*, No. 36, OECD, Paris, *www.oecd.org/dataoecd/22/2/33638319.pdf*.

Nicoletti, G. and S. Scarpetta (2005), "Product market reforms and employment in OECD countries", OECD *Economics Department Working Papers*, No. 472, OECD, Paris.

OECD (2002a), *OECD Economic Surveys: Russian Federation*, OECD, Paris.

OECD (2002b), *Regulatory Policies in OECD Countries: From Interventionism to Regulatory Governance*, OECD, Paris.

OECD (2004), *OECD Economic Surveys: Russian Federation*, OECD, Paris.

OECD (2005a), *Corporate Governance of State Owned Enterprises: a Survey of OECD Countries*, OECD, Paris.

OECD (2005b), *OECD Guidelines on Corporate Governance of State Owned Enterprises*, OECD, Paris.

OECD (2005c), *OECD Reviews of Regulatory Reform: Russia: Building Rules for the Market*, OECD, Paris.

OECD (2006), *OECD Economic Surveys: Russian Federation*, OECD, Paris.

OECD (2007), *OECD Economic Surveys: Ukraine Economic Assessment*, OECD, Paris.

OECD (2008a), *Measuring Entrepreneurship: a Digest of Indicators. OECD Eurostat Entrepreneurship Indicators Program*, OECD, Paris.

OECD (2008b), *OECD Investment Policy review: Russian Federation – Strengthening the Policy Framework for Investment*, OECD, Paris.

Renaissance Capital (2009), "Russia: electricity generation – InterRAO moves on to TGK11", *Renaissance Capital Utilities Research*, 5 March.

Shepotylo, O. and D. Tarr (2007), "The Structure of Import Tariffs in the Russian Federation: 2001 2005", *World Bank Policy Research Working Papers*, No. 4265.

Sprenger, C. (2008), "The Role of State Owned Enterprises in the Russian Economy", paper written for the OECD Roundtable on Corporate Governance of SOEs.

Srinivasan, T.N. and J. Bhagwati (1999), "Outward orientation and Development: Are Revisionists Right?", *Economic Growth Center Discussion Papers* No. 806, Yale University, Cambridge, MA.

Tarr, D. (2002), "On the Design of Tariff Policy: Arguments for and Against Uniform Tariffs," in Hoekman, B, A. Mattoo and P. English (eds.), *Development, Trade and the WTO: A Handbook*, World Bank, Washington, DC, 2002, available at *http://siteresources.worldbank.org/INTRANETTRADE/Resources/WBI-Training/288464-1162851806581/Tarr_Tariff_Uniformity_eng_paper.pdf*.

Troika Dialog (2008), "Who Owns Russia?", *Corporate Governance Annual 2008*.

Tompson, W. (2002), "Privatisation in Russia: Scope, Methods and Impact", *mimeo*, University of London, October.

UNCTAD (2007), *World Investment Report 2007*, p. 30, UNCTAD, New York/Geneva, 2007.

Wölfl, A., et al. (2009), "Ten Years of Product Market Reform in OECD Countries – Insights from a Revised PMR Indicator", *OECD Economics Department Working Papers*, No. 695, OECD, Paris, *www.oecd.org/dataoecd/29/41/42779045.pdf*.

Yakovlev, E., and E. Zhuravskaya (2008), "Reforms in Business Regulation: Evidence from Russia", CEFIR *Working Papers*, 2008.

ANNEX 5.A1

Regulation in the Russian electricity sector

Beginning in 2003, the Russian electricity sector has undergone an extensive period of regulatory reform and restructuring. The overriding objectives of reform have been to improve the operational efficiency of the sector and encourage large-scale private-sector investment to meet demand shortfalls.

The key aspects of the power sector reforms to date and current arrangements in the sector are:

- The potentially competitive and monopoly segments of the market have been separated by vertically unbundling the incumbent operator – RAO UES – into generation, transmission and supply companies. RAO UES has since been disbanded and independent generation and retail companies have been privatised to some extent.
- The transmission assets of RAO UES have been transferred to the Federal Grid Company (FGC), which is owned by the government. The FGC is prohibited from trading electricity and is required to enter into contracts with eligible market participants. Access tariffs are adjusted annually and set on a cost-plus methodology. An independent national system operator has been established to manage electricity flows on the transmission grid serving the wholesale market.
- Eleven Interregional Distribution Grid Companies (IDGCs) are being formed to own and manage the regional electricity distribution networks. The government has 52% equity holding in the IDGCs. The configuration of the IDGCs has changed considerably over the course of the reforms and the process of asset restructuring is still ongoing.
- A wholesale power market has been introduced and is expected to be fully operational by 2011. Currently, 70 to 75% of wholesale electricity is sold at regulated prices. This amount is expected to fall to 35 to 40% by 2010. By 2011, all electricity on the wholesale market is expected to be sold at unregulated prices. The retail market is expected to be fully liberalised by 2014.
- A range of market institutions and regulators have been established. The Federal Tariff Service (FTS) develops pricing principles and imposes regulated tariffs in the wholesale market. The Regional Tariff Services (RTS) perform analogous roles in the regional distribution networks, subject to thresholds set by the FTS. The Ministry of Energy also plays a key regulatory role in the sector while the Federal Antimonopoly Service (FAS) is responsible for competition supervision and regulating non-discriminatory access to network services. It also regulates the activities of the Administrator of Trade System (ATS), which operates the wholesale market.

In principle, the direction of reform in the Russian electricity market is consistent with the establishment of competitive wholesale and retail markets based on transparent prices that accurately reflect costs. Indeed, many of the recent reforms are in line with recommendations made in the *2004 OECD Economic Survey of Russia (OECD, 2004) and the IEA's study on electricity reform in Russia* (IEA, 2005). In practice, however, there are a number of ongoing issues that pose a threat to the establishment of competitive electricity markets.

Market structure

Generation

Six Wholesale Generation Companies (WGCs) emerged as part of the unbundling of RAO UES and were assigned generation assets in different energy zones within Russia. In addition, 14 Territorial Generation Companies (TGCs) acquired generation plants that predominantly supply local businesses and household consumers. Collectively, the WGCs and TGCs each account for around 25% of total installed capacity. As well as the WGCs and the TGCs, a number of independent power companies with well-established customers were partially unbundled as part of the reform process, but maintain control of local networks.

Despite these reforms, electricity generation in some energy zones remains reasonably concentrated with a few large players that are sometimes highly locally concentrated. In addition, despite a law signed into effect by President Putin in 2003 calling for the state to exit the power generation sector, the Russian government still retains significant ownership of generation assets. According to one estimate, the state currently owns 51% and controls 65% of national generation capacity and is an active force for consolidation in the sector.[1] Diversified ownership is clearly a prerequisite for meaningful competition and ongoing state involvement in electricity generation poses a major threat to an orderly transition to competitive electricity markets. If it is serious about increasing the efficiency of the electricity market and encouraging private sector participation, the state needs to exit the generation sector.

Increasing vertical integration into the fuel supply market poses another serious threat to competition in the generation sector. In particular, as a result of recent acquisitions, the natural gas monopoly Gazprom controls a significant proportion of thermal generation capacity in the European zone, while the major coal producer SUEK controls a large part of thermal generation in the Siberian zone.[2] At the same time, both of these companies are the primary fuel supplier to the electricity generation sector. These arrangements could easily result in obstacles in accessing fuel supplies for other generators. This highlights the need for strong and independent regulation in the sector to ensure that fuel is supplied to thermal power generators is on a non-discriminatory basis. In addition, the substantial state holding in Gazprom again calls into question the government's commitment to exit the generation sector.

Retail markets

There are currently around 370 retail companies in Russia supplying more than 80 000 small and medium-sized business and approximately 40 million households. However, despite a large number of market participants, there are currently no clear rules for consumer switching, implying a risk of localised monopoly retail suppliers. In addition, with consumer tariffs regulated until 2014, there is currently limited scope for competition in the sector. This acts as a barrier to entry for independent supply companies and blocks the benefits of reform from flowing through to the end user. Consumer choice is a prerequisite for a competitive retail market and needs to be instigated as soon as is feasible.

Cross-subsidies in electricity markets also act as a deterrent to market entry and investment. Currently, cross-subsidies are estimated to be in the order of RUB 120 billion per year. The government has recognised that these need to be eliminated. Towards the end of 2007, the Ministry of Economic Development entered into an agreement to subsidies electricity directly from the state budget. This practice needs to be extended with all cross-subsidies replaced by direct subsidies from the state budget. In the longer term, subsidies need to be eliminated completely. Transparent price signals that reflect costs create incentives for efficient behaviour and are an essential ingredient for successful market reform.

Regulatory arrangements

Good regulation requires good governance. The founding laws on electricity reform provide a good basis for establishing effective governance and regulatory arrangements. However, the specific roles of the various regulatory bodies are not always clear, increasing regulatory uncertainty for private-sector investors. The government must continue improving the regulatory framework to clearly specify the powers of regulators and the sanctions they are able to impose to perform their functions in a predictable and transparent manner consistent with strategic policy objectives.

At the same time, the regulatory framework must allow regulators sufficient flexibility to make micro regulatory decisions on technical matters. Where discretion is granted to executive bodies, the legislative framework should clearly prescribe the nature, scope and limits of discretionary powers. Equally important are mechanisms to uphold legal rights and enforce accountability, and procedures for changing the market rules. Moreover, a system of checks and balances needs to be in place to ensure that the decisions of the regulators and market institutions can be appealed.

A clear separation of regulatory function is also important for ensuring clear rules of the game for market participants. At present, there are several regulators with overlapping powers to regulate different aspects of the electricity market. In particular, the regulatory activities of the Ministry of Energy (MoE) and the Committee of the Market, which is supposed to develop market rules independently from the MoE, need to be coordinated to ensure that complementary regulatory arrangements are established.

Given significant market concentration in electricity generation in some regions and the ownership structure in energy markets, effective antimonopoly regulation is likely to be extremely important in the Russian context. Accordingly, the Federal Antimonopoly Service needs to be sufficiently well resourced and have the capacity to effectively monitor the electricity market. The administrative capacities of the other regulatory agencies also need to be enhanced to ensure effectively monitoring and dispute resolution. The Committee of the Market needs to be bolstered so that it can evolve into independent regulatory body for the power sector.

Notes

1. Renaissance Capital (2009).
2. As of June 2009, Gazprom group owns 57% of WGC-2, 60% of WGC-6, 46% of TGC-1 and 53% of TGC-3 (Mosenergo).

ANNEX 5.A2

Results of the 2008 PMR assessment of the Russian Federation

The *scope of the public enterprise sector* indicator measures the pervasiveness of state ownership across business sectors. It reflects the proportion of major sectors in which the state holds an equity stake in at least one firm. With a pervasive state-owned enterprise sector, Russia performs poorly in this area.

Figure 5.A2.1. **Scope of the public enterprise sector**

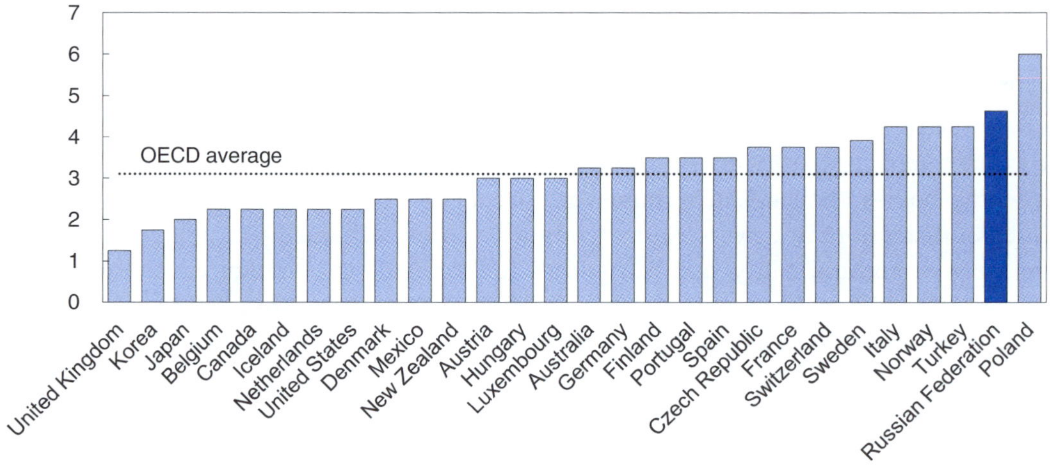

StatLink http://dx.doi.org/10.1787/650616483767

Figure 5.A2.2. **Direct control over business enterprises**

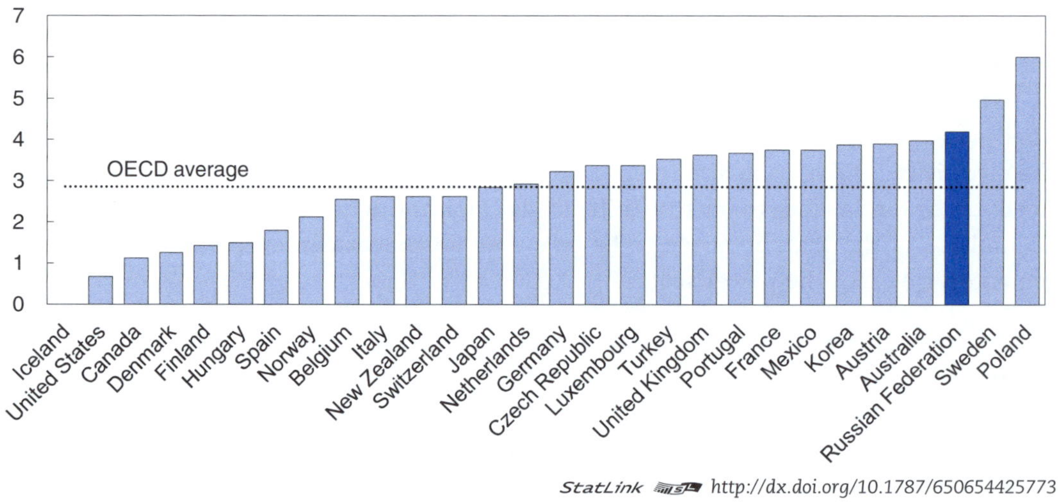

StatLink http://dx.doi.org/10.1787/650654425773

Figure 5.A2.3. **Government involvement in network sectors**

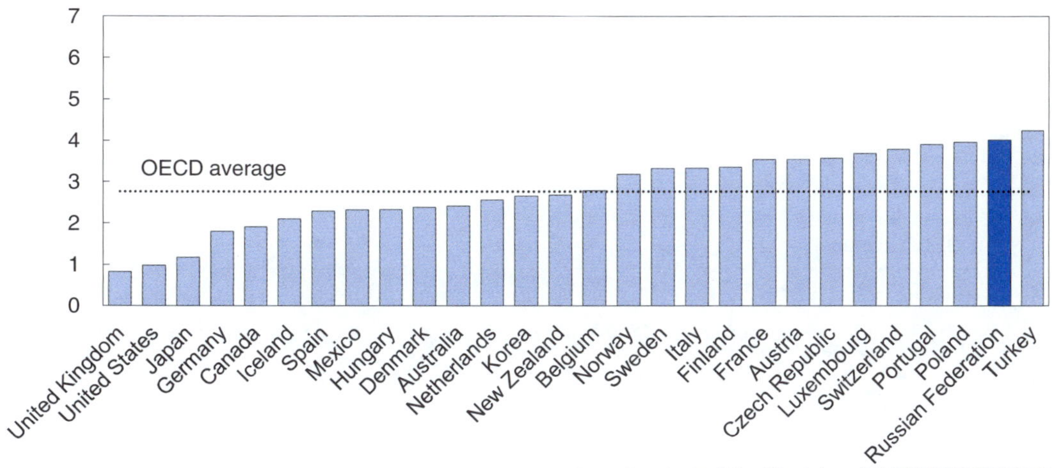

StatLink http://dx.doi.org/10.1787/650656415676

Direct control over business enterprises measures across sectors the existence of government special voting rights in privately owned firms, constraints on the sale of state-owned equity stakes, and the extent to which legislative bodies control the strategic choices of public enterprises. Russia performs poorly here reflecting restrictions on share sales for firms in "strategic sectors", extensive special voting rights, etc.

The indicator of *government involvement in network sectors* generally measures the extent of public ownership in the network sectors (gas, electricity, rail, air transport, postal services and telecommunications). Reflecting high levels of government ownership, even in the reformed electricity sector, Russia does not score well on this indicator.

The use of command and control regulation indicator measures the extent to which the authorities use coercive (as opposed to incentive-based) regulation, both in general and in specific service sectors.

The *price controls* indicator reflects the extent of price controls in specific sectors. Despite improvements in this area, the Russian government still imposes price controls in several competitive sectors, hence the high indicator value.

Figure 5.A2.4. **The use of command and control regulation**

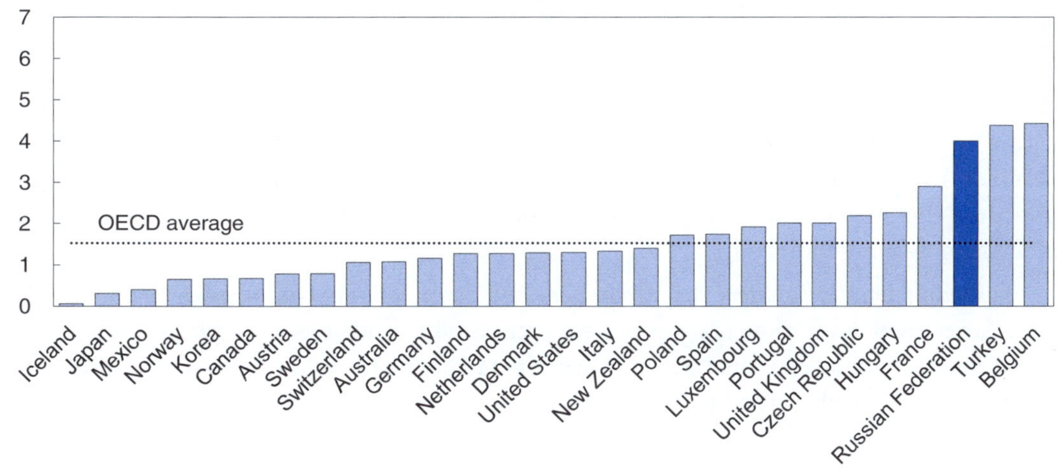

StatLink http://dx.doi.org/10.1787/650746212385

Figure 5.A2.5. **Price controls**

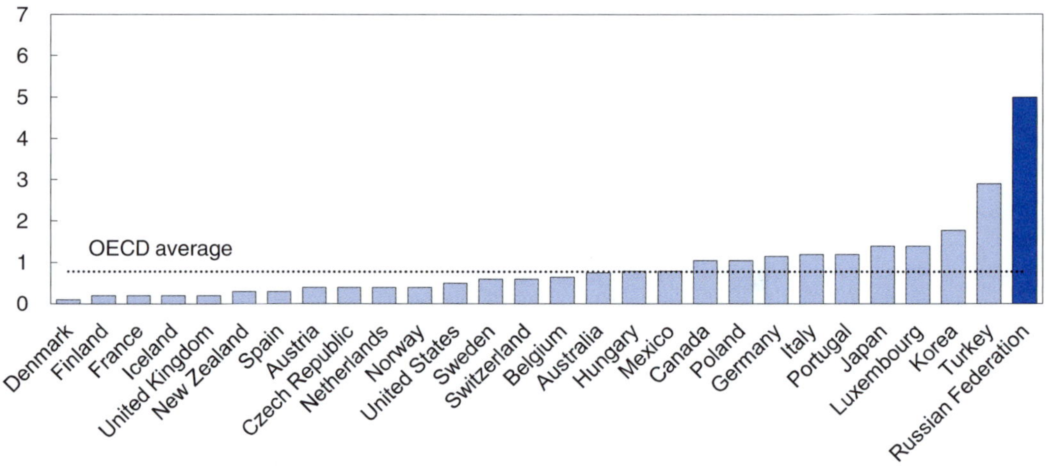

StatLink http://dx.doi.org/10.1787/650757220831

Figure 5.A2.6. **The licences and permits system**

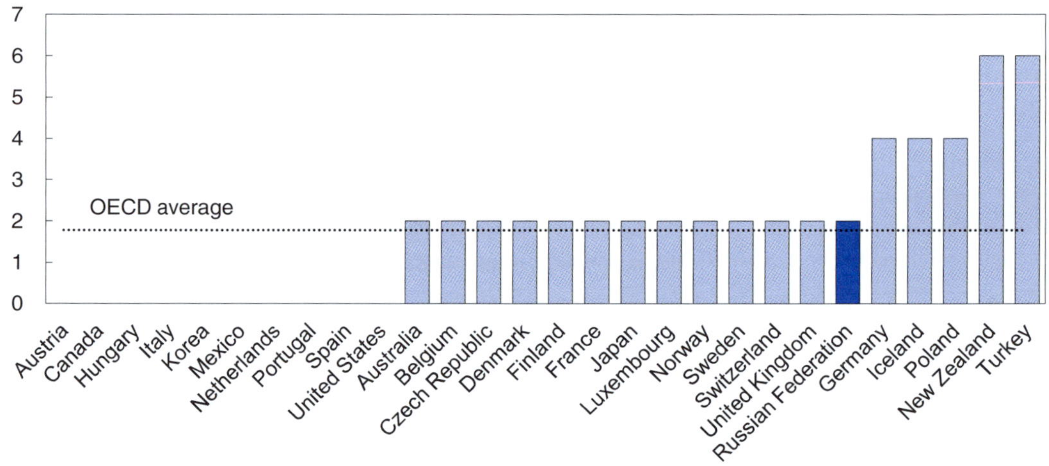

StatLink http://dx.doi.org/10.1787/650784764574

The *licenses and permits* indicator reflects the presence or absence of such devices as "one-stop shops" and "silence is consent" rules for getting information on, and issuing, licenses and permits. Russia does comparatively well here, reflecting the introduction of one-stop shops.

The indicator of *communication and simplification of rules and procedures* refers to aspects of the government's communication strategy and efforts to reduce/simplify the administrative burden of acting with government. Russia performs well in this regard reflecting the introduction of plain language drafting and systematic procedures for publicising new regulations.

The *administrative burdens for corporations* indicator reflects the number of mandatory procedures involved in the creation of new companies, as well as the number of agencies involved and the total cost of start-up procedures in both time and money. Costs have been converted at PPP exchange rates.

Figure 5.A2.7. **Communication and simplification of rules and procedures**

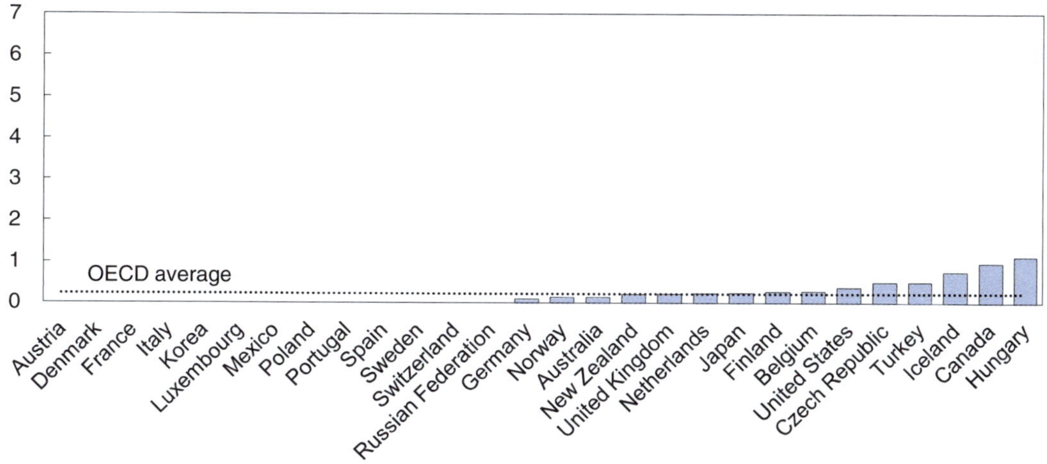

StatLink http://dx.doi.org/10.1787/650803548024

Figure 5.A2.8. **Administrative burdens for corporations**

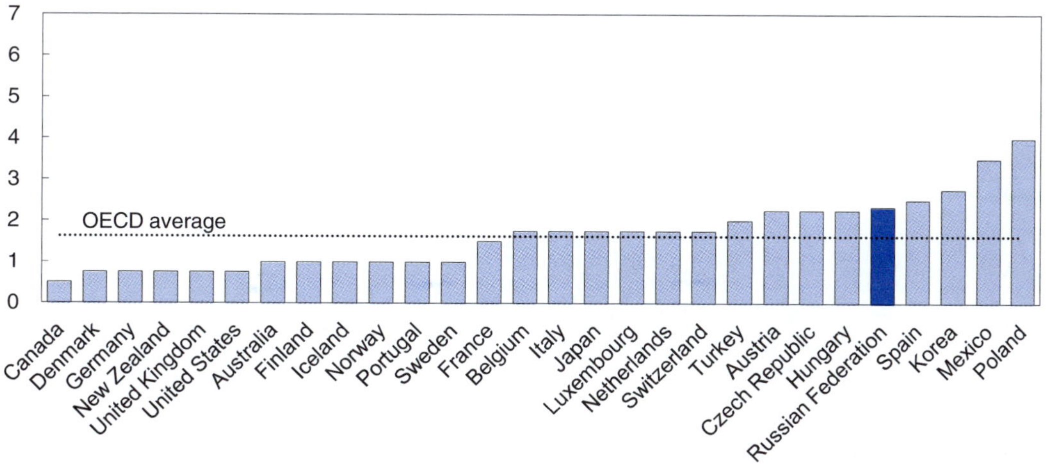

StatLink http://dx.doi.org/10.1787/650804040888

Figure 5.A2.9. **Administrative burdens for sole proprietor firms**

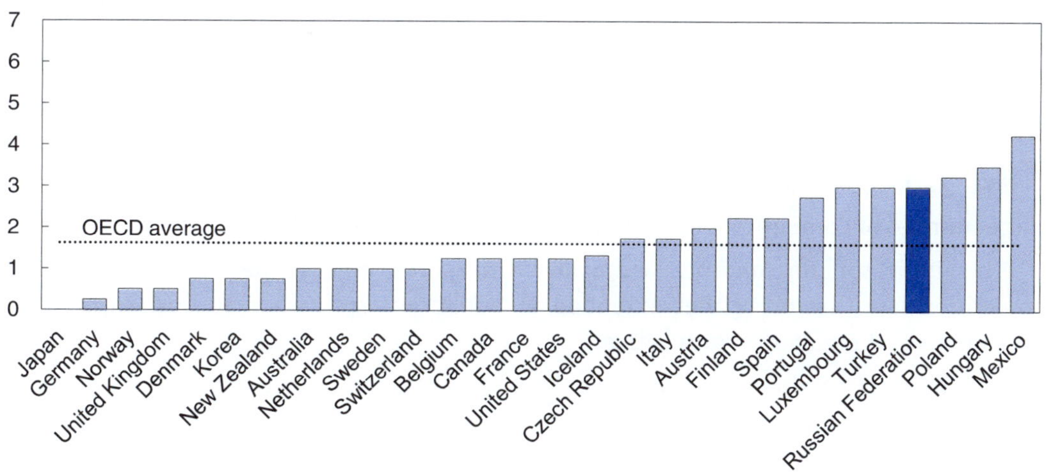

StatLink http://dx.doi.org/10.1787/650826245180

The *administrative burdens for sole proprietors* indicator is constructed in a more or less identical fashion to the indicator for new companies but is concerned with unincorporated small businesses. Again, costs have been converted at PPP exchange rates.

The *sector-specific administrative burdens* indicator reflects administrative burdens in the road transport and retail distribution sectors.

Figure 5.A2.10. **Sector-specific administrative burdens**

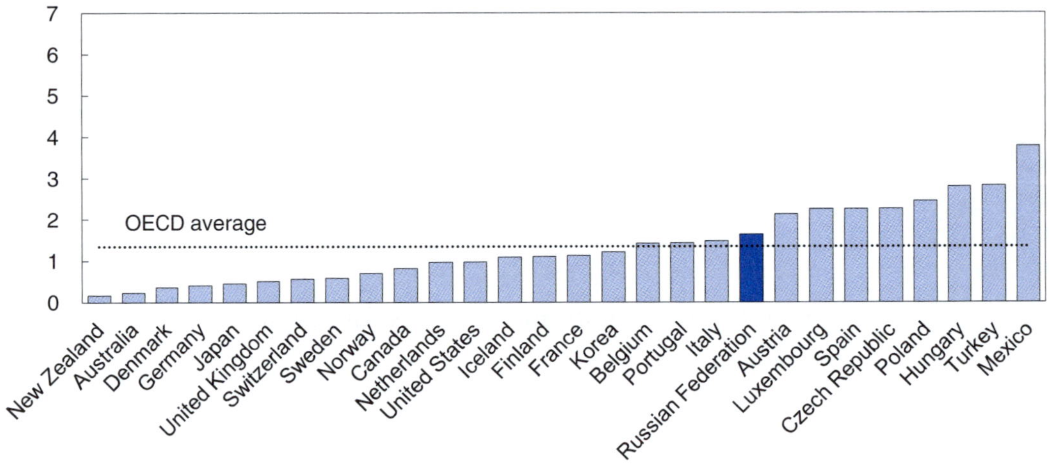

StatLink http://dx.doi.org/10.1787/650880480545

Figure 5.A2.11. **Legal barriers**

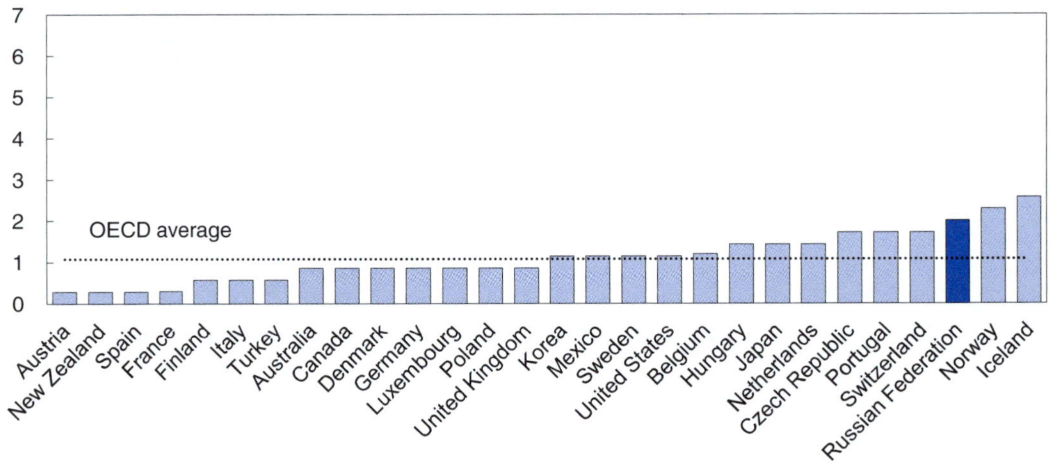

StatLink http://dx.doi.org/10.1787/651023478622

The *legal barriers* indicator refers specifically to the scope of explicit legal limitations on the number of competitors allowed in a wide range of business sectors or subsectors.

The indicator for *antitrust exemptions* measures the scope of exemptions to competition law that are either extended to public enterprises or authorised by other government and regulatory authorities.

The indicator of *barriers in network sectors* reflects a range of regulations that govern the entry of private-sector firms and vertical integration in the network sectors (gas, electricity, rail, air transport, postal services and telecommunications). Russia performs comparatively well here reflecting recent reforms in the electricity sector.

 OECD ECONOMIC SURVEYS: RUSSIAN FEDERATION – ISBN 978-92-64-05433-2 – © OECD 200

Figure 5.A2.12. **Antitrust exemptions**

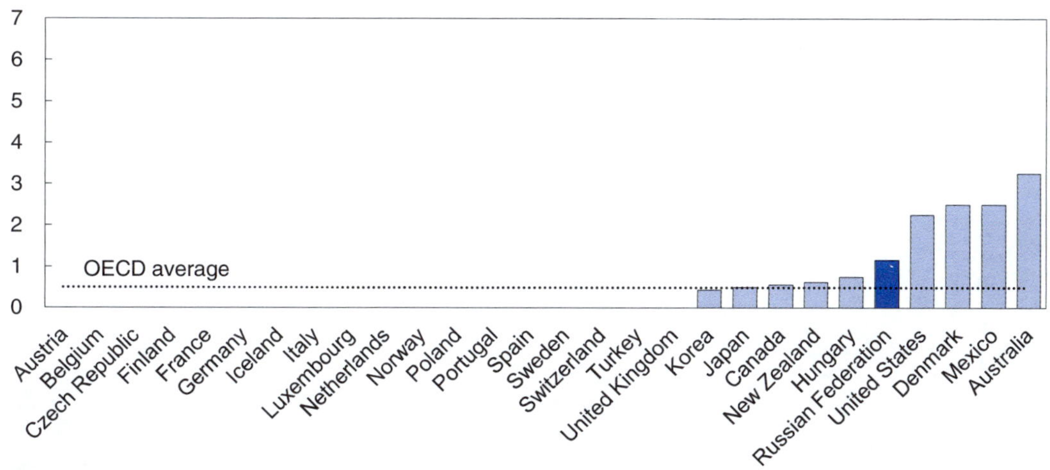

StatLink http://dx.doi.org/10.1787/651122351008

Figure 5.A2.13. **Barriers in network sectors**

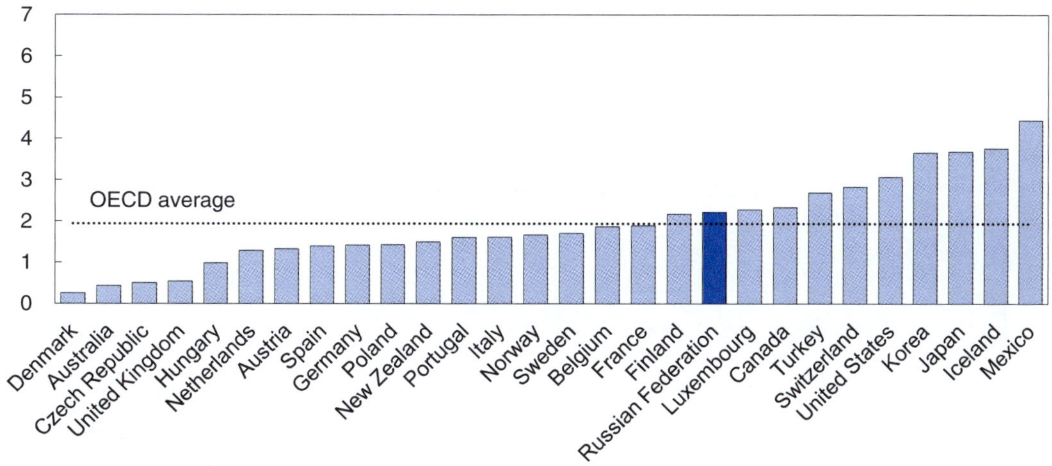

StatLink http://dx.doi.org/10.1787/651125817827

Figure 5.A2.14. **Barriers to entry in services**

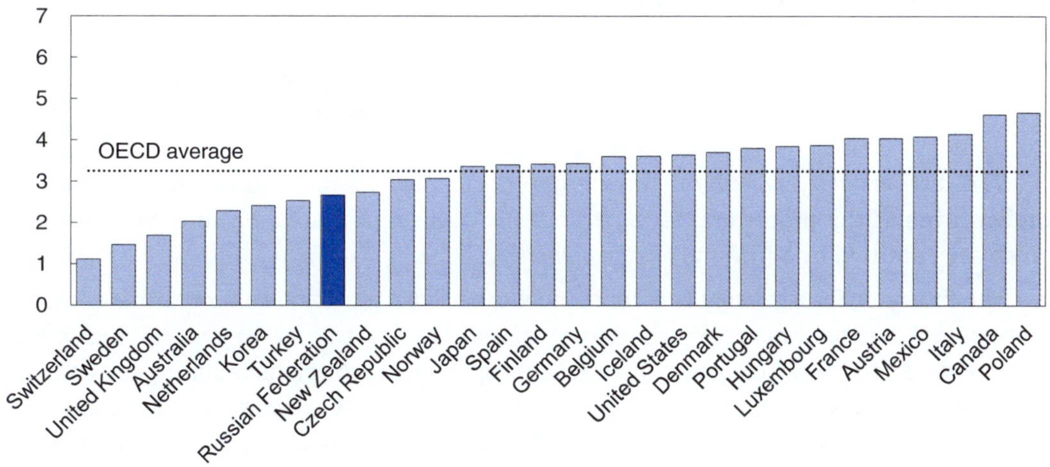

StatLink http://dx.doi.org/10.1787/651134820501

Barriers to entry in services covers regulations governing the entry of private-sector firms in the professional services and retail trade.

The indicator for *barriers to foreign direct investment* measures the extent to which legal restrictions apply on foreign acquisition of equity in public and private firms in general, and in the telecommunications and airlines sectors in particular.

Figure 5.A2.15. **Barriers to FDI (foreign ownership)**

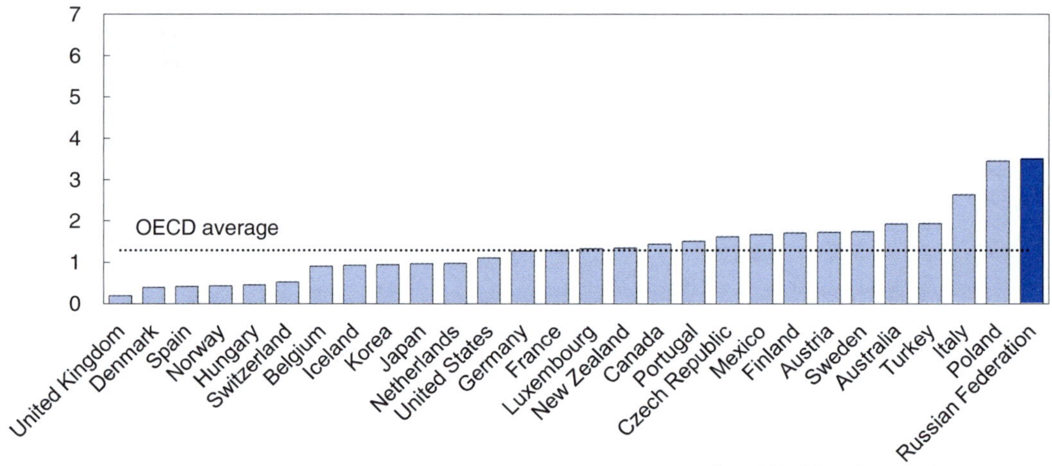

StatLink http://dx.doi.org/10.1787/651138083054

Figure 5.A2.16. **Discriminatory procedures**

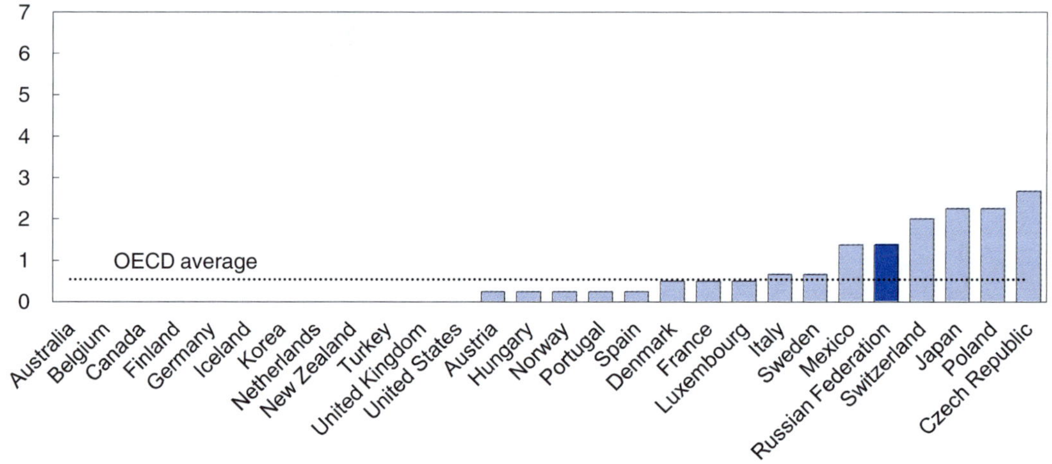

StatLink http://dx.doi.org/10.1787/651147653123

The *discriminatory procedures* indicator reflects the extent of discrimination against foreign firms at the procedural level. It does *not* cover restrictions on foreign ownership, which are captured by *barriers to foreign ownership*.

The indicator for *regulatory barriers* reflects other barriers to international trade, such as international harmonisation of standards and regulatory norms or mutual recognition agreements. Russia performs poorly here reflecting a lack of provisions requiring regulators to recognise the equivalence of regulatory measures in other countries, use internationally harmonised standards and certification procedures or avoid unnecessary trade restrictiveness.

Tariffs reflect the (simple) average of a country's most-favoured-nation tariffs.

Figure 5.A2.17. **Regulatory barriers**

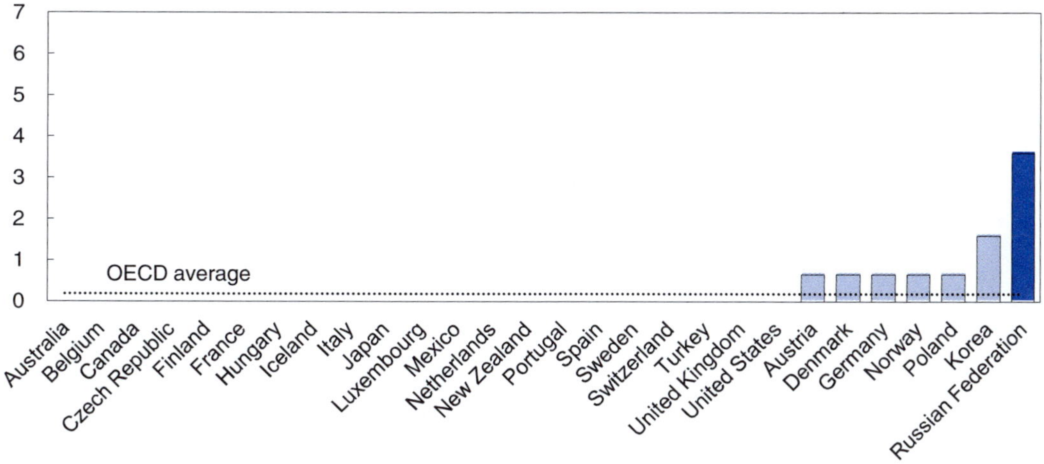

StatLink http://dx.doi.org/10.1787/651165337715

Figure 5.A2.18. **Tariffs**

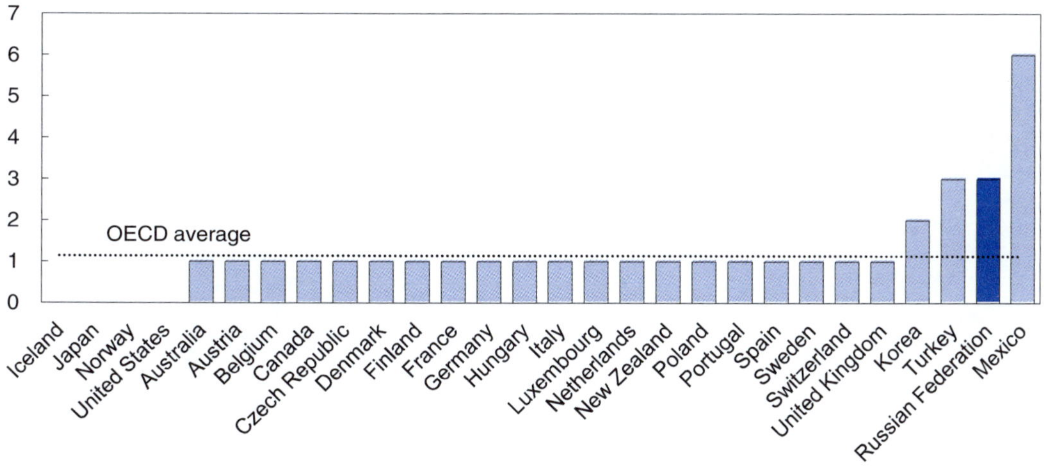

StatLink http://dx.doi.org/10.1787/651171343224

ISBN 978-92-64-05433-2
OECD Economic Surveys: Russia

GLOSSARY

ARDL	Auto-regressive distributed lag
CBR	Central Bank of Russia
CPI	Consumer Price Index
EU	European Union
FDI	Foreign direct investment
FGC	Federal Grid Company
FTS	Federal Tariff Service
GDP	Gross Domestic Product
GKO	Government Treasury Bill
HHI	Herfindahl-Hirschmann Index
ICT	Information and Communication Technologies
IDGC	Interregional Distribution Grid Company
IFRS	International Financial Reporting Standards
ILO	International Labour Organisation
IMF	International Monetary Fund
MET	Mineral Extraction Tax
MoE	Ministry of Energy
NWF	National Welfare Fund
OSS	"One-stop shop"
PMR	Product market regulation
PPP	Purchasing power parity
RAO UES	Russian joint stock company Unified Energy Systems
RAS	Russian Accounting Standards
REER	Real effective exchange rate
RIA	Regulatory impact analysis
RTS	Russian Trading System
RVCA	Russian Venture Capital Association
SEZ	Special economic zone
SOE	State-owned enterprise
SMEs	Small and medium-sized enterprises
TFP	Total factor productivity
TGC	Territorial Generation Company
TI	Transparency International
VEB	Vnesheconombank
VTB	Vneshtorgbank
VRR	VAT Revenue Ratio
WGC	Wholesale Generation Company
WTO	World Trade Organisation

OECD PUBLISHING, 2, rue André-Pascal, 75775 PARIS CEDEX 16
PRINTED IN FRANCE
(10 2009 06 1 P) ISBN 978-92-64-05433-2 – No. 56855 2009